KT-461-927

The 'Chandos Portrait' of William Shakespeare.
By courtesy of the National Gallery, London.

SHAKESPEARE
THE BASICS

The way in which Shakespeare's plays are studied has undergone considerable change in recent years. The new edition of this best-selling guide, aimed squarely at the student new to Shakespeare, is based on the exciting novel approaches shaping Shakespeare studies. This volume provides a thorough general introduction to the plays and a refreshingly clear guide to:

- Shakespeare's language
- The plays as performance texts
- The cultural and political contexts of the plays
- Early modern theatre practice
- New understandings of the major genres

Sean McEvoy illustrates how interpretations of Shakespeare are linked to cultural and political contexts and provides readings of the most frequently studied plays in the light of contemporary critical thought.

Now fully updated to include discussion of criticism and performance in the last five years, a new chapter on Shakespeare on film, and a broader critical approach, this book is the essential resource for all students of Shakespeare.

Sean McEvoy teaches English and Drama at Varndean College, Brighton, UK and on the Shakespeare MA at Royal Holloway, University of London. He is editor of the *Hamlet* volume in the *Routledge Guides to Literature* series, and of a forthcoming study of Ben Jonson's plays.

ALSO AVAILABLE FROM ROUTLEDGE

SHAKESPEARE
THE BASICS

SECOND EDITION

Sean McEvoy

LONDON AND NEW YORK

First edition published 2000
by Routledge

This edition published 2006
2 Park Square, Milton Park, Oxon OX14 4RN

Simultaneously published in the USA and Canada
by Routledge
270 Madison Avenue, New York, NY 10016

Routledge is an imprint of the Taylor & Francis Group, an informa business

© 2006 Sean McEvoy

Typeset in Aldus Roman and Scala Sans by
Taylor & Francis Books
Printed and bound in Great Britain by
MPG Books Ltd, Bodmin

British Library Cataloguing in Publication Data
A catalogue record for this book is available from the British Library

Library of Congress Cataloging in Publication Data
A catalog record for this book has been requested

ISBN10 0-415-36245-8   ISBN13 978-0-415-36245-0 (hbk)
ISBN10 0-415-36246-6   ISBN13 978-0-415-36246-7 (pbk)
ISBN10 0-203-01275-5   ISBN13 978-0-203-01275-8 (ebk)

For Mum and Dad

CONTENTS

ILLUSTRATIONS

ACKNOWLEDGEMENTS

The advice of Dr Elizabeth Clark, Professor Stuart Sim and Dr Nigel Smith was much appreciated during the early stages of the work on the first edition. The detailed comments of a number of readers at a later stage were invaluable, and in particular those of Dr Jerry Brotton, Professor Rob Pope and Professor Peter Thomson. Dr Ewan Fernie has also been most helpful and supportive. Jordan Savage was an invaluable consultant on Hollywood high-school films. I also want to thank Joe Moshenska and Dr Clare Wilkinson-Weber for their particular assistance. I am most grateful to Professor Yoshitoshi Murasato, this book's Japanese translator, for valuable comments and corrections.

I would also particularly like to thank Alan Jenkins, Principal of Varndean College, Brighton, and the Warden and Fellows of Keble College, Oxford, without whose offer of an Education Fellowship in the summer of 1997 this book would never originally have been written.

Quotations from Shakespeare's plays are taken from the *Riverside Shakespeare*, second edition (1997), edited by G. Blakemore Evans, copyright of Houghton Mifflin Inc., Boston.

Credits for illustrations are as follows: the emblems on pp. 27 and 28 are from Geoffrey Whitney (1586) A *Choice of Emblems*, Leyden, and Ripa (1600) *Iconologia*; Mander and Mitchenson Theatre Collection and John Haynes for p. 89; Mander and Mitchenson Theatre Collection for p. 93; Cheek by Jowl, John Haynes and the Lyric Theatre, Hammersmith, for p. 95; the Kobal Collection for p. 110; by courtesy of The National Portrait Gallery, London, for the portrait which appears as the frontispiece; and C.

Walter Hodges for p. 80. Jane Russell drew the map on p. 163. The sources for the map are Picard (2003: plate 7) and Gurr (1992). I would also like to thank Linda Nicol at Cambridge University Press for her help with the illustrations.

Talia Rodgers and Liz Thompson at Routledge were brilliant when I first wrote this book. Rosie Waters has been a terrific editor for this second edition, ably understudied by Andrea Harthill. I am extremely grateful for their support, advice and encouragement. Liz's creativity and tactful criticism made an enormous difference to the finished first edition. Finally, I must thank Nicky yet again for her patience and support; and, for her delightful interruptions, our own sprightly first edition, Julia.

INTRODUCTION

In the course of the last twenty-five years there have been great changes in the way Shakespeare is studied at undergraduate level and above. These changes are only now beginning to take hold in schools and colleges, where character, plot and theme – ideas that rarely appear in contemporary Shakespeare studies – have until the very recent past been dominant. This can mean that when students arrive at university, they feel unprepared and surprised at what they encounter when they start to work on Shakespeare. This book attempts to address the gap between the old and the new approaches by providing a thorough general introduction to Shakespeare which is based on the way his plays are often understood at the beginning of the twenty-first century.

WHY SHAKESPEARE STUDIES CHANGED

You might wonder why it is that the older way of studying Shakespeare in terms of his plays' themes, characters, plots and imagery has been superseded. The answer lies in the changes in philosophical and political viewpoints that have taken place, particularly in the universities, since the late 1960s.

One very influential modern idea is that everything takes place in space and time, 'in history', and that consequently there are no 'timeless' or eternal qualities which endure unchanged. The notion of a 'theme', such as 'love', assumes that love is something which is constant and abstract. A play will 'illustrate' or 'deal with' love, it is said, but love isn't located *in* the play itself. Love is assumed to be the same abstract notion for both Romeo and Juliet in sixteenth-century Verona and for two young people who live in twenty-first century London, or Tokyo or Seattle. But love does not stand outside of history. It is an emotion felt by people in actual time. The nature of that emotion depends a great deal upon the kind of society in which they live, and upon its practices and beliefs. It is the same *kind* of emotion; but it is not the same idea existing independently through time *outside* its historical context. Shakespeare seems to recognize this in *Romeo and Juliet*. The lovers' affair is so fairy-tale and theatrical, and also *literary* in its conduct, that it is clearly out of place in the feuding world of cynical Veronese politics, and is therefore doomed.

Character criticism is often based on a number of assumptions. 'Characters' are supposed to be accurate portraits of imaginary *real* people who can be treated as unified individuals. Thus Hamlet is an intellectual who thinks so much that he cannot make up his mind; Othello is a 'noble' Moor who is prone to terrible jealousy. But this is not even what *real* people are like. These assumptions wilfully ignore the complex, contradictory and indefinable mass of ideas, feelings and desires that actually constitute a person. Influential modern thinkers have emphasized the subconscious, that part of us which is an unknowable but important motivating part of our psychological make-up. They have also suggested that we are created as individuals by the forms of language in which we think and express ourselves. Such ideas undermine the notion of character as something unique, unified and definable; if we are to a significant extent constituted by language, we do well to remember that language is always social and shared. Modern criticism looks first to society and social relations. Individuals are understood only in that context. And in any case the concept of 'character' in the sense that we understand it when talking about, say, nineteenth-century novels was not current in Shakespeare's time. Individuals were not seen as unique, but rather as variations on a basic template of form and substance common to all humans. Furthermore, influential writers like the French thinker Michel de Montaigne (1533–92) taught that there is no stability or consistency in our sense of who we are, in any case. The ancient writer Plutarch, whose *Lives of the Noble Grecians and Romans* in Sir Thomas North's 1579 translation was the source for Shakespeare's *Julius Caesar, Antony and Cleopatra, Coriolanus* and *Timon of Athens,* sought in his biographies to bring out the contradictions and uncertainties of human consciousness:

> we are engendered* many, according as the matter glideth* ... For were it not so, but that we continue still the same, how is it that we take delight now in these things, whereas before we joyed in others? How is it that we love and hate, praise and dispraise contrary things? ... retain not the same visage*, one countenance, one mind and one thought?
>
> (quoted in Neill 1994: 82)

> * *engendered* created; *according as the matter glideth* depending on how things turn out; *visage* facial expression; *countenance* bearing, attitude

It is often suggested in traditional criticism that the action of the play flows out of the character, rather than seeing the role as being an expression or function of the society and culture depicted in the play. Thus character critics say that Macbeth kills King Duncan because 'he is ambitious', not because he lives in a society where status and manliness depend on committing acts of daring and violence, and where loyalty is a constantly shifting thing, depending on the balance of power between warriors (see p. 217). Character criticism is ultimately unenlightening and often contains all sorts of unspoken value judgements. What is wrong, in itself, we might ask, in aspiring above your station in life, particularly in a society as rigid as Scotland's in *Macbeth*?

As for plot, just telling the story is clearly too basic for advanced study. Imagery can be understood to be pictures in the reader's mind formed by the words (see below, p. 22ff.). Its study can certainly have its uses (see, for example, pp. 203ff.) so long as we do not regard the images as timeless symbols of eternal qualities ('the flower'; 'the snake'), as happened in the past.

DID SHAKESPEARE REALLY MEAN ALL THIS?

One other important point. If you are not used to contemporary criticism you may find yourself asking 'Yes, but is that what Shakespeare really meant?'. There are two responses I would want to make here to that question. The first is the obvious one, that the only proof of what the playwright *meant* is in the words that he wrote. We have no other evidence; we cannot ask him what he was thinking at the time. But why would we want to do that anyway? Once those words have passed down to us, in the present day, all that they *can* mean is what they mean now, to us, from our own modern perspectives. Connected with this is my second response. When Shakespeare wrote, he could express the ideas and beliefs of his time only in the language of his time. These ideas, beliefs and words were formed by the society and power structures of the world he lived in. Instead of the rather fruitless game of trying to work out what was in his head when he wrote, it is much more useful and interesting to examine what it is that his plays can tell us about those ideas and beliefs. We should also consider seriously the possibility that no author might *ever* be in control of *all* the meanings in the text he or she produces, anyway.

Of course, if *he* could express himself only according to the ideas and beliefs of his time, the same constraint applies to us. When we read or see a Shakespeare play, we can understand the texts only from where we are now, with our own ideas and beliefs. Contemporary criticism therefore finds its own political and social concerns in Shakespeare's plays, and expresses these concerns in the way that it reads the plays. Feminism was a powerful force for social change in the twentieth century, and much Shakespeare criticism looks with great interest at the way women are written about in the plays. There are other contemporary issues that are important in the way we read Shakespeare today: how power is exercised in society; the nature of social justice; how language shapes the world; questions of sexuality.

To find these ideas in 400-year-old plays should not really be surprising. Shakespeare was writing at the time when the modern world and its structures of power and authority were being formed. In English literature of the late-sixteenth and early-seventeenth centuries we can see the modern world under construction, for good or for ill.

HOW TO USE THIS BOOK

Shakespeare: The Basics is in two parts, both of which will be useful to anyone studying any of the plays.

Part I sets out to explain why Shakespeare's plays were written in the way that they were. The intention is not only to help you to read the plays more easily, but to provide you with ideas that will help you to undertake the kind of close reading of a passage required for many examinations. It explains also why the plays are to be seen as scripts written for *performance*, whose full meanings are actually realized only on stage.

Part II takes in turn the plays' different types or *genres* and explains how modern critics read them. You may well want to read only those sections which include the plays you are studying, but I would encourage you to read the *whole* of the relevant section, not just the paragraphs which mention your play. Your understanding of one text is *always* enhanced by a grasp of other texts of the same type; I hope it will make you want to go on and read or see these other plays, too. I have taken examples from those most frequently studied on undergraduate courses, but what is written in each section could apply to *any* of Shakespeare's plays of that genre.

There are sections throughout the book that seek to put the plays very firmly in their historical context, by giving relevant information about social and political life in England during Shakespeare's time, and by explaining the sort of theatre for which he wrote. In these sections you will find tinted text 'boxes' in which I anchor the plays within their historical context, emphasizing the value of regarding the plays themselves as historical documents. These history boxes are not *background*, and for this reason they are not lumped together at the beginning of the book. The plays are also documents from which we can learn about the past that produced them. They are to be viewed as products of their period, not as standing out separately from it. To reflect this, I introduce the historical information in the boxes at relevant points in my discussion of the plays. At the same time, if you want to find only historical details, these boxes, which are clearly indicated in the Table of Contents, are easily recognizable as you flick through the text. The boxes also give you some information about Shakespeare's own life, in its historical and social context. There is a chronology that brings together all such information at the end of the book. There is also a glossary where some technical terms are defined and explained.

Throughout the discussion of these different aspects of the modern study of Shakespeare, I hope that I never lose sight of how exciting and beautiful these plays can be today, both in the theatre and in the classroom.

Whichever of the plays you are studying, you will find the sections on language and performance useful. You may, however, want to read only the genre chapter dealing with the particular play you are studying. Realizing that students may well dip in and out of the book in this way, I have tried to ensure that discussion of certain points is briefly repeated so that no-one using the book in this way misses anything important. If you use the book for information about specific aspects relating to one or other of the plays, it would be a good idea to read the whole of the section containing that information, so that you understand how it contributes to the broader discussion.

At the end of each genre chapter I sum up the main points you should have grasped and suggest some further areas to explore in your own thinking and study. I also suggest what to read next, offering comments on the suitability and difficulty of the different books and articles which I mention. In keeping with the usual scholarly practice I give references to the other books I have used. This is done by listing, in brackets, the author, the date of publication and the page number referred to (e.g. Ryan 2002: 48). The authors and their works are listed, in alphabetical order, in the References. Simply look for an author's surname and the year of publication, and you will find the title and other details that will help you to find the book, should you wish to consult it for yourself (a long dash instead of a name indicates that the book is by the last-named author).

For the sake of consistency, all quotations of Shakespeare's plays, unless otherwise stated, come from the *Riverside Shakespeare* (Boston, MA: Houghton Mifflin, 2nd edition, 1997). The reference I give to Act, Scene and line after each quotation will probably be very close to the format in the edition you are using. These appear as, for example, II 2 9–12, which means Act Two (II), Scene Two (2), lines nine to twelve. When I quote Shakespeare, I have glossed the difficult words and phrases. Words marked with an asterisk are explained in indented passages following the speech or speeches quoted; the number of the line in which the asterisked words occur is given in square brackets.

THIS BOOK OUTLINES ONLY ONE WAY OF STUDYING SHAKESPEARE

In this book I mostly follow one type of criticism, which happens to be the one you are most likely to meet at university. It is probably the most influential, too. This approach always sets the plays firmly in the context of the time in which they were written and in the time in which they are read. It is also influenced by certain feminist ideas. Contrasting versions of the approach are known as *new* historicism and cultural materialism. I want to stress, however, that this is certainly not the only way Shakespeare is read today, and in this second edition I have introduced some material from other kinds of criticism. There is a whole range of other critical approaches based, for example, on psychoanalysis or on gender studies, or on performance study, or on other ideas. Such critical strategies are just as interesting and just as valuable. I hope you will go on to explore these exciting ideas for yourself, once you have finished this book. No book can cover every approach to Shakespeare, and one of my main aims in this book is to give you an idea of just how many different approaches can be taken.

This book is in large part an attempt to bring together, in a form accessible to those of you beginning advanced study of Shakespeare, important work by contemporary scholars. I hope that *they* will forgive my occasional simplification of their arguments and that the book will give you, the reader, the confidence to turn to these original thinkers, and so take your study beyond the basics.

PART I

UNDERSTANDING THE TEXT

SHAKESPEARE'S LANGUAGE (1)

Your first Shakespeare play is the hardest. People sometimes talk as if reading a 400-year-old play were a process similar to reading a modern novel. They have forgotten how different a piece of writing *Macbeth* or *Julius Caesar* is from almost anything you might have read before. This opening part of the book aims to explain those differences clearly, so that you will find it easier to understand why Shakespeare can be difficult. It gives you practical advice on how to read Shakespeare's plays on your own. Finally, it goes into detail about the ways in which Shakespeare's language is constructed, which will help you analyse his work, and so increase your appreciation of it.

WRITING FOR A THEATRE AUDIENCE

This is an obvious point to start with, but a very important one. William Shakespeare, just like all the other playwrights of his time working in the London playhouses, did not write with *readers* in mind. He wrote lines for the actors to speak which had to be understood as soon as they were heard by the audience. He had no sense that he was writing for a future readership, although of course texts of the plays were occasionally published without his explicit consent in a sort of 'paperback' ('Quarto') form (see Box 1.2, p. 23). There is also considerable evidence that Shakespeare imagined that his plays

BOX 1.1 SHAKESPEARE'S AUDIENCES

In 1600 about 15–20 per cent of those living within reach of London's theatres were regular playgoers. There is considerable dispute about the make-up of the audiences at the public playhouses, but it seems that the theatre was not solely an aristocratic and middle-class interest, although the gentry did attend. Many of the middle class were in fact Puritans and opposed the theatre. Recent research indicates that a good number of playgoers would have been relatively uneducated: clerks, artisans, apprentices, women.

A skilled London worker would earn about six shillings (30p) a week. The penny entrance fee for 'the pit' was inexpensive entertainment compared to the potential cost of gambling, drinking or whoring. An afternoon at the theatre, complete with beer and hazelnuts, was affordable for many people, even if not for London's teeming poor.

It has sometimes been assumed that those who paid for standing space in the pit came along only for the spectacle, the language being beyond their comprehension. But Hamlet is clearly teasing those standing only a few feet away in III 2 9–12 in his advice to the actors. Other evidence indicates a higher level of understanding on the part of those who stood watching and listening in the pits. The most popular plays – *Hamlet, King Henry IV Parts I and II*, Marlowe's *Dr Faustus* and Kyd's *The Spanish Tragedy* – combined action and spectacle with discussion of philosophical and political ideas, which hardly indicates an ignorant, sensation-seeking audience.

There is no evidence that audiences were particularly badly behaved, or that they booed and hissed the villains. There were occasional disturbances, but it would appear that audiences on the whole listened carefully, applauding or laughing appropriately, though individuals would perhaps have been more talkative than a modern audience. Writers complain about spectators not appreciating their plays, not about them throwing fruit or storming the stage.

With the opening of the first indoor theatre at Blackfriars in 1608, audiences began to fragment. A new kind of 'aristocratic' repertoire developed for the more exclusive audience at

Blackfriars. While Shakespeare's company continued to present the same plays at this new indoor theatre and at the Globe, other outdoor theatres began to produce plays of a more populist style for their predominantly working-class audiences. Some argue that this was the beginning of the class-based theatrical tradition in the United Kingdom.

might be published together after his death and revised them with this in mind (though some scholars disagree). But that came much later. When he wrote the words to be spoken by a character, he would have had in mind an actor whom he actually knew. That man had to learn and then perform those words in a crowded, bustling, open-air theatre located in a busy and rather seedy urban environment.

It might be thought that writing which is meant to be heard, not read, would be simpler to understand than writing intended for publication. After all, the audience cannot go back to the beginning of a speech if they lose track of what is happening. But this is not necessarily so. What actually happens is that the language gets more *patterned*: it tends to have distinctive rhythms and repetitions of words, phrases and ways of saying things. This patterning helps the audience keep track of the sense of what they are hearing. Think for a moment about a joke or a political speech. A joke may often have three similar events or characters, each described in very similar words, moving towards the punchline the third time round. A political 'sound bite' will often use a memorable phrase, perhaps employing repetitions and contrasts and a satisfying and forceful rhythm ('Ask not what your country can do for you – ask what you can do for your country'). How Shakespeare's language works through this distinctive patterning is the main focus of this section.

In the modern media we are unused to long speeches, complex language and extended dialogue. Consider any contemporary film or TV programme. The speaker in a conversation in a TV drama tends to change after no more than a couple of sentences. An interviewee on a news programme is rarely allowed much more than this without being interrupted. In Shakespeare's time people were much more used than we are to listening to long and (to us) demanding passages of speech. It has been estimated that in 1600 72 per cent of men and 92 per cent of women were unable even to sign their own names (Williams 1995: 394). Because most of the audience could not read, their ability to take in spoken language had to be more developed than ours. If they did not *hear* a piece of information, there was no way they could check it by the written record. In addition, very many of those who could read could only read aloud. The ability to read silently, in your head, which we learn while still small children, had been developed by only a small minority of people.

Another difference between ourselves and Shakespeare's audience is that we live in a culture crammed with visual signs. We are surrounded by TV and computer screens, by advertising boards, by magazines, graphics and posters. Companies identify themselves by logos, increasingly, rather than names. Yet in 1600 people saw relatively few pictures or visual signs. Printing was very expensive, and woodcuts and engravings were the only means of reproducing pictures. Paintings – apart from surviving murals on the interior walls of churches – were never seen by the overwhelming majority of people, who did not enter the houses of the great. 'Emblems' (see below, pp. 27–8), printed pictures which expressed a moral of some sort, were probably the only kind of illustration regularly seen by most people. For these people the spoken word was practically the only means of communication. Thus they were better at listening than we are. It is no wonder we find that these plays take some getting used to in the theatre, let alone on the page.

CHANGES IN VOCABULARY

There is a second reason why Shakespeare can be hard to read: our language has changed in the last 400 years. While grammar – the internal structures of the language that determine which words and forms of words can be used together in order to make sense – changes very slowly over time, *vocabulary* – the words which make up a language – is constantly changing.

Vocabulary can change in three ways. Firstly, individual words can disappear altogether. Secondly, and more commonly, the meanings of words can change. Thirdly, new words are being created all the time and Shakespeare himself was not afraid to make up a word occasionally when no existing word served his purpose.

In 1500 English speakers would have understood that the word *eek* meant 'also'. Few people outside of those who have studied the history of the language would understand this word today. Before a word passes out of use altogether, however, it goes through the stage of being *archaic*: we still understand what it means, but we immediately recognize its use as self-consciously old-fashioned. If I tell you that I have just *bade* farewell to my *damsel*, boarded an *omnibus* to the *hostelry*, then *quaffed* a tankard of foaming ale, you would understand that I had just said goodbye to my girlfriend, got on a bus to a bar and drunk some beer. You would, however, realize that I was using these old-fashioned words for effect. Shakespeare is, not surprisingly, full of words which are on the way out of the language. In fact, many archaic words have been kept in use solely because people have learnt them in school when studying Shakespeare.

Linguistic conservatives are constantly trying to prevent words changing their meaning, but change is a normal and constant feature of all language, particularly where social relations are concerned. In the 1920s it was considered ill-mannered, but not illegal as it is now, for a man to *make love to* a woman in public; but what has changed is the meaning of the expression (in those days it meant to chat someone up), not the law on public decency. New readers of Shakespeare are often flummoxed by such changes in word meaning, particularly those subtle changes where the new meaning is related to the old one. For example, Hecate, the leader of the witches in *Macbeth*, says that they are going to deceive the tyrant king Macbeth into thinking he is invincible, so that when fate finally turns against him and destroys him, the blow will be all the harder. She reminds the other witches:

Hecate   You all know security
          Is mortals' chiefest enemy

(III 5 32–3)

She is using 'security' not in its modern sense of 'being safe' – clearly that would not make sense – but in its 1604 sense of 'complacency', a groundless feeling that nothing can touch you, so confident do you feel. There is a subtle but important difference. Less confusingly, although we still use the word 'chief' to mean 'most significant', 'chiefest' is an archaic form – we can see immediately what it means, but we would not say it today.

We can miss some important nuances of meaning in the plays, if we are unaware of a particular change in the English language since 1600. 'Thou' and 'you' (and their other grammatical forms thee, thy, thine, your, etc.) had distinct uses. 'Thou' was used by parents to children, and by masters to servants, and to inferiors in general. 'You' was the more respectful form, used by children to parents and servants to masters, or to social superiors (similar to the 'tu' / 'vous' distinction in French). But 'thou' was also used to those with whom you were intimate. In 1600 it was not usual to say 'I love you'. 'Thou' and 'thee' were what lovers called each other.

As for new words, Shakespeare's period was a time of great innovation. Some call the sixteenth and seventeenth centuries the 'early modern' period, which I think is useful because it suggests that Shakespeare's time stands at the beginning of the modern era in which we still live and was different from the medieval period which preceded it (see the discussion of feudalism, pp. 175ff.). Others call the period the Renaissance, meaning 'rebirth'. This is taken to imply that the art and culture of that period were in some way vastly superior to those of the 'Middle Ages', a questionable value judgement but again an indication of a marked change. Whatever we call the period, it was a time when education, scientific knowledge and contact with other countries and cultures were all rapidly increasing. Words from Greek, Latin, Italian, Spanish, Dutch and other tongues were finding their way into the language to enable people to describe and understand the new horizons – geographical, social, political, philosophical and scientific – which were opening up before them. The vocabulary of English grew at a faster rate than at any time before or since. The language grew and developed so quickly that by the early 1600s it was as different from the English spoken in 1500 as it is from the English spoken in Britain today (White 1998: 3).

As well as reflecting the changing language of his period, Shakespeare's works have a considerable influence on contemporary English. Because the plays have long had a major role in education and culture in English-speaking countries, many of the words and idioms (distinctive ways of saying things) that were new when Shakespeare was writing have found their way into the standard vocabulary of English as a world language today.

SOME WORDS IN SHAKESPEARE THAT HAVE GONE FROM OUR LANGUAGE

aroint	*go away*
beshrew	*a curse upon*
cautelous	*crafty*
decoct	*heat up*
hest	*a command*
lobe	*chilblain*
murrain	*plague*
neb	*mouth or nose*
reck	*pay attention to*
strossers	*trousers*

SOME WORDS WITH THE SAME PRIMARY MEANING, BUT WHICH IN SHAKESPEARE HAVE AN ALTERNATIVE MEANING WHICH HAS NOW PASSED AWAY

clown	*peasant*
colour	*disguise*
round	*frank*
use	*interest gained from lending money*
union	*a pearl*

SOME WORDS IN SHAKESPEARE WITH DIFFERENT MEANINGS NOW

anchor	*hermit*
boot	*something extra*
clip	*embrace*
diffidence	*mistrust*
doom	*opinion, judgement*
fond	*stupid, silly*
gentle	*of high birth*
habit	*clothes, costume*
incontinent	*at once*
nice	*shy, fastidious*
physical	*good for the health*
quick	*alive*
reprove	*disprove*
success	*outcome, whether positive or negative*
tomboy	*prostitute*

On the previous page are some examples of the kinds of difference in vocabulary you may find in reading the plays. You will have to rely on a good modern edition with clear explanatory notes on these changes. I would recommend the Oxford Shakespeare, the New Cambridge Shakespeare and the third series Arden Shakespeare.

REGISTERS OF LANGUAGE

Sometimes new readers of Shakespeare think that they are having trouble understanding the text simply because it is Shakespeare. In fact, the problem often arises because Shakespeare is deliberately making the language difficult in order to express what the character in the play is trying to do. Consider these two brief passages. In the first example, King Lear, a very old man, is waking up from a long sleep. Before he fell asleep, he was raving mad, lost on a heath in a storm and deserted by almost all those who owed him respect. He has not seen his youngest and best-loved daughter Cordelia since he banished her in a fit of rage.

King Lear   Pray do not mock me:
　　　　I am a very foolish fond old man,
　　　　Fourscore and upward, not an hour more nor less;　　60
　　　　And to deal plainly,
　　　　I fear I am not in my perfect mind.
　　　　Methinks I should know you and know this man,
　　　　Yet I am doubtful: for I am mainly ignorant
　　　　What place this is, and all the skill I have　　65
　　　　Remembers not these garments; nor I know not
　　　　Where I did lodge last night. Do not laugh at me,
　　　　For, as I am a man, I think this lady
　　　　To be my child Cordelia.

(IV 7 58–69)

It may be worth checking two words against the notes at the bottom of the page in the edition you are using: *fond* (59) means silly, not affectionate; *fourscore* (60) means eighty. Otherwise the ␣ge is clear, simple and powerful. But that is because the play ␣es King Lear to come across as having a clear mind at last.

The simple language is dramatically effective and moving in its plainness. This is a play where language has been used, up to this point, for flattering and lying, or for riddles, or to express the confused meanderings of madmen's minds. Clear, simple speech comes as a striking relief. But it shows also that Shakespeare can be very simple when that is what the dramatic situation requires.

Consider in contrast this speech from *Troilus and Cressida*. For the first time, the audience sees Agamemnon, the leader of the mighty Greek forces which have been unsuccessfully besieging the city of Troy for seven long years. What then will bring them ultimate victory? He addresses his generals:

Agamemnon Princes:
> What grief hath set these jaundies o'er your cheeks?
> The ample proposition that hope makes
> In all designs begun on earth below
> Fails in the promis'd largeness. Checks and disasters   5
> Grow in the veins of actions highest reared,
> As knots, by the conflux of meeting sap,
> Infects the sound pine and diverts his grain,
> Tortive and errant, from his course of growth.

(I 3 1–9)

Agamemnon is saying, in essence: 'It's no surprise we haven't taken Troy yet. The things we do never turn out as we expect them to.' In the first place, this less than inspiring message to the Greek high command is conveyed in a convoluted word order: the words do not come in the order which would make the overall meaning as clear as possible. Then the main ideas are conveyed in unusual ways: for example, '*ample* proposition' (3) means 'good prospects'; 'actions *highest reared*' (6) means 'important actions'. The comparison with the grain of a pine tree is not an obvious one, to say the least, and the vocabulary uses a Latin word instead of an English one whenever possible. *Conflux* (7), meaning 'flowing together', and *tortive* (9), 'twisted', were pretentious new English words adapted from the Latin by Shakespeare. This is the first time they are seen in English. He even describes the commanders' glum expressions by using a medical term: 'jaundies' (2) means 'jaundice'.

He goes on to repeat this message in the next six lines, and then says that the gods send us difficulties so that we can see who the superior men really are (i.e. himself). Yet he is proposing to do precisely nothing. The complexity and difficulty of Agamemnon's language masks the stupidity of what he is actually saying. Either he is deliberately putting up a smokescreen for fear that the other leaders will see that he has run out of ideas, or he is so pompous and vacuously self-important that he fails to realize what high-sounding nonsense is coming from his mouth. Whichever is true, the language reveals him to be an inadequate leader.

Whenever Shakespeare's language gets difficult, and the explanatory notes at the bottom of the page multiply accordingly, there is usually some reason connected with what the drama is trying to do. Shakespeare is attempting to produce a particular effect on his audience. Sometimes it will be because he is reproducing the street-language of the poor; at others, because he is sending up self-important schoolteachers or blindly passionate lovers, or stupid, brutal soldiers. These different styles or modes of language are sometimes called *registers*.

Sometimes, of course, the language is complex, as you would expect, because Shakespeare is trying to reproduce complex states of mind or feelings. If a character is trying to come to terms with, for example, the fact that his lover had betrayed him – a lover on whom he depended for his whole sense of personal identity – the complexity of the language will reflect the complexity of the thoughts and feelings it describes. Look, for example, at Troilus' speech from *Troilus and Cressida*, where the sight of Cressida's infidelity makes him lose all faith in the principles of logic itself:

Troilus	This was not she. O madness of discourse,	
	That cause sets up with and against itself!	
	Bi-fold authority,* where reason can revolt*	
	Without perdition,* and loss* assume all reason	145
	Without revolt.* This is, and is not Cressid!	

(V 2 142–6)

* [144] *Bi-fold authority* divided basis of thought; *revolt* contradict itself
[145] *perdition* loss [of sense]; *loss* loss of sense [146] *revolt* contradiction

BALANCE AND ANTITHESIS

What comes next is some advice about the structure and patterns of Shakespeare's thought. Very often the key to getting a clear understanding of a speech depends on recognizing which words or phrases are being spoken in direct connection with certain other words and phrases in the sentence. Usually the two connected words are contrasted in some way. Perhaps they are opposites in meaning; maybe one indicates a state of time later than the other; maybe they refer to different people or situations. The full sense of both words depends upon the balancing effect of each upon the other. If you stress the contrasted or balancing words as you read the speech aloud, the sense is usually made plain. This balancing of words and ideas is very common. When it involves a contrast of terms with conflicting meaning it is known as *antithesis*.

Here is an example from *Romeo and Juliet*. I have chosen it because it expresses a common Christian way of thinking in the early modern period. A single thing (including an individual human being) has an equal capacity for good or ill. The Christian world was strictly divided between God and the Devil, the saved and the damned, the good and the evil. It is hardly surprising that antithetical thinking was so common.

Friar Lawrence is a monk with a good knowledge of the natural powers of herbs and plants. At his first appearance he lets the audience in on some of his lore (the superscript numbers indicate which words are paired together by contrast, e.g. mother[1] / tomb[1] and grave[3] / womb[3]):

Friar   The earth that's nature's **mother**[1] is her **tomb**[1];
        What[2] is her burying **grave**[3], **that**[2] is her **womb**[3];   10
        As from her womb children of divers kind*
        We sucking on her natural bosom find:
        Many[4] for many virtues excellent,
        None[5] but for **some**[4], and yet **all**[5] different.
        O, mickle* is the powerful grace that lies   15
        In plants, herbs, stones and their true qualities;
        For **naught**[6]* so vile but **on**[7] the earth doth live
        That **to**[7] the earth some special good doth give;
        Nor **aught**[6]* so good but, strained* from that **fair use**[8],
        Revolts[9] from **true**[9] birth, stumbling on **abuse**.[8]   20

> **Virtue**[10] itself turns **vice**[10] being misapplied,
> And **vice**[11] sometime by **actions**[11] dignified.

> (II 3 10–22)

* [11] *divers kind* different or many kinds [15] *mickle* great [17] *naught*
nothing [19] *aught* anything; *strained* led astray

If you read this rather difficult speech aloud, stressing the words in bold type, it will make more sense. If, at the same time, you always make it sound as if the first of each numbered pair needs the second of that pair to complete the sense, the passage will be even more intelligible. Find the balancing words, read them with the right emphasis, and the pattern of logic and thought will become clear.

Two other points to notice about this speech. First, the fact that it is in rhyme has an important effect on its meaning. In English folk-culture, well-known sayings which encapsulate some wisdom are often expressed in rhyme: *Red sky at night, shepherd's delight* is a banal example. In early modern plays, rhyming couplets which express opinions often carry with them this appearance of wisdom which has rubbed off from this oral tradition. These rhyming statements are referred to by the Latin word *sententiae*.

Second, the pattern of balancing words is actually quite varied. For example, you will often find a second balancing pair completed before the first term has been matched: *a* is followed by *b*, then *b* is repeated before we reach *a* again (look at lines 19–20 in the passage above, for example). After all, if the pattern of the balancing pairs was the same all the way through, the verse would be monotonous and tedious in sound and rhythm. The skill of the writer here consists in using the conventions of early modern verse drama in a varied way according to the effects he wishes to produce.

COMPARISONS, IMAGES AND ANALOGIES

The language of early modern drama is not generally that of plain description. A great deal of the written English of the time was in verse form, and the use of *figurative* language, which is particularly characteristic of poetry, was common. By *figurative* I mean language that describes one thing by comparing it, directly or indirectly, to something else. As a simple example, to say that a freezing cold day

BOX 1.2 PLAY-TEXTS IN SHAKESPEARE'S TIME

A popular play might be printed in *Quarto* format (a paper pamphlet about 250cm by 200cm in size), but theatre companies opposed this practice, as it made the texts available to other performers. After Shakespeare's death, however, his friends John Hemmings and Henry Condell published in 1623 the so-called First Folio of his plays (a folio is a large leather-bound book). Some of the plays of Shakespeare exist only in this volume; others exist in both the Folio and the Quarto form, and there are often considerable variations between the versions.

Throughout the nineteenth and much of the twentieth century most scholars assumed that there was one perfect (but lost) original text on which both Quarto and Folio are based: what Shakespeare *really* wrote. Where several versions of a play like *Hamlet* existed, an amalgamated ('conflated') version, considered to represent what Shakespeare must have written, was produced.

A modern view is that it is a mistake to regard a play as existing in a single perfect form. Shakespeare was a working playwright well used to the fact that performances vary from one staging to the next. A popular play like *Hamlet* or *King Lear* would be adapted each time it was performed. Government censorship also required alteration of texts. Since 1559 a licence has been required to perform a play, available then from an official called the Master of the Revels. In 1606 the same official was granted the right also to license the printing of plays. The Master of the Revels could and did insist on certain cuts before a performance could take place. For example, the scene where Richard abdicates in *King Richard II* was thought too subversive at the time, when Elizabeth was increasingly infirm, but found its way into the Folio version after her death. When a play toured with a small cast, cuts would be made. In *King Lear* the differences between the Quarto and the Folio text are so significant that the Oxford Shakespeare offers two plays, *The History of King Lear* and *The Tragedy of King Lear*. The point is that there is no 'pure' text. A play-script is a blueprint for live performances, all different, and none the true version.

has an *icy grip* on you is to speak figuratively: the air is likened to a cold hand firmly grabbing hold of you. A significant part of the dramatic and the poetic effect in Shakespeare's plays is the result of carefully developed comparisons which, when they work to create a particular picture in the audience's mind, are known as *imagery*. It has been a feature of poetic writing since the time of the ancient Greeks, but in Shakespeare it gains a sophistication and a precision which call for comment.

Here is another passage from Shakespeare's Trojan War play *Troilus and Cressida*. Troilus, one of the many sons of Priam, King of Troy, is in love with Cressida. He has not spoken to her yet; he has only admired her from afar. He is employing her uncle, Pandarus, as a go-between to sing his praises to Cressida in the hope that she will agree to a meeting with him. The first time he is on stage alone with the audience he describes his situation to them in a particularly striking image:

Troilus   Her bed is India, there she lies, a pearl: 100
          Between our Ilium* and where she resides,
          Let it be called the wild and wand'ring flood;*
          Ourself the merchant, and this sailing Pandar
          Our doubtful hope, our convoy and our bark.*

                                                          (I 1 100–4)

* [101] *Ilium* another name for Troy [102] *flood* the sea [104] *bark* a ship

The image of Cressida as a pearl lying in a bed conveys a great deal about Troilus' idea of her. Firstly, her whiteness. In 1600 the fairer the skin the greater the beauty; white skin connoted goodness, and black skin wickedness in the racial thinking of the time, too. The image also suggests her feminine roundness and her exotic strangeness as a woman ('India'). A pearl is hard and unyielding, too, of course, as well as perfect in a way that no human being ever is. From the start he idealizes her impossibly. An erotic charge is clearly an ingredient. He is already imagining her in bed.

A pearl is also a thing of great value, difficult and perhaps dangerous to obtain. But he does not cast himself in the role of the adventurer who crosses the sea to win the prize. Instead he is the speculator who remains at home and waits for the employee in whom he has invested his money to do the work for him. Thus Troilus, despite the extravagant lover's language of the first part of the image, sees Cressida as an object or possession to be purchased at only material – financial – risk. Subtly, a great deal of information about his attitude to her (which will foreshadow the course of their affair) is contained in this image.

As was pointed out above (see p. 14), early modern audiences were familiar with a limited range of visual representations. An emblem was a picture which symbolized, usually allegorically, a piece of wisdom or a belief about life. The illustrations in Figure 1.1 contain some examples. 'Chapbooks', cheaply produced and roughly printed unbound editions, were often composed solely of woodcut emblems. In a society of widespread illiteracy, cheap emblem sheets were as close as you got to genuine popular literature. We know that the pages of such books were often fixed to the walls of even humble cottages. There was a whole set of well-known emblems on which 'theatrical' pictures – both on the stage itself and in the language – would draw to enhance their meaning. Queen Elizabeth was portrayed holding a sieve, not to boast her prowess in the kitchen, but because it was associated with the chaste Roman virgin Tuccia, who proved her chastity by her ability to run with a sieve full of water without losing a drop, and also with an emblem which symbolized true judgement. It implies that she could sieve good counsel from bad (White 1998: 9). The people of the time must also have been used to doing this sort of analysis on mental pictures.

Shakespeare uses allegorical images as emblems to make a moral or political point (by *allegorical* I mean telling one story in terms of another in order to pass comment on the first story). To return to King Lear: when the old king is out on the heath, deserted by his family and his court, homeless and despised, he sinks into madness. Yet in his mad ravings there is a kind of wisdom. He has seen that a king is just a man. He has experienced the sufferings of the poorest. He comes to see the nature of the power held by the rich over the poor.

King Lear   Through tattered clothes small vices do appear:
           Robes and furred gowns hide all. Plate* sin with gold,   165
           And the strong lance of justice hurtless breaks;

> Arm it in rags, a pygmy's straw does pierce it.
> None does offend, none, I say none. I'll able 'em.*

> (IV 6 164–8)

* [165] *plate* i.e. put in plate, sheet metal, armour [168] *I'll able 'em* I can vouch for this from my own experience

There are two images or emblems here. In the first we see two men, a poor man in rags and a rich man in expensive clothes. Both do wrong to others, but we cannot see the offence of the rich man because his wealth conceals it. The image is of the sores and rashes – external markers of internal moral disease – visible through the rags of the poor man but hidden by the robes of the rich. The poor and desperate who turn to crime, on the other hand, are caught and condemned. In the second emblem, wickedness is depicted as encased in a suit of golden armour: money. Even the strong lance of the state's justice cannot pierce it. Clothe wrong-doing in rags, and even the straw of a puny man can punish it. The image is saying that if you are rich, you are far more likely to get away with illegal, even wicked, behaviour than if you are poor.

Lear has, in the past, abused his power as a monarch. Now that he is poor and outcast, he can see how right and wrong in society tend to be defined by those with wealth and power. Blaming our ills on the crimes of the poor as if only they did wrong will get us nowhere. The idea that we need a better way of organizing our society is suggested by the play. Notice how a political argument is expressed in a verbally realized visual image. This is characteristic of how early modern English drama works. This sort of analysis could be replicated thousands of times for the complex images which throng the plays. Many plays contain complex patterns of repeated images which convey and explore key ideas in the drama (see, for example, pp. 203ff. below).

It is important to remember that Shakespeare and his contemporaries were working in a climate of ideas and beliefs very different from our own. Medieval thinking had been dominated by the idea that God had organized the world into a series of linked hierarchies, so that human beings were ranked as inferior to the angels but superior to animals, which in turn were superior to plants, and so on. Within these hierarchies, or 'domains', lay

(a)

(b)

(c)

Figure 1.1: Three emblems from contemporary collections

Note Each suggests a moral message of some sort:

(a) Even the most wealthy, proud and youthful will die one day.

(b) The serpent and the flower: beware the superficially attractive; danger may well lurk beneath it (see *Macbeth*, I 5 65–6).

(c) Occasio or Fortuna, an emblem of the goddess of luck. Good fortune is a beautiful woman (because she is desirable, but also proverbially fickle in her affections). She has only one lock of hair because you have only one chance to grab her as she goes by. She stands upon a wheel because fortune moves in a circular fashion: when you are at the height of your good luck, there is only one way to go, down – and vice versa (see *Hamlet*, II 2 228–36 and 492–7).

further hierarchies. A king was at the top of the human pyramid, a lion above all beasts and an eagle above all birds. While ideas were changing in Shakespeare's time, this type of thinking was still influential, and this means that we, from our modern perspectives, might find some of his analogies or comparisons surprising. For example, in medieval thought an eagle had far more in common with a king or a lion (as the chief creatures in their own domains)

BOX 1.3 THE GREAT CHAIN OF BEING AND RADICAL POLITICS

The medieval idea of the Great Chain of Being organized the world into a fixed order, with God at the top, descending successively through angels, men, women, animals, birds, fishes, insects, trees and plants to stones. There were nine orders of angels. Men were organized in a fixed order from king down to serf.

Such domains within the greater hierarchy meant that the structure of each class of being reflected the structure of creation as a whole. Even parts of the human body corresponded to other elements in society: the head was the king, the arms warriors, the hands workers, and so on. Each 'link' in the chain had power over the link below. To disobey those in authority was thus to defy the divine plan. Superiors had to be obeyed even when they seemed to do wrong (Ulysses in *Troilus and Cressida* expresses this view [I 3 75–124]).

In Shakespeare's time, those who were in positions of power wanted everyone else, including royal government, to know their rightful place, and so argued that this medieval hierarchy was divinely ordained. But in London, where a merchant class was making its own way to wealth and power, not everyone was convinced. The rise of individuals through business undermined the theory that a person is born into a particular class and must remain there. Some even argued that sovereignty lay in the people, not the monarch. At the same time, science was developing, and men like Copernicus, Galileo and Francis Bacon showed that observation and experiment could explain the world in new ways. Copernicus' proof that the earth went around the sun, and not vice versa, was known in London at this time: man was no longer at the centre of the universe. There was also a small but influential group of 'sceptical intellectuals' who made it their work to doubt everything, discarding worn-out beliefs. The writings of one such thinker, the Frenchman Michel de Montaigne (1533–92), were read by many, including Shakespeare himself. Hamlet's soliloquy (III 1 55–87) doubting the Christian idea of the afterlife can be seen as an example of how a radically minded student may have thought at this time.

Puritanism also had a significant impact. Puritans argued that a poor man's reading of the Bible was as valid as a rich man's, building upon a radical popular tradition which for hundreds of years had argued that all people should be equal. The Puritans' commitment was to God first, and to civil authority only thereafter, so that the king was no longer necessarily God's mouthpiece. Much of the age's political conflict can be ascribed to this moment when obeying God and obeying the monarch became two different things. By 1642 a king who did not behave in a godly way was no longer a king to be obeyed, and civil war followed.

than it did with other birds. Such correspondences were simply the way God had organized the world. Many thinkers still believed that there were occult, quasi-magical connections between things which resembled each other which could be harnessed for medical and other uses. The extensive use of comparison and analogy in the plays of the time reveals the way in which people might seek to acknowledge the links in what was known as the 'Great Chain of Being' and to exploit these for effect. The images become increasingly complex because, of course, Shakespeare was living in post-medieval times (and even in medieval times there were those who did not agree or act in accordance with the Great Chain and analogical thinking). Old ways of thinking were becoming mixed with new views of the way the world worked. As the example from *King Lear* shows, politics was no longer a simple question of obeying the king and accepting your place in a God-given hierarchy.

Comparative-analogical thinking of this kind came much more naturally to Shakespeare's audiences than it does to the modern reader or audience member. The creation of verbal images was also very powerful, achieving subtle, sometimes political, effects. Today we are sophisticated readers of the visual image. The challenge in reading and watching early modern drama is to hear and feel the mental pictures created by the language with the same sort of sophistication.

SHAKESPEARE'S LANGUAGE (2)

VERSE AND PROSE

When you flick through a Shakespeare play, you immediately notice the different ways in which the language is set out on the page. The majority of all but a few of the plays are written in verse, but a significant amount of all but one (*King Richard II*) is written in prose. Prose, broadly speaking, is any sort of writing which is not poetry; this book is written in prose. When writing prose, a new line is started when the text reaches the edge of the page, except in the case of a new paragraph. In verse, the poet begins a new line whenever the effect which he or she is trying to produce calls for it. Often this is because the poet wishes to keep his or her lines to a regular length. In Shakespeare this is usually a standard five-beat line (see p. 34 below).

Verse is the principal means of expression in Shakespeare, though prose is used in particular circumstances. Here I want to point out certain of the effects that are achieved by shifting between verse and prose. Generally, prose is of lower status than verse: poetry is 'elevated', noble; prose is 'prosaic', ordinary. Working-class and comic characters usually speak prose, their 'betters', the serious characters, verse, by and large. Domestic scenes between women tend to be in prose, too. And, finally, when one character has to work hard to persuade another on stage, prose tends to be used.

But that does not mean there is something unrefined and second rate about prose speech. Here is an important moment from one of the funniest and most exciting of all the plays, *King Henry IV Part I*. At the end of the play, King Henry finally engages his rebel enemies in battle. His wayward son Prince Hal (Henry or Harry) has spent many of his scenes in the play in a London tavern, drinking and jesting with a boastful, cowardly but very funny fat old knight called Sir John Falstaff. In this final battle the prince, now reconciled with his father, comes face to face with the rebels' greatest warrior, Harry Hotspur, son of the Duke of Northumberland. During their fight to the death, on which the fate of the crown depends, Sir John Falstaff waddles on stage to cheer from the sidelines. To his horror, he himself is attacked by Douglas, Hotspur's Scottish ally. No warrior, Falstaff falls down 'dead'. Douglas leaves him lying there, and leaves the stage. Hal eventually kills Hotspur and speaks nobly, in verse, over his enemy's body. Then he notices the 'corpse' of his fat old friend.

Prince Harry   What, old acquaintance! Could not all this flesh
 Keep in a little life? Poor Jack, farewell!
 I could have better spar'd a better man.
 O, I should have a heavy miss of thee,   105
 If I were much in love with vanity!*
 Death hath not struck so fat a deer to-day,
 Though many dearer, in this bloody fray.*
 Embowell'd* will I see thee by and by.
 Till then in blood by noble Percy lie. *Exit*   110
 Falstaff riseth up
Falstaff   Embowell'd? If thou embowel me today, I'll
 give you leave to powder* me and eat me too,
 tomorrow. 'Sblood,* 'twas time to counterfeit, or that hot
 termagant* Scot had paid me, scot and lot, too.
 Counterfeit? I lie, I am no counterfeit. To die is to be a 115
 counterfeit, for he is but the counterfeit of a man who
 hath not the life of the man; but to counterfeit dying,
 when a man thereby liveth, is to be no counterfeit, but

the true and perfect image of life indeed. The better part   120
of valour is discretion, in the which better part
I have saved my life.

(V 4 102–21)

* [106] *vanity* spending your time on pleasure [108] *fray* fight, battle [109]
Embowell'd Hal means buried, put in the 'bowels' of the earth, though
Falstaff takes it to mean 'disembowel', to gut, as you would an animal
before eating it. The portly Sir John certainly is 'embowelled' – possessed of
ample guts [112] *powder* season with salt and pepper [113] '*Sblood* a swear-
word, 'by God's blood' [114] *termagant* a boastful, blustering, hot-tempered
character from the old religious 'Mystery' Plays

Sir John's attitude in this speech to the audience comes across as more like common sense than the sentiment of a coward. The honour and nobility of the duel between the rival Harrys has left one of them dead on the ground. Prince Hal, speaking over the body of Falstaff, cannot resist making jokes about his size. There is an almost offensive lack of respect in the way that Hal mocks his friend, even in death. The prince uses heroic language, but there is an aristocratically arrogant harshness about it, despite its poetic qualities, even with the final rhyming couplet. In some productions of the play the audience is made even less sympathetic to Hal by having Falstaff's face, unseen by the prince, turned towards the audience so that the actor can respond to what he is hearing by his silent changes of expression. Or sometimes the 'fight' between Douglas and Falstaff is played in such a way as to make the audience think that Sir John really is dead. Hal exits at line 110. There is then a pause before Falstaff, still supine, roars the word 'Embowell——'d!' before sitting bolt upright. Audiences sometimes cheer at this point. Verse can be uplifting and beautiful, and also witty and full of energy; but it can also lose the common touch, the audience contact, that prose can give.

The point again is that we should be aware of the conventional uses of language in order to see how the writer exploits these uses for dramatic effect. When the duke enters to quell the street-fight between the Montagues and the Capulets at the beginning of *Romeo and Juliet*, he speaks the first sustained verse in the play (I 1 78–100). The earlier insults and squabbling (between the servants – see I 1

1–62) were conducted first in prose and then in two-line snatches of verse as the nobility become involved (I 1 63–77). Here, with the duke's entrance, extended verse conveys order, dignity and authority. This is the normal use. As readers, we have to identify these conventions in order to see when the dramatic situation needs to turn them on their heads.

Indeed, prose is often used purely for its dramatic impact without reference to the social status of the speaker. Sometimes it is used to break the pattern of a scene which has been running in verse, so marking the end of a particular event or atmosphere. Alternatively, it can signal the beginning of a new dramatic moment. Falstaff's shift into prose (in line 111 above), given the situation, would be just as effective whatever the social status of the speaker.

VERSE

The majority of the time, however, Shakespeare writes in *blank verse*. This term refers to lines of unrhymed poetry, each of which has five stressed syllables. The stress conventionally falls on the second, fourth, sixth, eighth and tenth syllables. The classical name for this verse form is *iambic pentameter*: each line of verse consists of five iambic 'feet' (a 'foot' being in this case a two-syllable unit comprising an unstressed syllable followed by a stressed syllable). This requires explanation.

English pronunciation requires the speaker to put emphasis on certain syllables rather than others. The writer's name is pronounced *Shake*speare, not Shake*speare*. Poetry often organizes the stressed syllables in regular patterns to create rhythm and musicality. The characteristic rhythm of the (five-stress) iambic pentameter is de-**dum**-de-**dum**-de-**dum**-de-**dum**-de-**dum**. This pattern of line is found in Chaucer, then in the poets and playwrights of Shakespeare's time, then in the work of many important subsequent poets: Milton, Pope, Keats and Tennyson for example, but also in many contemporary poets. In other words, it is the standard line in English poetry. Chaucer made his pentameters rhyme. The first writer to use unrhymed pentameters was the Earl of Surrey in his 1557 translation of the Latin epic poem *The Aeneid*. By the time Shakespeare started writing, Kyd and Marlowe had made it the standard verse form for drama, and it remained so until the writing of verse drama went out of fashion in the eighteenth century.

Here is a line of Shakespeare with the stresses just where you would expect to find them. It is Hamlet's advice to his mother soon after he has seen his father's ghost for the second time. She should be sorry, he says, for marrying Claudius and by being so avoid the vengeance that is coming:

Hamlet   Re**pent** what's **past**, a**void** what **is** to **come**.

(III 4 150)

As you can see when you read it, the second, fourth, sixth, eighth and tenth syllables are stressed. Some are long sounds ('past') and some are short sounds ('is'). Of course, if every single line had this regular pattern of stress, over the course of a three-hour play it would get rather monotonous. What happens is that the writer uses this as a framework, and then varies from it in all sorts of subtle ways. This not only gives the sound of the language interest and variety but produces particular effects which add to the meaning of what the character is saying. So, on many occasions, the pattern of the stress is irregular: this is known as *modulation*. Sometimes the actual length of the line varies, too. It all depends on the overall impact the speech is supposed to have within the context of the play.

Look now at a speech from *Hamlet*. Old Hamlet, the King of Denmark, has been murdered by his brother Claudius so that he could seize both the crown and the hand of Queen Gertrude. The murdered monarch's ghost appears to Prince Hamlet, his son, in the middle of the night. The prince has been told that a ghost looking like his father was seen walking the castle battlements, but until now he has not seen it for himself and remains unsure what the ghost is. If it is his father's unsettled spirit, it may well mean that there is some act of revenge required of the prince before the ghost can find rest. The ghost identifies itself and tells him of its sufferings in purgatory (according to Roman Catholicism, the place where the souls of the dead go, if they had committed sins not grievous enough for hell. They suffer there until the penalty for their misdeeds is paid, and then they can go to heaven.)

I have marked the text to show the actual way in which an actor or reader would stress these lines in contrast to where you would expect the regular stress to fall. The italicized syllables show where the stresses regularly fall in blank verse. The bold syllables show where I think the stresses of the line, when actually spoken, do not coincide with the normal stress pattern of the five-beat line. You might see a slightly different pattern (there is no absolutely right answer here) but my suggestions are in line with 'standard' British English speech patterns, both in 'received [dictionary] pronunciation' and in most British regional accents. In other words, as you read it, you naturally stress the underlined syllables (but you will stress the bold syllables as well). This modulation – deliberate variation from the normal de-dum-de-dum-de-dum-de-dum-de-dum pattern – gives more than variety and musicality to the line. The ear is expecting a certain regular pattern of stresses, so that when this expectation is unrealized, the words which you did not expect to hear stressed call attention to themselves and stand out. Usually (but not actually in every case) these words have significance in the dramatic impact of the speech overall. Look at the stressed words marked in bold, which fall outside the normal stress pattern.

Ghost   **I** *am* thy *fath*er's *spir*it,

> **Doom'd** *for* a *cer*tain *term* to *walk* the *night*   10
> And *for* the *day* con*fin'd* to *fast** in *fires*,
> **Till** *the* foul *crimes* **done** *in* my *days* of *na*ture
> Are *burnt* and *purged** a*way*. **But** *that* I *am* for*bid*
> To *tell* the *se*crets *of* my *pri*son-*house*,
> I *could* a *tale* un*fold* whose *light*est *word*   15
> Would *har*row *up** thy *soul*, **freeze** thy *young* *blood*,
> Make *thy* two *eyes* like *stars* **start** *from* their *spheres,**
> Thy *knot*ty *and* com*bined* *locks* to *part*,
> And *each* par*tic*ular *hair* to *stand* on *end*,
> Like *quills* up*on* the *fret*ful* *por*cupine.   20

(I 5 9–20)

* [11] *fast* go hungry [13] *purged* cleansed; *But* except [16] *harrow up* torment [17] *spheres* sockets [20] *fretful* bad-tempered

The first word in line 9 ('I') is unconventionally stressed. In theory this is true of the first syllable in a blank verse. But of course, for Hamlet, this is a terribly important syllable. With it the ghost identifies itself and satisfies the question both Hamlet and the audience have been asking. The first word of the next line ('Doomed') is not only unconventionally stressed but very long in sound. When a stress, particularly an irregular one, falls on a word with a long vowel sound, as here, the word has even more force and impact in the sentence. The fact that the ghost is inescapably condemned to years of horrific torture and fretful unrest is power-fully conveyed in that word through its place in the stress patterning of the line. To me it sounds as if the ghost is feeling particularly sorry for itself, but it could also be said in a way which scares. The fact that the ghost is eagerly looking forward to the point at which its sufferings will stop, and regrets the sins it committed on earth which have condemned it to this fate, is conveyed in the next words which stand out: 'Till' and 'done' in line 12. The next irregularly stressed word, 'But' in line 13, is an example of how modulation sometimes does not bring out the meanings of words so much as stress the overall logical development of a speech. Here the main effect is strongly to signal the beginning of a new sentence; but I suppose it also indicates the force of the divine prohibition on telling the truth about purgatory. The final two irregularly stressed words have the effect of making the physical impact of hearing the ghost's account of the horrors of the afterlife even more striking. The sudden icing-up of Hamlet's young blood is brought out in the emphasis on 'freeze'; the word 'start' jumps out at you. Indeed, this is what 'start' means here. Hamlet's eyes would jump from their sockets in shock, if he saw the torments his father must face in purgatory.

I am not, of course, suggesting that a full appreciation of Shakespeare's verse requires this sort of detailed awareness of vari-ations in the stress patterning all the time. The variations work almost subconsciously, just as, no doubt, the writer put them in without consciously striving for technical effect. But when you are looking closely at a passage from a play this is certainly something you need to be aware of in order fully to grasp how the language achieves the meanings it does.

Here is another, most dramatic, example. At the end of *King Lear*, the heartbroken old king holds in his arms the dead body of his daughter Cordelia, killed before news of her reprieve from execution could reach her. The speech includes these lines:

Lear   **Why** *should* a *dog*, a *horse*, a *rat* have *life*,
 And *thou* no *breath* at *all?* Thou'lt *come* no *more*,
 Ne*ver*, **ne***ver*, **ne***ver*, **ne***ver*, ne*ver*.

(V 3 307–9)

In a moment of terminal grief, Lear speaks a line the stress pattern of which is wholly inverted. This comes after two very nearly regular lines, apart from the powerful question posed by the irregularly stressed 'Why' in line 307. In this way it is forcefully brought home to the audience that Lear's world really has been turned upside down. Chaos is here.

Modulation of stress patterning is an important way in which the writer manipulates the rules of blank verse to produce particular effects. Altering the line length is another way of doing this. As Shakespeare developed as a dramatist, this is something he did more and more. Take, for example, the first line of the ghost's speech: 'I *am* thy *fa*ther's *spi*rit'. This is two stresses short of the standard five. There are, in fact, three syllables (dum-de-dum) missing from the full blank verse line. What this does, of course, is make the actor pause to preserve the rhythm pattern. This silence is dramatically required for the ghost's announcement to sink in. The actor playing Hamlet no doubt reacts physically, and this two-beat pause gives the audience a space to become aware of the prince's reaction.

Line 13, on the other hand, has an extra stress. It is a six-beat line, technically called an *alexandrine*. Clearly, its irregularity emphasizes its meaning: to tell more is forbidden, and that is underlined by the way 'forbid' stands out. But it is a disturbed line, with a heavy full stop followed by the irregularly stressed 'but', and it does not flow at all smoothly. Consequently, it conveys the ghost's turmoil as it contemplates the horrors and the loneliness of its predicament: being unable to share with Prince Hamlet the nature of its suffering. In order to lessen the damage to the overall rhythm, the actor may well pause for a couple of seconds at the full stop here. In the 1623 Folio text there is a question mark instead of a full stop (at the time a question-mark was used as we today would use an exclamation mark, as well as to indicate a question). Clearly, excitement and mental disturbance are to be conveyed here.

One of the commonest modulations involves stressing the first syllable (or even missing out the first unstressed syllable, the so-called 'headless' line) in order to give more impact to the opening of the line. Another is to add an extra unstressed syllable to the end of the line to give it a softer, falling, ending. Such line-ends are called 'feminine' (as distinct from the hard-stressed ending of a line, which is predictably called 'masculine').

Another verse technique used by Shakespeare concerns the interplay between sentences and lines. In the early years of the Elizabethan theatre an idea expressed in verse would sometimes have its sense clumsily completed at the end of the line, so-called 'end-stopping'. In *Hamlet* a play is put on for the court in which the characters are made to speak in old-fashioned, rhyming, end-stopped lines. It is possible that the players' language is a deliberate parody of Christopher Marlowe's dramatic verse (Marlowe died some seven years earlier, but his plays were still performed by the principal rivals of Shakespeare's company.) Here is the Player King in the *Murder of Gonzago*, as performed before the Danish court, telling his wife that he does not wish to hold her to her promise that she would never remarry after his death:

Player King   I do believe you think what now you speak,
But what we do determine* oft we break.
Purpose* is but the slave to memory,
Of violent birth, but poor validity.

(III 2 186–9)

* [187] *determine* decide [188] *Purpose* intention

End-stopping can be lumbering in its effects; but even this old-fashioned (for 1600) use can have weight and dignity, as is appropriate for the *sententia*-like wisdom (see above, p. 22) which the Player King is passing on. Had Hamlet listened to his advice, events would certainly have turned out differently.

End-stopping can be powerfully dramatic when combined with rhetorical figures (see below, pp. 44–54). Look at the famous abdication speech from *King Richard II*. King Richard, an indecisive and rash monarch open to the influence of favourites, alienates important noblemen on whom he depends for support. One of them,

Henry Bolingbroke, rightful Duke of Lancaster, first exiled by Richard, then deprived of both lands and titles, returns home to reclaim them. Richard panics and hands over power to Bolingbroke without the latter even asking for it (though neither does he refuse it). This is the moment when Richard gives in:

> King Richard   Now mark me how I will undo myself:
>   I give this heavy weight from off my head,
>   And this unwieldy sceptre from my hand,   205
>   The pride of kingly sway* from out my heart;
>   With mine own tears I wash away my balm*
>   With mine own tears I give away my crown,
>   With mine own tongue deny my sacred state,
>   With mine own breath release all duteous oaths;   210
>   All pomp and majesty I do forswear;*
>   My acts, decrees and statutes* I deny.

(IV 1 203–12)

* [206] *sway* rule [207] *balm* the sacred ointment applied to kings during the coronation ritual [211] *forswear* deny, cast off [212] *statutes* laws made in parliament

The powerful finality of each of Richard's actions is reinforced in the way the meaning is linked with the conclusive ending of each line. Contrast the way Richard's language runs on between the lines in this speech, a few scenes earlier. The king has fallen into a depressive state, fearing that he is about to lose his throne:

> King Richard   For God's sake, let us sit upon the ground   155
>   And tell sad stories of the death of kings:
>   How some have been deposed, some slain in war,
>   Some haunted by the ghosts they have deposed,
>   Some poisoned by their wives, some sleeping kill'd,
>   All murdered – for within the hollow crown   160
>   That rounds* the mortal temples of a king
>   Keeps Death his court; and there the antic* sits,
>   Scoffing his state and grinning at his pomp,
>   Allowing him a breath, a little scene,
>   To monarchise, be fear'd, and kill with looks,   165

BOX 2.1 KINGS AND QUEENS

Thirty years before Shakespeare was born, Henry VIII had nationalized the possessions of the Roman Catholic Church and created the Protestant Church of England, of which he was Supreme Head. His daughter, Elizabeth I (1558–1603), was queen for most of Shakespeare's lifetime. The early part of her reign was a time of relative peace and stability. She largely completed the process begun by her father and grandfather (Henry VII) of centralizing power and of breaking the independent fiefdoms of lords and nobles. She brought about a truce between the different wings of the Church and beat off a Spanish invasion fleet in 1588. In the years following, however, bad harvests, increasing poverty and social unrest made England a much less peaceful place. Britain, in its modern sense, did not then exist. Elizabeth I was Queen of England (and of Wales, which had been brought under the English crown by the Acts of Union of 1536 and 1543). Irish resistance to English power continued throughout Shakespeare's life. Scotland was an independent country and another hostile neighbour. Elizabeth was succeeded in 1603 by the King of Scotland, who became James I of Great Britain (1603–25). James had a more autocratic style than Elizabeth and faced opposition from Catholic rebels (the Gunpowder Plot of 1605, for instance) and from the Puritans in parliament. He and his son Charles I (1625–49) adopted a new political belief, most powerfully expressed in Catholic monarchies: *absolutism*. A feudal monarch respected the honour and rights of other lords, but the absolute monarchs saw themselves as God's sole representative on earth. Their will was absolute and they owed respect to no one. Public and court display under James I moved their emphasis increasingly away from the idea of the country as a single body, with each part carrying out its proper function, towards that of a divine king separate from the kingdom below him. The Civil War (1642–5) put an end to this idea.

Some writers ended up in prison for slandering monarchs, aristocrats or foreign dignitaries, including Shakespeare's friend Ben Jonson. Shakespeare, however, seemed to have a great deal of political acumen. In February 1601 the Earl of Essex asked for a special performance of (probably) *Richard II* to signal his impending rebellion against the queen. Shakespeare's company complied, and two members of the company were later questioned by government law officers. But they clearly did not lose royal favour in consequence; they performed before Elizabeth on the eve of the earl's execution. All of this has caused much ultimately fruitless speculation about the company's political sympathies.

Infusing* him with self and vain conceit,
As if this flesh which walls about our life
Were brass impregnable; and humoured thus,
Comes at the last, and with a little pin
Bores through his castle wall, and farewell, king!   170
                                                                    (III 2 155–70)

* [161] *rounds* surrounds [162] *antic* joker, teaser [166] *Infusing* filling up

The first sentence, listing the ways monarchs have lost their lives, runs over four lines. Then it ends suddenly and heavily in the middle of line 160: 'All murdered'. A line of blank verse has a natural pause, a *caesura*, which tends to come after the second beat, but obviously can be placed anywhere for effect. The dash falling on the caesura makes the realization strike even harder: that, rather than living happily ever after, kings are usually done to death. This feature of verse, when the sense runs on from one line into the next, is called *enjambment*. When it happens, emphasis tends to get thrown on to the word which ends the line whose sense overruns its ending, or on to the first word of the next line. This can be seen at the ends of lines 167 – 'as if this flesh which walls about our life / Were brass impregnable' – and 169 – 'with a little pin / Bores through his castle wall'. In the first case, the emphasis on the word 'life', left exposed and hanging on the end of the line before the hard and rumbling sound of 'brass impregnable', makes it seem all the more vulnerable. In the second, the word 'pin' seems similarly to be left hanging: it appears all the tinier, so that its effect, in killing a king through his castle wall, is to make the king appear more fragile still. Again, a political idea is expressed through a visual image, created verbally.

Blank verse is not blank when it rhymes. As his career progressed, Shakespeare used rhyme less and less, but there are two distinctive uses of rhyme in the plays. Most notable is the use of a pair of rhyming lines, a 'rhyming couplet', to signal the end of a scene or the whole play. The rhyming couplet seems to give a sense of completeness. *King Lear* ends with four consecutive couplets (V 3 320–7), perhaps ironically if one considers the deeply ambiguous ending of that tragedy. When a play ends without a rhyming couplet, as does *The Winter's Tale* (V 3 154–5), a sense of incompleteness is bestowed on the conclusion. Indeed, since the ending of that play presents a 'statue' coming to life as a woman who was supposed to have died sixteen years earlier, the lack of a concluding couplet is part of the general air of strangeness and provisionality surrounding the end of that play.

The other use of rhyme is to mark out a passage as distinctive from the rest of the blank verse and prose around it. It can be used to give to a saying or maxim the appearance of folk-wisdom, as in the Player King's speech quoted above (p. 39). Alternatively, it can be used in rapid dialogue to give energy, combined with a backwards and forwards movement. In an early play, *The Comedy of Errors*, two sisters, Adriana and Luciana, are arguing about men. They are waiting for Adriana's husband Antipholus to come home for dinner. He is late, and Adriana feels aggrieved at the way men feel they can make women wait at their leisure. The younger and unmarried Luciana takes the man's point of view:

Adriana	Why should their liberty than ours be more?	10
Luciana	Because their business still lies out a'door.*	
Adriana	Look when I serve him so,* he takes it ill.	
Luciana	O, know he is the bridle of your will.	
Adriana	There's none but asses will be bridled so.	
Luciana	Why, headstrong liberty* is lashed with woe:	15
	There's nothing situate under heaven's eye	
	But hath his* bound in earth, in sea, in sky.	
	The beasts, the fishes and the winged fowls	
	Are their males' subjects and at their controls:	

Man, more divine, the master of all these,   20
Lord of the wide world and wild wat'ry seas,
Indued with intellectual sense* and souls,
Of more pre-eminence than fish and fowls,
Are masters to their females and their lords:
Then let your will attend on their accords.*   25

(I 310–25)

* [1 1] *still lies out a'door* is always away from home [12] *serve him so* treat him in the same way [15] *headstrong liberty* wilful self-assertion [17] *his* its [22] *intellectual sense* reason [25] *accords* wishes

The rhyme in lines 10–13 gives the dialogue something of the quality of a ball-game, with language being lobbed from one player to the other. But do the rhyming couplets of Luciana's speech (15–25) give its sentiments an air of wisdom? Or is it that by putting in rhyme these very conventional Renaissance ideas about male natural superiority, Shakespeare makes them seem glib and naive, particularly in the mouth of the inexperienced Luciana?

RHETORIC

Consider these two items of twentieth-century language:

(a) Beanz Meanz Heinz.
(b) We shall not flag or fail. We shall go on to the end. We shall fight in France, we shall fight on the seas and oceans, we shall fight with growing confidence and strength in the air, we shall defend our island whatever the cost may be. We shall fight on the beaches, we shall fight on the landing grounds, we shall fight in the fields and in the streets, we shall fight in the hills; we shall never surrender.

The advertising copywriter of (a) has written a slogan which combines humour, a memorable jingle of sounds, and three words which build to a climax. Similarly with (b): the British Prime Minister Winston Churchill would not have inspired much resistance to the threat of German invasion in 1940 without the speech's carefully structured repetitions building towards a conclusion. It is

BOX 2.2 SOME RHETORICAL FIGURES AND TROPES

Here is a very small selection from the scores of common rhetorical figures and tropes found in Shakespeare. It will be evident that in effective rhetoric different figures and tropes can combine in the same sentence for great effect; my example of tricolon is also an example of parison and interrogatio. All the examples come from *Julius Caesar*. The republican conspirators led by Brutus and Cassius murder Caesar because they fear he is about to become monarch of Rome. Caesar's lieutenant, Mark Antony, succeeds in turning the Roman crowd against the conspirators after an inflammatory speech at Caesar's funeral.

Rhetorical figures	Definition	Example
Alliteration	Repetition of consonant sounds	'This was the most unkindest cut of all;' (Antony on the wound made by Brutus on Caesar's body, III 2 183)
Anadiplosis	Repetition of a word at the end of a line or clause at the beginning of the following line or clause	'The noble Brutus Hath told you that Caesar was ambitious. If it were so, it was a grievous fault And grievously has Caesar answered it.' (Mark Antony on the murdered Caesar, III 2 77–80)
Anaphora	Repetition of a word at the beginning of a succession of lines, clauses, etc.	'And do you now put on your best attire? And do you now cull out a holiday? And do you now strew flowers in his way That comes in triumph over Pompey's blood?' (The tribune Murellus chides the Roman crowd for cheering Caesar through the streets, I 1 48–51)

(continued on next page)

Rhetorical figures	Definition	Example
Asyndeton	Piling together words, phrases, clauses without conjunctions	'"Speak, strike, redress!"' (From the 'anonymous' letter thrown through Brutus' window urging him to action, II 1 47)
Hendiadys	One idea is expressed through two nouns	'You have some sick offence within your mind, Which by the right and virtue of my place, I ought to know of;' (Portia persuading her husband Brutus to explain his troubled behaviour, II 1 268–70)
Parison	A sequence of phrases with similar structure	'As Caesar lov'd me, I weep for him; as he was fortunate, I rejoice at it; as he was valiant, I honour him; but, as he was ambitious, I slew him.' (Brutus on the murdered Caesar, III 2 24–7)
Paronomasia	Words with similar sounds but different meanings put in opposition	'Now is it Rome indeed, and room enough, When there is in it but one only man.' (Cassius on Caesar, I 2 156–7)
Ploce	Repetition of a word in the same line or clause	'I did mark How he did shake – 'tis true, this god did shake;' (Cassius on Caesar, I 2 120–1)

(continued on next page)

Rhetorical tropes	Definition	Example
Antithesis	Words set up in opposition to each other in nearby lines or clauses	'I come to bury Caesar, not to praise him.' (Mark Antony on the murdered Caesar, III 2 74)
Hyperbole	Exaggeration	'Why, man, he doth bestride the narrow world Like a Colossus, and we petty men Walk under his huge legs, and peep about To find ourselves dishonourable graves.' (Cassius on Caesar, I 2 135 –8)
Personification	Attributing human qualities to non - human things	'See what a rent the envious Casca made; Through this the well -beloved Brutus stabb'd; And as he pluck'd his cursed steel away, Mark how the blood of Caesar followed it, As rushing out of doors to be resolv'd If Brutus so unkindly knocked or no.' (Antony on Caesar's corpse, III 2 175 –80)
Metaphor	An implicit comparison	'Poor man! I know he would not be a wolf, But that he sees the Romans are but sheep; He were no lion, were not the Romans hinds.' (Casca on Caesar, I 3 104 –6)

(continued on next page)

Rhetorical tropes	Definition	Example
Interrogation: the rhetorical question	A question which does not require an answer	'He hath brought many captives home to Rome Whose ransoms did the general coffers fill; Did this in Caesar seem ambitious?' (Mark Antony on the murdered Caesar, III 2 88–90)
Tricolon	A climax of three words or phrases	'Who is here so base that would be a bondman? If any, speak for him I have offended. Who is here so rude that will not be a Roman? If any, speak for him I have offended. Who is here so vile that will not love his country? If any, speak for him I have offended.' (Brutus justifying his actions at Caesar's funeral, III 2 29–34)

the form of this part of the speech, as much as the sentiment it contained, which makes it memorable after so many years.

It was believed, both in ancient times and in sixteenth-century Europe, that certain linguistic effects can naturally produce emotional reactions in both speakers and hearers. The study of these effects is known as *rhetoric*. From the fifth century BC the different forms and structures into which speakers crafted their language to make it persuasive, memorable or moving were listed, taught and learned in schools and universities. In the sixteenth century it was a major part of the curriculum. Skill in rhetoric was the essential quality of a public man.

Outside of academic philosophy, the word today has acquired a generally bad press: we us the phrase 'just rhetoric' to mean bluster empty of reason and logic. But, in fact, we use rhetoric all the time in our speech and writing, and nowhere more so than in advertising. In Shakespeare's time there was no pretence that rhetoric was anything other than an essential part of all literary writing. Without it, wrote George Puttenham in his *Art of English Poesy* (1589), language is 'but as our ordinary talk'. The skilful writer picks the effects that naturally inspire certain feelings and reactions, and refines them to be both elegant and appropriate to the subject matter. 'Nature herself suggesteth the figure in this or that form: but Art aideth the judgement of his use and application' (Puttenham 1936: 298).

A *figure* is one of the two main types of rhetorical effect. It is concerned mostly with the placing and positioning of words in the sentence to produce particular patterns, usually by use of repetition and its effects. Scholars catalogued very many different types of repetition, giving them Greek names such as *anaphora*, *parison*, *ploce* and *anadiplosis* (see Box 2.2). It is the overall effect of these figures, rather than their particular differences, that I want to examine. 'Figures' also include devices where the speaker exclaims and emphatically addresses his hearers (*apostrophe*), or asks of them the so-called 'rhetorical question', the answer to which is obviously implied (*interrogatio*).

The other type of rhetorical effect, the *trope*, is concerned with effects created by changing the meaning of a word. These effects are distinguished by the familiar terms by which style is analysed: metaphor, simile, irony; understatement; exaggeration; allegory (see above, p. 25); and by such less-familiar terms as synecdoche (where the part stands for the whole – 'hand' for a worker) and metonymy (where the greater is substituted for the lesser – calling a king 'England', for example).

In the plays, rhetorical figures are used by characters who are overtly seeking to persuade, but they are also a common feature of the language of verse drama.

Look at another speech from *King Richard II*. Richard has recently stepped down, and Bolingbroke is about to ascend the throne and become King Henry IV – Prince Hal's father, in fact. The Bishop of Carlisle, who is attending proceedings, objects strongly. Richard, who was God's chosen representative on earth, is still alive, but absent. No man, the bishop argues, has the right to depose God's anointed ruler. Bolingbroke (who is called 'Herford' here – 'Duke of

Hereford' was one of his titles) is no more than a thief. God will punish England for this sacrilege and condemn the country to generations of civil war. The other speaker involved, Northumberland, is one of Bolingbroke's temporary allies.

Bishop of Carlisle   I speak to subjects, and a subject speaks,
          Stirred up by God thus boldly for his king.
          My lord of Herford here, whom you call king,
          Is a foul traitor to Herford's king,   135
          And, if you crown him, let me prophesy,
          The blood of English shall manure* the ground,
          And future ages groan for this foul act.
          Peace shall go sleep with Turks and infidels,*
          And in this seat of peace tumultuous wars   140
          Shall kin* with kin and kind* with kind confound.*
          Disorder, fear, horror and mutiny
          Shall here inhabit, and this land be call'd
          The field of Golgotha* and dead man's skulls.
          O, if you rear* this house against this house,   145
          It will the woefullest division prove
          That ever fell upon this cursed earth.
          Prevent, resist it; let it not be so,
          Lest child, child's children cry against you 'woe!'
Northumberland   Well have you argued, sir, and for your pains   150
          Of capital* treason we arrest you here.

                                                        (IV 1 132–51)

    * [137] *manure* fertilize [139] *infidels* non-Christians [141] *kin* family; *kind* race; *confound* mix together in opposition [144] *Golgotha* the 'place of the skull', where Jesus was crucified [145] *rear* rear up, like a horse [151] *capital* punishable by death

It was indeed believed by some sixteenth-century historians that the furious civil wars of the fifteenth century had been a divine punishment for the usurpation of Richard's throne by Henry Bolingbroke. Two things are clear about the way the bishop's speech is written. First, we can see how Carlisle's rhetoric seeks to persuade by making it clear that the unnaturalness of the act will lead to a horrific future. Second, we can see how the bishop's faltering

BOX 2.3   SOCIAL MOBILITY

The period during which Shakespeare was writing saw great hardship for many people, but it was also a time of new social mobility. In the countryside class divisions were still pronounced. Men and women alike worked on the land, either as servants or day-labourers. Those able to rent land were known as husbandmen. If they could also afford to employ servants and labourers, they were called yeomen. Above the yeomen were the gentry and the aristocracy, whose incomes came mostly from the land which they owned.

Unemployment and hunger were generally seen as the results of laziness or greed, although parishes made some effort to help the poor. Leaving one's parish to look for work was risky. Under the 1597 Poor Law, 'masterless men' could be classed as vagabonds and sentenced to be whipped until bloody, and then returned to their home parish. Poor Tom in *King Lear* would have been a recognizable figure to audiences. Despite the risk, around 6,000 people a year entered London looking for work. Both in the capital and in the towns obedience to social superiors was still very important, but increasingly many people were making their way in the world by their own efforts. Merchants didn't always have a 'gentle' background, but commerce made them the most powerful social group in London. They made up the council of aldermen which administered the city.

Those whose livelihood was the theatre also demonstrated a certain social mobility. Shakespeare was not born into a prosperous, well-educated, land-owning family. His father John Shakespeare dealt and traded in whatever was profitably passing through Stratford-upon-Avon, including animal skins, coal, corn and malt for beer. He was probably a butcher, too. At one time chief alderman of Stratford, he was eventually arrested for debt. William Shakespeare turned out to be a far more successful businessman. He became a shareholder in the theatrical companies for which he wrote and performed, and began to acquire some wealth. In October 1596 he secured a coat of arms for his father and with it the rank of gentleman.

When the Lord Chamberlain's Company became The King's Men in May 1603, royal patronage confirmed Shakespeare's social status. Around 1613 he was able to retire to Stratford a reasonably wealthy man. He had bought the largest private house in the town, a rambling old building called New Place, and was clearly regarded as a local worthy.

control over the techniques of persuasive language will give the audience an impression of how desperate and forlorn his attempt to stop Bolingbroke is. There are many subtle uses of repetition for effect here. I shall focus on just a few.

Each of lines 133–5 uses the word 'king'. The first is genuinely meant, and refers to Richard, Carlisle's true king. The second refers, sarcastically, to Bolingbroke. The third refers back to Richard, but in a clinching way. In rhetoric the third term in a repetition tends to act as a climax. This is tricolon, 'the rule of three'. Richard is *really* 'proud Herford's king'. This is asserted by the movement of the language towards this third use. So how can Hereford-Bolingbroke be king?

The repetition of 'foul' – used first in line 135 to describe Bolingbroke – in line 138 to describe his act of taking the throne not only connects the abstraction *sacred kingship* with this ambitious personality but, coming as it does after the strange description of blood as 'manure', gives a strong impression of an England where blood and kingship have literally been turned to shit. Bolingbroke is an execrable man, and fouling will be the result of his sitting on *this* throne.

The harsh reality of civil war is well conveyed in line 141. 'Shall kin with kin and kind with kind confound' alternates a hard-*k* sound with a hard-*n* sound five times in ten syllables. Words which refer to welcoming and gentle relationships are rubbed up against each other in harsh-sounding syllables. Family relationships are turned into bruising conflicts: this much the repetition of sound and word suggests.

But after this Carlisle begins to lose his way. Just as students were taught the effective and appropriate use of rhetoric, so they were taught also to see where it is badly used. On stage, Carlisle is facing massed ranks of hard-faced and ruthless Bolingbroke supporters. As the speech unfolds, their jaws drop and their stares harden at the bishop's politically innocent effrontery. The bishop begins to realize that he is out of his depth. His language becomes more extreme, uncontrolled and less effective. The reference to Golgotha (line 44) in fact picks up the idea, expressed in certain images earlier in the play, of Richard as Christ, but the repetition of 'and dead man's skulls' would in this case be seen as unnecessary – *Golgotha* means 'place of the skull', as both the on-stage and off-stage audiences would have been aware. 'Woefullest division' is both clumsy and inadequate to describe the apocalyptic civil war predicted. The repetition in the final line, 'Lest child, child's children, cry against you woe', sounds ugly and is weak and hard to understand. In this one speech we see rhetoric working to move us; then the dramatic situation changes and the crafted balance of word and sound breaks down, as the bishop's confidence collapses.

Rhetorical effects are not all about the language of political persuasion. Sometimes they are effective in communicating the most profound emotions, too. In Act I of *Antony and Cleopatra*, Mark Antony, the great Roman general, has fallen in love with the sensual Queen of Egypt, Cleopatra. They are both mature and experienced people, but there is in their feelings for each other an intensity more commonly encountered in the expressions of those less used to such passions, which is totally absorbing. Antony has, in fact, been neglecting his responsibilities as one of the three joint-rulers of the Roman Empire and has to leave Cleopatra in Egypt to recover his political position in Rome. Cleopatra teases and irritates him. Then she relents and strives to put her feelings into words:

Antony   I'll leave you, lady.
Cleopatra   Courteous lord, one word:
       Sir, you and I must part, but that's not it.
       Sir, you and I have loved, but there's not it;
       That you know well. Something it is I would –   90
       O, my oblivion* is a very Antony,
       And I am all forgotten.

                                   (I 3 87–92)

                            * [90] *oblivion* forgetting

The structure of Cleopatra's speech is fully as rhetorical as the Bishop of Carlisle's. Yet it has an intimate, personal quality that is quite different. She is trying to find the words to express her feelings for Antony in the face of his departure. She knows she is losing something precious but cannot say clearly what it is. It might perhaps be a sense of foreboding that she is about to be abandoned and forgotten by Antony. The repetitions of line 89 seek to modify her first attempt to express herself: it is not their parting; it is not the love they have experienced together. It is something she feels, but cannot say. It is the rhythms and sounds of the repetition that communicate this, not just the words themselves. It is as full a use of rhetoric as any more obviously persuasive speech.

SUMMARY

- I have outlined the features of Shakespeare's language which you need to understand to read it with appreciation and understanding.
- I hope I have made clear that it is the *sound* of the language, in specific crafted ways, that is crucial to its meaning. This is quite unlike the characteristic modern experience of reading prose silently in your head.
- You need to be aware also of how the structure of verse and prose, and the use of rhetorical features and imagery, contribute essentially to the meaning conveyed by spoken language.

FURTHER READING

Adamson *et al.* (2001) is an excellent introduction to Shakespeare's language as speech crafted for the stage, and to the early modern English of the plays. Kermode (2000) is a very readable play-by-play exploration of Shakespeare's language. An older but very good introduction is Brook (1976). McDonald (2001) is thorough and very readable, and stresses the historical context to very good effect. Blake (1983) provides a very comprehensive account of the subject. Vickers (1971) is a good introduction to Shakespeare's rhetoric.

TYPES OF STAGE ACTION

Most drama watched today is on TV, film, DVD and video. In comparison to those media, what can actually happen in a Shakespeare play acted on stage is quite limited. The physical resources of the theatre, the number of actors involved and the size and nature of the stage constrain what can be shown to audiences. In Shakespeare's time, the types of stage activity deployed by playwrights were consequently limited in number.

Broadly speaking, what happens on stage in a Shakespeare play will consist of such elements as the following:

- dialogue involving two or more characters who ignore the audience's presence;
- dialogue involving two or more characters who occasionally speak to the audience in 'asides', or who are in some sense only partially within the 'fiction' of the play;
- soliloquy – one character alone on stage talking to the audience;
- a spectacle of some sort – a sword fight, a masque, a dumbshow, a tavern scene, a song, a dance or similar; sometimes the spectacle is watched by other characters who form an on-stage audience;
- a direct address to the audience by a chorus figure.

The first of these is a dramatic form with which we are very familiar. Our constant exposure to popular TV programmes, film and naturalistic theatre has attuned us to think that naturalism is 'proper' drama. Indeed, a significant proportion of Shakespeare's plays consists of action of this sort, the actors making no overt acknowledgement that an audience is observing them. But, as you can see from the list above, a great deal of the on-stage action tends to involve a direct recognition of the audience's presence, and as a consequence apparently loses its claim to be some sort of simple representation of reality. As the actors perform, they constantly signal to us that they know they are actors in role. If you are used to film-style naturalism, where we praise most highly acting that conveys 'realism', this acknowledgement of role awareness will seem unusual.

It seems, in fact, that the actors constantly varied their styles of performance. Sometimes they could be depicting the thoughts and feelings of characters so vividly that the audience is swept along with, and emotionally affected by, the 'reality' of what is being portrayed. Richard Burbage, who played many of the leads in Shakespeare's plays, was described by a near contemporary as capable of 'wholly transforming himself into his part and putting himself off with his clothes' (White 1998: 59). The theatre's Puritan enemies (see Boxes 3.1 and 8.1, pp. 57 and 178) regarded this ability to enchant and ensnare through the truthfulness of its representation of human behaviour as one of the stage's most dangerous qualities. They felt that wicked deeds were presented in so convincing and attractive a way that some of the audience would want to copy them.

A range of acting styles was deployed. Sometimes the style was naturalistic; sometimes actors delivered a speech formally, as an orator would at court; at other times the actors used a style which made it very clear that they acknowledged both the presence of the audience and the fictionality of what was happening on stage. Often these styles would follow one after another in the space of a few minutes. Just as the shocking and the tragic lived side by side with the silly, the absurd and the smutty in the same scene, so the style of acting would have to shift and change in an instant. Consistency, whether of character, style or mood, was not a salient characteristic of the English stage at this time. Narrative drive, engaging the audience and dramatic impact were always more important than 'consistency'; in fact, many plays glory in their inappropriately juxtaposed, but nonetheless connected, moments. Look at the way the action of *The Winter's Tale* shifts from pathos and sentimentality to horror, absurdity and smuttiness, then to mockery of that horror, all in the space of the fifty lines around the stage direction

BOX 3.1 EARLY MODERN VIEWS ON THEATRE

The Council of London Aldermen would not allow playhouses to be established in areas under their direct control. Many of the reasons they gave were practical. Those who attended the afternoon performances should have been working, so the theatre damaged the city's economy. The crowds that gathered caused disturbance. They attracted criminals and prostitutes, and they spread infectious diseases.

All this was true. But the mostly Puritan aldermen had more profound objections. Acting was not a 'respectable' but an artisan profession. Actors were associated with travelling jesters and jugglers. Any actor had to be licensed, or he would be classed as a vagabond and become subject to the harsh laws applied to vagrants. Women did not take the stage: performing *for* men would be an admission of whoredom. Successful actors seeking social advancement were mocked, even by others in the theatre. It was said that because they made their living pretending to be what they were not, actors were inherently untrustworthy people. On stage, boys pretended to be women, and common men kings. Players were thus usurping God's role in deciding how people should appear on earth. The clothes worn were often those of real lords and bishops, left to a servant who had sold them on to a company. Until 1604 the law prescribed the types of fabric and the colours which people could wear, depending on their class and income. A further complaint against actors, therefore, was that some of them overturned social distinctions by dressing in a forbidden manner. The theatre was seen to show social rank to be merely conventional and, therefore, to teach a subversive message. What is more, it encouraged crime and disobedience through the 'copy-cat' effect it would have on its audience.

'*Exit pursued by a bear*' (III 3 51–107; see p. 260). Look at the way Hamlet explicitly reminds us that the voice under the ground is not that of his tormented father's soul in purgatory, whose suffering we have just heard horrifically described (I 5 13–19), but that of a boy actor moving around the stage 'cellarage' below their feet (I 5 150–1, 162). This is how the theatre worked.

REPRESENTATION ON THE EARLY MODERN STAGE

Writers and audiences in 1600 understood the relationship between what is physically happening on stage and what those real events are supposed to represent in an 'imaginary world' in a different way from the dominant forms of representation today. The German critic Robert Weimann usefully calls these two concepts 'the play in the world' and 'the world in the play' (Weimann 2000: 12). Generally (but by no means exclusively) in modern culture we are used to thinking of 'the world in the play' (or film or TV programme) as a separate and alternative reality of which we are privileged and unseen spectators. In the late nineteenth and early twentieth centuries most theatre strove to persuade the audience that it was watching just such a piece of reality unfold: as if the fourth wall of a room had been removed so that everything within was 'revealed'. In the theatre this is known as *naturalism*, though in film and TV, which have in the main adopted the same style, it tends to be known as *realism*. But on the early modern stage there was no clear divide between these two worlds. There is never the sense that the on-stage action is in a totally different realm like that on the other side of the cinema screen or behind the proscenium arch in naturalistic drama. Actors acknowledge the fact that the audience are watching, or that they are themselves aware that they are actors playing a role. It may well be the case, as Weimann argues (see below, p. 82) that the front of the stage in the public playhouses was the conventional place for the most overt acknowledgement of the audience, but even in the most apparently 'naturalistic' scenes played upstage there could still be asides, and lines could be played 'knowingly' as lines written for the audience's appreciation and not as the 'natural' speech of the character. Furthermore, the British critic Bridget Escolme has persuasively argued that certain superficially 'naturalistic' parts in Shakespeare are written to require – indeed are incomprehensible without – the character's motivations for action arising from their relationship with the audience, for example Cressida in *Troilus and Cressida* (Escolme 2005: 39).

This is similar to, but not the same as, those forms of twentieth-century theatre that sought to break the theatrical illusion and 'estrange' their audience. Writers like Bertolt Brecht and Edward Bond strove to produce an 'epic' theatre which does not want to evoke mere unthinking emotional escapism in its audience. It does not want its audience so lost in sympathetic identification with the characters as to be unable to reflect upon the morality and politics of what is being enacted. Instead, these dramatists wanted audiences to maintain a distance and be constantly aware of the fictionality of what was portrayed. In one of Brecht's plays, for instance, a character will suddenly come out of role, come down to the front of the stage and sing a song to the audience about the on-stage situation. But in Shakespeare the audience do not need the illusion broken, because it is never complete. As Pauline Kiernan puts it, mere imitation of life is a 'dehumanising' process. Shakespeare's self-consciously aware fictional theatre is 'used to explore reality, not imitate it; realities can only be explored with such force through reality'. There is emotional engagement, too: 'we engage emotionally with a fiction, not with an imitation of life' (Kiernan 1996: 98–9).

The response expected from audiences was quite different from what is standard now. Our TV and film culture is built around star lead actors, and we are typically asked to identify with them and their 'personal' problems. Shakespeare's plays don't set out to examine the character traits and the problems of individuals as such and without reference to the wider issues. On the public stage, in front of a mixed audience, plays aimed to show a whole society at work together with the problems of people within that society. That is why in a single play there are kings and servants, warriors and jesters, noblewomen and whores, and all their lives are shown to be interconnected. It is the why and how of the events on stage that evoke the emotions and the laughter. There is no single vantage point, no one dominant character, from whose perspective we are asked to view the action of the whole play. We are given many different voices and many different perspectives between which we are asked to judge.

There is a further point. This was a largely oral culture, with limited literacy (see above, p. 13). We usually think of acting as the rendering of a written text into a fundamentally *imitative* action, but in this culture performance for its own sake, not *of* anything at all but perhaps just to show off or to delight, 'undoubtedly functioned as a crucial element in that society's whole way of life' (Hawkes 2002: 112).

There are several formal strategies in the writing which are important in this style of theatrical representation. The play is made to refer explicitly to its own status as a play.

REFLEXIVITY

The way in which the on-stage action keeps referring back to itself is known as its reflexivity. Self-reference is obvious from the language itself, with its puns and word-plays drawing attention to how a particular word or phrase is being used, as when Hamlet tells Claudius that he is 'too much in the sun ["son"]' (I 2 67; see p. 73). It is also evident in the constant playing with the conventions of verse forms and rhetoric (see p. 44 above). The delivery of the lines in live performance will bring out this self-consciousness even more clearly than when the text is merely read. But more obviously it is also there in the plays' habit of setting up *other* performances on stage and turning some characters into a second audience which the paying audience observes watching. Look, for example, at the hidden Othello observing what he *thinks* is his lieutenant Cassio boasting about taking Othello's wife, Desdemona, as his mistress (IV 1 74–170). Shakespeare's theatre was fascinated with representation. How is it that we can depict fictional men and women on stage in such a way as to make that 'world-in-the-play' a recognizable simulation of 'reality'? What happens when we do that? What is revealed about our views and ideas by our choice to represent a black man, a whore, a bishop, a legendary hero or a famous historical character on stage? The plays seem self-consciously to be constantly watching themselves at work both critically and ironically, and yet always playfully.

Here are three of the principal techniques by which the audience is made to think in these ways. They are not unique to early modern English theatre, but they are among its important constituents.

SOLILOQUIES AND ASIDES

A soliloquy is addressed by a character, alone on stage, directly to the audience. An aside is a remark or speech directed at the audience and *unheard* by the other characters on stage at the time, and is usually quite short. Depending upon how it is played, when Macbeth voices his doubts about going ahead with King Duncan's murder (I 7 1–28), the audience is either hearing what Macbeth is saying to himself or, more effectively in my opinion, being *told* by him what he is thinking. Many film versions of Shakespeare deal with the soliloquy by using the 'voice-over' convention of cinema, which we take to represent what is going through a character's mind (see below, p. 108). But this is to assume that the character is real and has 'inner thoughts'. The plays are not naturalistic and the character knows that the audience is there. We sometimes think that because a soliloquy is addressed to us, the audience, rather than to another character, it must have some special authority. But why should it? All speeches reveal 'states of mind', and in fact a character is just as capable of seducing and misleading an audience as he or she is of seducing and misleading another character.

Because asides and soliloquies involve a character talking to the audience, some sort of relationship is established between that character and the audience. Sometimes the whole audience will share one view of that character; more often individual audience members will react in different ways. In any case, we are being asked again to make a judgement about whether we accept what is being said to us, or of the credibility of the character as a reporter. Audiences will often laugh at pompous or foolish characters who confide in them. The actors sometimes respond in character to this laughter. Audiences can find themselves siding with the 'darker' forces in a play through these means, too.

Soliloquies and asides also make us complicit in what the speakers are doing. We share their viewpoints for a moment, or longer, even if we cannot agree with what they say. It is another means of making us aware that no single viewpoint predominates in a play. Here is a soliloquy from *Othello* spoken by Iago. Othello is a very successful Moorish general working for the state of Venice. He has just promoted an officer, Cassio, to be his lieutenant. This has dashed the hopes of another of his junior officers, Iago, a man in whom Othello has complete trust. We know from the first moments of the play that Iago hates his general, not least because he is black. Othello has just eloped with and married Desdemona, the daughter of a rich Venetian, against her father's wishes. Iago has secretly done his best to wreck the marriage, but the Moor's credit with the Venetian government is such that the state ignores her father's disapproval and the marriage is blessed in spite of the difference in their age and race. At the end of the third scene Iago comes, alone, to the front of the stage to share his plans for a more thorough revenge.

Iago   I hate the Moor,
              And it is thought abroad that 'twixt my sheets
              He has done my office.* I know not if it be true,
              But I, for mere suspicion in that kind,
              Will do as if for surety.* He holds* me well,   390
              The better will my purpose work on him.
              Cassio's a proper man. Let me see now:
              To get his place, and to plume up my will
              In double knavery – How, how? Let's see –
              After some time to abuse* Othello's ear   395
              That he* is too familiar with his wife.
              He hath a person and a smooth dispose
              To be suspected* – framed to make women false.
              The Moor is of a free* and open nature,
              That thinks men honest that but seem to be so,   400
              And will as tenderly be led by th' nose
              As asses are.
              I have't.* It is ingendered.* Hell and night
              Must bring this monstrous birth to the world's light.
              Exit

(I 3 386–404)

* [388] *done my office* had sex with my wife [390] *Will do as if for surety* Will act as if I were sure it is true; *holds* regards [395] *abuse* deceive [396] *he* Cassio [397–8] *He hath a person and a smooth dispose / To be suspected* His attractive appearance and smooth manners make it easy to suspect him of being a womanizer [399] *free* generous [403] *have't* have it; *ingendered* conceived

Iago's outrageous suggestion that he will act as if Othello has slept with his wife even though he's not sure it's true (388–9) might be done with a cynical leer; it might also be done with a deranged expression. Either way, the audience becomes complicit in Iago's intention and, like it or not, is soon involved in his vengeful plotting.

He actually asks them what he should do ('How, how? Let's see' [394]). Many actors who have played the part have been capable of getting members of the audience to share Iago's delight in his own powers of evil invention. We may well laugh at his accurate description of Cassio, perhaps accompanied by a comic impression (392; 397–8). Iago has an energy, an affability, a dash of that common humanity which the distant, heroic, wordy Othello lacks. We will be forced to think about the connection between male *bonhomie* – for Iago is certainly, in a colloquial British phrase, 'one of the lads' – and decent behaviour in general. What is there in his language which makes his racism, his contempt for women and his lying have an energy that proves attractive, both now and then? This is how the soliloquy works at a more significant, audience-implicating level than that of just revealing 'character'.

ON-STAGE PLAYS

We have already noted that Shakespeare depicts a group of actors putting on a play for the Danish court right at the centre of *Hamlet*. The prince has persuaded the group to insert some action into the play which mimics the murder of his father as described by the ghost. Hamlet is watching his uncle Claudius closely to see how he reacts to this dramatic re-enactment. If he shows fear or embarrassment, he thinks that it will prove the ghost's words to be true, and he can then confidently take his violent revenge. Yet the words the actors speak in the on-stage play are advising the prince *not* to act on resolutions made in passion (III 2 187–97), and warning us that our actions often have unseen consequences (III 2 210–13). Hamlet himself gets so excited during the performance that he keeps interrupting it and has to spell out the plot of the play to Claudius to make sure he gets the reference (III 2 261–4).

It is unclear from the text how Claudius reacts – it is a matter for the actor and director to decide what reaction the king actually shows. But it is clear that Hamlet thinks that drama can make us regret our actions. It can, indeed, have a *political* impact on us; but, that said, what is the effect of *Hamlet* on its audiences? Is it suggesting that it is acceptable to murder a wicked king? Is revenge always justified? But, if drama can teach moral and political lessons, why is it that Hamlet pays no attention to what the Player King is telling him? And why does the play need Hamlet as a 'chorus' (III 2 245) to interpret its meaning for the audience? Here again the very nature of stage representation is put up for our scrutiny.

Similar reflections are prompted by the performance of *Pyramus and Thisbe* by Bottom's company at the end of *A Midsummer Night's Dream* (V 1 32–355). On this occasion it is questions about dreams and art which are raised. We are asked to think about the connection between love itself and the stories we tell about love, and the contrast between the life an audience leads and the sort of world represented on the stage. When you read these lines or see them on stage, you also might think it hard to regard the Athenian men with much sympathy after their reactions to the workmen's play. There are also fully staged performances of different sorts in *The Tempest* (IV 1 60–142), *Henry VI Part II* (I 4 1–40) and *Pericles* (II 2); and there is an hilarious improvised play in *Henry IV Part I* (II 4 376–480). To these plays one could add the numerous disguises and roles played by characters pretending to be other people in Shakespeare's other plays, from Viola pretending to be the eunuch Cesario in *Twelfth Night* to the Duke's disguise as Friar Lodowick in *Measure for Measure*. Actors in Shakespeare must expect not only to play someone else but also to play someone playing someone else again: they need to learn how to portray acting. This may well mean having to think about what it actually means to *act*.

SUB-PLOT AND JUXTAPOSITION

Eighteenth-century neo-classical writers criticized Shakespeare because he disobeyed the *Dramatic Unities*. These ideas originated with the Greek philosopher Aristotle, but it was the commentaries of the Italian Ludovico Castelvetro (1505–71) that came to influence authoritatively how plays should be written. According to Aristotle and Castelvetro, the action of a play should occur in one setting (the unity of place) over the course of a single day (the unity of time); and there should be only one plot (unity of action). Shakespeare must have known of these rules, for other playwrights like Ben Jonson made a point of not breaking them; see, for example, the Prologue (lines 31–2) to *Volpone* (1606). But Shakespeare had no intention of keeping to them; nor had many of his contemporaries. His plays set out to depict a society at work, not the small group of kings, gods and heroes who are the subject of Greek tragedy.

BOX 3.2 WOMEN AND SEX

In Shakespeare's time, upper-class women had to be virgins at marriage. Property usually was passed on to a man's first-born legitimate son, and virginity was proof, in theory, that the first born was the husband's offspring. Women of other classes, too, were supposed to marry as virgins, but sex before marriage, using primitive though sometimes effective forms of contraception, was the norm. People generally married when they were in their mid-twenties, allowing couples the time to have built up some sort of reserve of property or capital. If a woman became pregnant, marriage followed irrespective of age, and this seems to have been the sequence for a large number of early modern brides. Anne Hathaway was two months' pregnant when Shakespeare married her in November 1582. He was 18, young to marry, while his bride was 26.

The high mortality rate meant that many of both sexes were widowed at a relatively young age. Remarriage was common. A widow bequeathed her husband's property was in an unusual position, as this was the only situation in which a woman might legally own and dispose of goods and estate. Otherwise women lacked the legal rights of men. In fact, according to the law a son need no longer obey his mother, once he had ceased to be a minor at the age of eight.

Many writers of the time asserted women's inferiority to men. Some drew on the medieval tradition that blamed mankind's fall on Eve. The same tradition saw a woman as a temptress, sexually insatiable once she had lost her virginity. Others thought of a woman as an incomplete man, lacking the faculty of reason and the ability to control her emotions. She was controlled, like the tides, by the fickle moon, as her menstrual cycle showed. Fluidity and excess were qualities often attributed to women in literature (see pp. 246f.). A woman's inability to control her tongue elevated silence to the position of highest female virtue. Yet all this stands against the many intelligent, witty and determined women we find in the plays of the period. And for most of Shakespeare's life the monarch was a woman.

Adultery by the wife was considered wrongful, but it was a particular disgrace on the man to be thus 'cuckolded' by his wife. On the other hand, male infidelity was, it seems, almost excused. In London brothels were plentiful and were frequented by men of all classes. While no particular shame was associated with this, there was also no cure for the venereal diseases caught there.

Reading the works of Shakespeare and his contemporaries, it seems that, outside of Puritan households, men and women were perhaps much more sexually frank than they are today. This was a society in which, after all, very little privacy was to be had. Bedrooms, even beds, were very commonly shared by family members other than the husband and wife.

Sometimes new students of Shakespeare wonder about the purpose of the minor plots in the plays. It is usual in a play for there to be a main line of action involving the noble characters, and one or more subsidiary plot lines which at first glance might be seen to be of no immediate relevance to the main narrative. They are, however, crucial to the play's overall impact. In Chapter 2 I explained how in *King Richard II* Henry Bolingbroke, Duke of Lancaster and Hereford, had taken the throne that rightfully belonged to his cousin Richard II (see pp. 39 and 49). In *King Henry IV Part I*, a group of Bolingbroke's former allies led by the Duke of Northumberland and his son Harry Hotspur are attempting, in their turn, to depose King Henry and put *their* claimant on the throne. The sub-plot of the play concerns Sir John Falstaff and his relationship with King Henry's son Prince Hal.

Falstaff is on one level Hal's alternative father, one who represents a life devoted to pleasure, irresponsibility and self-centredness. He might be seen as the sort of over-indulgent parent who has not grown up himself. He is a real contrast to the king's own stern seriousness and sense of vast responsibility. Both men show Hal affection in their different ways. Yet Falstaff is also, in a positive way, the opposite of Hotspur, England's greatest warrior, for whom honour is the most important thing in life. Indeed, with his dying breath he tells Hal that the dishonour of his defeat in single combat matters more to him than the loss of his life (V 4 78–80). Yet

Hotspur's defeat and death at Shrewsbury are the product of his own naive worship of that ideal honour. Hotspur's father, Northumberland, and his forces fail to arrive at Shrewsbury in time to fight. The rebels consider not facing the royal army in battle because they are outnumbered. Hotspur insists they should fight against these overwhelming odds because it will increase the glory and honour won by their combat (IV 1 77–8). Yet his colleagues have no such sense of honour. Vernon and Worcester, his allies, keep from him King Henry's final offer to satisfy all the rebel grievances because they think he might accept them. They also know that the king is likely to forgive Hotspur, but never themselves (V 2 1–25).

Falstaff puts all this in context in a soliloquy spoken on the morning of the battle, immediately before Worcester and Vernon plan to deceive the valour-obsessed Hotspur:

Falstaff	I would 'twere bed-time, Hal, and all well.	125
Prince	Why, thou owest God a death.* *Exit*	
Falstaff	'Tis not due yet, I would be loath* to pay him	
	before his day. What need I be so forward with him	
	that calls not on me? Well, 'tis no matter, honour pricks*	
	me on. Yea, but how if honour prick me off* when	130
	I come on? How then? Can honour set to a leg? No.	
	Or an arm? No. Or take away the grief of a wound?	
	No. Honour hath no skill in surgery then? No. What	
	is honour? A word. What is in that word honour?	
	What is that honour? Air. A trim reckoning!*	135
	Who hath it? He that died a 'Wednesday. Doth he	
	feel it? No. Doth he hear it? No. 'Tis insensible*	
	then? Yea, to the dead. But will it not live with the	
	living? No. Why? Detraction* will not suffer it.	
	Therefore I'll none of it, honour is a mere scutcheon.*	140
	And so ends my catechism.*	

(V 1 125–138)

* [126] *death* probably pronounced nearly the same as 'debt', which would explain Falstaff's next remark [127] *loath* unwilling [129] *pricks* spurs [130] *prick me off* 'marks me off on a list', presumably of casualties; but there may also be an obscene play on words here [135] A *trim reckoning!* 'A neat

little amount that adds up to!' [137] *insensible* not detectable by the senses
[139] *Detraction* people gossiping and criticizing behind your back [140]
scutcheon the shield on a nobleman's tomb [141] *catechism* questions and
answers learnt by children when preparing for confirmation into the Roman
Catholic Church

Falstaff's palpable common sense serves to point out a more
sensible and human way of living, which takes into account the
empty boastfulness and violence of the feudal code of honour. In
1600 Hotspur's ideals were shared still by many of the aristocracy.
But as values they had no real place in a world of professional
soldiers armed with pikes and muskets, and in a world where political leadership had long since ceased to be associated with skill in
battle.

But it is not just the characters in sub-plots who offer an alternative view of the values central to the main narrative: *events* in the
sub-plots also comment upon the main plot in an important way. In
Act I of *King Henry IV Part I* Falstaff hatches a plot to rob a party
of pilgrims at Gadshill on the way to Canterbury that night (see pp.
193). Hal and his friend Poins join the mugging party but disappear
just before the attack takes place. Once Falstaff and his cronies have
robbed the pilgrims, Hal and Poins appear in disguise and rob
Falstaff in turn (II 2). The idea behind Poins' joke is to hear the
'incomprehensible lies that this same fat rogue will tell us when we
meet at supper, how thirty at least he fought with . . . ' (I 1 187–8),
which they can then expose as lies. But of course these events echo
the events of the main plot. The 'martyred' Richard (Canterbury
was the shrine of the martyr Thomas à Becket) was robbed of the
crown by Henry Bolingbroke (Falstaff, Hal's alternative father);
now there is another group of robbers (Hal and Poins, mirroring
Hotspur, Northumberland and Worcester) out to rob the robber. As
in the main plot, these robbers are apparently the friends of their
intended victims.

What is being said by this parallel narrative? An equivalence is
being established between highway robbers and warring medieval
barons. In a political world where military force actually decides the
right to rule, and might is right, what difference is there between its
exercise on a lawless highway and on a battlefield where the crown
is the prize? In another echo, in the final battle at Shrewsbury in

Act V the king dresses up several of his knights to look like him, perhaps so that he might appear to be everywhere in the battle. Disguise may not be honourable, but it is effective, whether at Shrewsbury or at Gadshill. The difference is that highway robbers and footpads are punished with death by the state. Robbers of the crown are in a position where no one can punish them, so long as they maintain the might which brought them to power in the first place. They can tell the story of their coming to power in a way that justifies it, as Falstaff does in the attempt to explain his defeat.

The parallel actions of non-noble characters in Shakespeare have the effect of undermining the acts of the nobles by exposing high politics to an unflattering comparison. The actions of characters like Falstaff reveal that the difference between their deeds and those of their social superiors is one of scale only. There is nothing special about the problems of the rich and powerful; it is just that sometimes they have the capacity to turn their wrongdoings into myths which glorify them. Sometimes the sub-plot is comic. Then it serves as a mockery, a parody, of the play's main concerns. But when we laugh at serious matters, we often reveal the real truth about them.

This placing together of contrasting scenes and events in order to bring into focus key points of comparison can be called juxtaposition. It is similar to the notion of montage in film studies, and in a Shakespeare play forms an important element in the way the many voices and characters from the different social groups combine to produce that drama's overall effect. Sometimes the sub-groups have a major part to play, as in *King Henry IV Part I*; at other times the role is less significant, as in *Othello*. Sometimes main-plot characters change their way of talking and behaving and become in effect the commentating sub-plot. This is what happens in *King Lear* (see pp. 25–6): when he is mad on the heath, the king joins the ranks of the homeless and destitute and thereby points out for the audience the direct connection which exists in the same society between the conduct of the rich and powerful and the fate of the poor (III 4 28–36; IV 6 150–66).

The ways in which the various plays use juxtaposition is a topic dealt with in subsequent chapters (see e.g. pp. 190 and 251 for discussions of *King Henry V* and *The Tempest*), in which juxtaposition is considered in terms of the plays' different types, or genres.

SUMMARY

In this chapter I have argued that Shakespeare's plays, rather than attempting to present a 'realistic' picture of life, are very often aware of themselves as fiction. The means employed to remind us of their fictional status include:

- remarks indicating that the actors are speaking lines from a play; actors speaking directly to the audience;
- staging a smaller play within the main play;
- juxtaposing contrasting scenes and plot lines to encourage us to reflect on the main action and judge the play's events.

FURTHER READING

Detailed discussions of the issues covered here can be found in White (1998: Chapters 3 and 6). More advanced is Kiernan (1996); see especially Chapter 5. A thorough exploration of the possibilities of Shakespearean representation can be found in Weimann (2000). Escolme (2005) illustrates superbly the key differences between how modern naturalistic theatre seeks to depict the 'real' world, and how Shakespeare's stage was often doing something quite different.

THE PLAYS IN

PERFORMANCE

The first three chapters have looked at the language and structure of Shakespeare's plays, with one eye fixed on their meaning for theatre audiences. The plays were written for performance. To that extent it is obvious that we are missing something very crucial, if we read them as if they were poems written in dialogue form or an unusual kind of novel. In fact, the study of the play-scripts *solely* as literary texts seems to miss the entire point of how and why they were written: they are blueprints for a live performance, not texts for reading and study. Yet that is how they were primarily regarded for a very long time, from roughly the late eighteenth century until the 1970s. Some nineteenth-century critics like Charles Lamb, and even the occasional twentieth-century critic like Harold Bloom, have felt that *any* staging sullies the ideal 'performance', which it is argued exists only in the reader's mind. But this view seems wilfully perverse. In a media studies course, students would not be expected to study the *scripts* of films except in so far as they are adjuncts to our understanding of the finished film. The text alone is an incomplete realization that leaves us with a two-dimensional account of the whole experience. What we should be studying, many modern critics say, is the *performance text*: that is, the play in actual performance as experienced by an audience.

As an indication of how much there is to be added to the depth and complexity of the play-script in front of us once we imagine an actual production of the text, we can look at a crucial moment in *Hamlet*. This will demonstrate the inadequacy and thinness of a purely text-based reading of the play. It will also throw up some of the difficulties and challenges of this way of reading a Shakespeare play.

Just after his long opening speech in Act I Scene 2, Claudius turns his attention to Prince Hamlet. The stage direction (see p. 226) indicates that Hamlet does not come on stage in his due place according to social rank, but enters last. Or does he? The stage direction I quote is from the *Riverside Shakespeare*, based on the Second Quarto of the play published in 1604. The 1623 First Folio text has Hamlet in his proper place, entering third in order behind the king and queen. This is not just a matter for dry textual scholarship. If, in such a status- and ritual-conscious society, Hamlet is out of his normal place in the procession as it enters the court, what is signalled is an imbalance in the court hierarchy prompted by his desire to rebel against convention. In fact, the Quarto text may preserve playhouse practice; the Folio, published after Shakespeare's death, could well have been 'tidied up' by someone else. In any case, Hamlet has to be positioned somewhere when he gets on stage. But whatever his location, whether he is sitting on a chair to his uncle's left and with Gertrude on his right, or whether he is downstage right or left with his back to the king (where his expressions will be clearly visible during all that precedes his first line), the audience will find it significant and interpret it accordingly.

It is important to notice, too, that there is no single 'true' text to guide us here. We have three different versions of the play published between 1601 and 1623. Even if some older editions of the play 'conflate' the three into a single version, to understand *Hamlet* means appreciating that there is no precisely fixed authoritative text. This should be understood of all the plays first produced in this period (see Box 1.2, p. 23).

If he is wearing black, as the text indicates he should be (I 2 68, 77), he will stand out against the wedding clothes of the king, queen and courtiers. This is something easily missed in a reading of the play. But what does Hamlet look like? On what basis should a casting decision be made? Is he a large mature man, as Burbage must have appeared? Or does he appear a youthful and laid-back student, dressed to appeal to the youth of his time, like David Warner in Peter Hall's 1965 Royal Shakespeare Company production in England? Is he good looking? When he speaks, does he sound royal and English or does he have a different accent? Is he black, like the Americans Ira Aldridge and Morgan Smith in the suburban London theatres of the 1860s? These are not mere trivialities of casting, and while they may not occur to us when we read the play, they *do* affect our response when we see it performed. It is also worth pointing out that the reactions of individual audience members to the portrayal of Prince Hamlet will vary according to their age, gender, sexual orientation and background.

King Claudius has been talking to Laertes, the son of his chief minister, and has just granted Laertes permission to return to France. Then he turns to Hamlet:

King   But now, my cousin Hamlet, and my son——
Hamlet (Aside)   A little more than kin, and less than kind.*   65
King   How is it that the clouds still hang on you?
Hamlet   Not so, my lord, I am too much in the sun.*
Queen   Good Hamlet, cast thy nighted colour off,
         And let thine eye look like a friend upon Denmark.*

(I 2 64–9)

* [65] *A little more than kin, and less than kind* There are two meanings here, one rude and one polite. Hamlet's idea seems to be that Claudius will not be able to acknowledge publicly any hidden insult, even if he hears it. The polite meaning is: 'I am more than just a relative [kin], but not actually your son [kind].' The rude meaning is: 'I am a close relative of yours [kin], but you do not exactly treat me with affection [less than kind]' [67] *too much in the sun* Again, there are two meanings. The first is: 'You are generous in lavishing your royal presence on me' (conventionally, the king was compared to the sun); the second is: 'You are treating me like your son when I am not and do not want to be' (a play on sound: *sun, son*) [69] *Denmark* the king

The stage direction '[*Aside*]' (line 65), which indicates that Hamlet speaks to the audience, is again from the *Riverside Shakespeare* version. In fact it is not an aside in any of the three known early seventeenth-century versions (First and Second Quartos and Folio) of the play. The direction was added by an editor, Theobald, in 1726, though it may have come down as a stage tradition from Shakespeare's time. It certainly works well when delivered as an aside. It immediately establishes a conspiratorial intimacy between Hamlet and the audience, as Iago does in *Othello* (see p. 61). If, on the other hand, it is spoken publicly, so that the whole court can hear it, we have a bold, provocative and cheeky rather than a joky and conspiratorial Hamlet. Does Hamlet rise and bow to deliver his next line, or is he already standing? Is Claudius so annoyed by his riddling that the Queen has to intervene uninvited (line 68) to prevent her new husband losing his temper in public? Is there any reaction on the part of the court? Is there bitterness in Hamlet's words, or is he looking for a snigger with his sarcastic tone? Are his arms folded defensively, or do they make theatrical gestures as he speaks? These are decisions the director will make with the actor, and each such detail helps define the significance of the moment. The responses from the audience will depend also on how well members know the play and how they have seen this scene done before.

I have spent some time on this moment and these questions to illustrate that once we start thinking about the text in performance (how the play would look and be received in the theatre) as distinct from reading it as an object of study, we quickly see that its full meaning depends on a series of interpretative decisions, and that these will differ from production to production, and even, perhaps, from performance to performance of the same production. Equally, the full meaning will tend to differ for each audience member. Despite the textual variation that often exists, the play in print, on the other hand, tends to be a very much more stable entity. When we strip away the performance possibilities, the play is much more manageable as a literary artefact; but to treat it as such is a distortion of what it really is. The solution lies, I think, in the recognition that when we study a play-script we are studying something provisional. A play-script is not the finished artistic product. Literary interpretations have to be made in order to understand and present the play, but they must go hand in hand with a constant awareness of how the play will operate in the theatre, and with all the possibilities of meaning that the play has to realize for different people.

There is, after all, a fairly stable heart to the text. The play cannot mean whatever you want it to mean. In studying the plays, we are looking at the possibilities for meanings in the theatre that the scripts open up. We are not looking for *the* truth about any particular text.

Since the conditions of both performance (see the next section) and audience reception were obviously very different in Shakespeare's time, it is likely that the plays meant something to the audiences then which is different, to a greater or lesser extent, from what they mean to audiences today. In looking at the conventions of the original staging, as far as we can recover them, we can in fact discover a great deal about *why* the plays were written the way they were, and this allows us to deal with some of the matters that puzzle the modern reader used to the conventions of naturalism.

The conventions of the early modern stage are considered next. Discussion then focuses on how, in a similarly conventional way, the plays' meanings in modern times have been produced by the active work of both performers and audience at particular historical moments.

PERFORMANCE *THEN*

We have already looked at the construction of the plays and the types of language and action employed, but there are many other features that are unlike the conventions of modern drama. If you are not familiar with these plays, the way in which, for instance, change in the location of the action or the passing of time is conveyed might seem to you very unrealistic. If there was no scenery or lighting in the modern sense, wasn't the presentation rather unconvincing? Did it get confusing, with actors doubling up on roles (as they must have done) to play the large number of parts required in many of the plays? And how could anyone take seriously a youth playing the female lead role, Lady Macbeth or Cleopatra?

But why do we think that our art forms are just like 'real life', and therefore superior? The American performance scholar Alan Dessen (1986: 87–8) has written very well about the strange cinematic conventions we have no difficulty in accepting:

Although to a modern sensibility cinema may embody the epitome of realism, what is 'real' about sitting in a darkened auditorium, watching figures larger than life (especially in close-ups) projected on to a flat screen and seen through camera angles that often do not correspond to our normal viewing range, while listening to voices, not from the lips of speakers, that boom around us in stereophonic sound accompanied by music from a full orchestra (and how many of us have thought through the implications for 'realism' of background music in cinema or television)?

Audiences, from early modern times to the present, have had their own expectations of what makes a representation credible. What mattered in Shakespeare's time was that the story was told and that the action kept moving. Costumes, hand-held props or extra characters would identify a place if location were necessary. If a jailer came on leading a prisoner in chains, it was clear where the action was situated. An actor with a napkin and a knife has clearly just been eating, and his entrance will establish the locale as outside a hall or private chamber. If necessary, the script just says where they are: 'This is Illyria, lady', says the sea captain (whose costume indicates that the action takes place at a port or on a beach) to Viola when she asks where she is (*Twelfth Night* I 2 1–2). No more was necessary. Scenes which take place in the dark might seem to be a problem in an outdoor theatre where all performances took place in daylight. But the convention of torches being carried, or that of characters appearing in night-gowns, for example, worked perfectly well. Very often the characters just said it was dark and acted accordingly. In fact, Alan Dessen argues, it had certain dramatic advantages compared to modern practices. In the moonlit scenes between the lovers in Acts II and III of *A Midsummer Night's Dream*, for example, the confusion produced by the blindness of love and its analogue, magic – not darkness – is underlined by the daylight setting (Dessen 1986: 96). At the indoor Blackfriars theatre there was candlelight, but the torch convention seems to have applied there, too – though with perhaps some lowering of the light level (White 1998: 150). The audience did not expect to see 'real life' as if the fourth wall of a room had been removed and they could see the action going on within, as in modern TV or conventional drama.

The theatre was a representation, a self-conscious fiction; but, in being so, it was also much *truer* than an art which pretends that it can copy nature exactly. Pauline Kiernan (1996) has argued that Shakespeare explicitly rejected such early modern views about art as those propounded by Sir Philip Sidney. Sidney considered art that produced an exact replica of nature to have surpassed nature itself because, unlike nature's offering, this artefact would be eternal and unchanging. Shakespeare realized, says Kiernan, that this is to produce something false. Art can never reproduce nature exactly because it is *not* nature. The truth of life and nature is mutability and change. By choosing to be a playwright, Shakespeare chose an art which puts the human body, not an invisible realm of ideas, at the centre. By constantly acknowledging that its representations were both physical and fictional manifestations in real time, Shakespeare's theatre emphasized the truth that only the physical present is real; that time moves on and the past is irrecoverable; that no representation can be 'true'. The more we strive to re-create the past exactly, the more the skill of the re-creation becomes what you notice (Kiernan 1996: 10–12). Either that, or we are fooled into believing that we are seeing what 'really' happened. Both these reactions, but particularly the first, are found in response to Hollywood historical blockbusters. In that sense Shakespeare's drama is far more real than any naturalistic, 'mimetic' art form.

But why should action require a specific location? Later editors often put a place identification at the beginning of each scene because they were assuming the use of realistic painted backdrops, the fashion in theatres in the eighteenth and nineteenth centuries. But as shown in Figure 4.1 (page 80–1), Shakespeare's public stages were open, perhaps based on the idea of a galleried inn yard with a central stage.

Spectators stood in the yard area or 'pit', while permanent galleried seating ran almost all the way round the stage. The theatrical experience was quite different in these conditions. On the open stage it is the drive of the story and the action which hold the audience, so that the specific location becomes irrelevant. If it matters to the action, place will be indicated; otherwise it will not. For example, the balcony above the stage, when not used for musicians or spectators, could become a separate acting area, indicating the walls of a besieged town or the balcony of a house (this is,

BOX 4.1: PLAYHOUSES

In 1576 James Burbage erected the first purpose-built permanent playhouse in Shoreditch, and called it The Theatre. His rival Philip Henslowe opened The Rose across the river in Southwark in 1587. The Swan was built nearby in 1595, then The Globe in 1599. The earliest companies had performed in the yards of galleried inns. A scaffold was put up, with a curtained booth behind as a backstage area. The audience would stand around the scaffold in the 'pit' or, in the case of the more wealthy, sit in the galleries above. These gallery balconies still exist at old English pubs like *The Eagle* (Cambridge) or *The George* (Southwark). The same arrangements were no doubt made when, in times of plague in London, the companies went off on regional tours. It was difficult, however, to collect money for a performance, since any passer-by was able to observe. Playhouse design reflected the yard-and-stage arrangement, but no-one could get in without paying.

Since plays were performed in full daylight, spectators could see one another as clearly as they could the actors, and vice versa. Audience reactions to events on stage would have been an integral part of the spectacle. Wealthier spectators in the galleries could not avoid seeing those in the pit, who were in fact clustered at the focal point of the building. Standers could see those in the galleries. There was no one privileged position for viewing (today it is the centre of the stalls). It was possible to move around the pit during the play to get different perspectives. The experience would have been much more communal and democratic than in later centuries.

In 1608 the first professional indoor theatre with all-year-round candlelit performances was opened: the Blackfriars Theatre. Shakespeare was one of the shareholders. Basically a large rectangular room, this was a very different type of playhouse, aimed at a more aristocratic audience. To stand at The Globe or The Swan cost a penny; access to the galleries cost a further penny and it was threepence to sit in the highest gallery of all. A curtained-off lord's room cost sixpence. In contrast, just to get into the Blackfriars Theatre cost sixpence. This paid for a place in one of the three wooden galleries that ran along three sides of the auditorium. For twice that, a shilling, a bench in the pit was available (there were no standing areas). For two shillings you could sit on the stage itself, which was twenty-five feet wide, the whole theatre being only sixty-six feet from the back of the stage to the auditorium. The Civil War in 1642 closed the public theatres, but the Blackfriars had provided a model for the theatres that would open after the Restoration (1660).

however, the least visible part of the acting space). It seems that flying effects were possible from the canopy over the stage, which was painted with the sun, moon and signs of the zodiac. Ghosts could appear from or disappear into a space below the stage via a trapdoor – or devils appear, as if from hell. It was also possible that there was a 'discovery space' in the tiring-house. This would be an alcove covered by a curtain which could be pulled back to reveal a particular scene, giving the sense of a hidden, perhaps interior, space being revealed. But we should also bear in mind that many scenes take place in no specifically represented space at all. The audience did not think in that way about what they were seeing.

If we accept the replica Globe on London's Bankside as a true approximation of an early modern theatre, the depth of the stage (30 feet/10 metres at the Globe) meant that actors entering from the tiring house would be visible to the audience for as much as the duration of two lines of speech before reaching the front of the stage where the action is taking place. This offered great comic and dramatic potential. The spaces in front of and to the sides of the two pillars were shut off from the main acting area, and long asides unheard by other characters would seem plausible. This was used as a generally unlocalized space from which the comic characters would interact with the audience. They may even have done this from the pit, in the midst of the audience (White 1998: 95). As well as unlocalized, this area was undefined, being both part of the play's space and in some sense part of the audience's real world, too. It was the focal point for the entire playhouse. In this position, so close to the 'understanders' that they could touch his feet, an actor delivering a soliloquy could command the attention of the entire audience, those farthest removed from the stage being no more

The Globe Playhouse,
1599–1613

A CONJECTURAL
RECONSTRUCTION

KEY

AA   Main entrance
B   The Yard
CC   Entrances to lowest gallery
D   Entrances to staircase and upper galleries
E   Corridor serving the different sections of the middle gallery
F   Middle gallery ('Twopenny Rooms')
G   'Gentlemen's Rooms' or 'Lords' Rooms'
H   The stage
J   The hanging being put up round the stage
K   The 'Hell' under the stage
L   The stage trap, leading down to the Hell
MM   Stage doors
N   Curtained 'place behind the stage'
O   Gallery above the stage, used as required sometimes by musicians, sometimes by spectators, and often as part of the play
P   Back-stage area (the tiring-house)
Q   Tiring-house door
R   Dressing-rooms
S   Wardrobe and storage
T   The hut housing the machine for lowering enthroned gods, etc., to the stage
U   The 'Heavens'
W   Hoisting the playhouse flag

Figure 4.1 C. Walter Hodges' reconstruction of The Globe playhouse

C. Walter Hodges
1965

on of Staircase

than 40 feet/13 metres away. This area seems to have been a privileged space wherein marginal characters could offer criticism of the central characters of the drama, or frame dispassionate evaluations of the conduct of the principal action. It was where behaviour and language which break the rules are allowed because the world of the play is at least partially left behind. It is where acting tended to be least 'realistic', and the performer's relationship with the audience was more like that of a modern 'stand-up' comedian, or even that of a musician displaying personal virtuosity. It is the space in which Iago, Feste and Falstaff are active for much of their time. The German critic Robert Weimann has called this area the *platea* (Latin: 'an open street', and therefore 'an unspecified place'), as distinct from the *locus* ('a specific place'), the realm of the fully localized and historical action further upstage (Weimann 2000: 181).

If it were possible for us to join an early-seventeenth-century audience watching a production, we would encounter two codes that would mean far less to us than they would to the rest of the audience. The first is the system of ritual poses and gestures which depicted certain emotions and states, perhaps partly derived from the formal gestures taught in schools and colleges as part of rhetoric. These poses would not have been slavishly followed (even by the very worst actors), but they constituted an effective shorthand and so offered a basis from which to develop a performance. They seem to have featured in the so-called 'dumbshows' (like that in Act III Scene 2 of *Hamlet*), which summarized the plot of the play or demonstrated some action which moves the plot along. The stage direction for the Player Queen to make 'passionate action' (III 2 135, stage direction [sd]) will have meant something specific to the boy playing the role. There are plenty of clues to some of these conventional gestures. Pulling your hat down over your face, as Macduff does when he hears the news of his slaughtered family in *Macbeth* (IV 3 208), seems to have indicated extreme grief. Having your arms wrapped around your chest in a 'sad knot', like Ferdinand in *The Tempest* (I 2 224), seems to have indicated melancholy. Good acting and subtle drama clearly would have played on these conventions in a knowing way. According to Ophelia's account of Hamlet's behaviour after he has burst into her chamber, he was displaying via the conventions of gesture and dress the emotions of a thwarted lover. She seems convinced by them, but because the audience would recognize these *theatrical* conventions, Hamlet's sincerity is clearly called into doubt at this point:

Ophelia	My lord, as I was sewing in my closet,	
	Lord Hamlet, with his doublet all unbraced,*	75
	No hat upon his head, his stockings fouled,	
	Ungartered, and down-gyved* to his ankle,	
	Pale as his shirt, his knees knocking each other,	
	And with a look so piteous in purport	
	As if he had been loosed out of hell	80
	To speak of horrors – he comes before me.	
Polonius	Mad for thy love?	
Ophelia	My lord, I do not know,	
	But truly I do fear it.	
Polonius	What said he?	
Ophelia	He took me by the wrist, and held me hard,	
	Then goes he to the length of all his arm,	85
	And with his other hand thus o'er his brow,	
	He falls to such perusal of my face	
	As 'a* would draw it.	

(II 1 74–88)

* [75] *his doublet all unbraced* his jacket all unfastened [77] *down-gyved* hanging around his ankles like leg-irons (shackles which connected prisoners' ankles with a chain) [88] '*a* he

The other convention we would probably miss are the stage formations that refer to emblems (see p. 25). Sometimes the shape the actors' bodies made on stage, combined with their dialogue, would add a level of meaning by reminding the audience of one or other of these proverbial images. The English theatrical scholar Martin White has identified one such moment in Thomas Kyd's play *The Spanish Tragedy* (1592), where two lovers embrace in a way that would remind the audience of the emblem of the vine supporting the elm and keeping it upright, even in extremities. The Latin motto for this emblem (*Amicitia, etiam post mortem durans*) translates: 'Love, enduring even after death'. This is both appropriate and grimly prophetic, as the male of the pair, Horatio, is about to be murdered and hung upon a bower (White 1998: 140–1). We would miss this reference and others like it, which are hard to reconstruct today. They belonged to the semiotics (sign system) of the theatre of the time and to its art in general. Another example is afforded by the colours of costumes, which had a symbolism nearly lost to us now. Black, white, gold and red seem to have been the most common colours; green could suggest happiness and blue honesty; yellow a jealous character.

If we could go back to a public playhouse in 1600, the aspect of the staging of a play that we would find strangest would be that all the female parts were played by males, usually teenage boys. What was the reason for this practice?

Women may well have appeared on stage in the guild plays of the Middle Ages. Actresses performed publicly in Italy, France and Spain in Shakespeare's time. We know also that when visiting Italian companies appeared at court, women took their places on stage alongside the men. So why were they banned from the public theatres? And what was the attitude of the audience watching these boys in women's clothes, often playing high tragic leading roles?

The evidence can be confusing, and considerable academic controversy abounds here. Some contemporaries of Shakespeare clearly disapproved of the practice. Puritan opponents of the theatre (see Box 3.1, p. 57) quoted biblical injunctions against cross-dressing (e.g. Deuteronomy 22:5). Following the idea then common that a man was a more developed type of being than a woman (because his sexual organs were on the outside rather than still hidden within his body, and also because he possessed reason and emotional control), the Puritans argued that such transvestism was forcing the male to regress to an inferior state. Worse, it encouraged lustful thoughts among men, who would, through their confused perception of them as women, become sexually attracted to boys. The British feminist critic Lisa Jardine has suggested that this is actually *why* it was popular. This gender confusion was particularly evident when boys playing women then disguise themselves as boys, as Viola does in *Twelfth Night* and Rosalind in *As You Like It*.

There is certainly evidence that some men found erotic this casting of boys as emotionally dependent creatures. The licensing of homosexual desire in this way was one of the attractions of the

BOX 4.2: HOMOSEXUALITY IN SHAKESPEARE'S TIME

In the ancient Greek tradition, love between men was seen as a pure and noble thing. While sexual acts between men were capital offences in Shakespeare's day, individuals were hardly ever prosecuted. Homosexual acts occurred, of course, both between men and between women. There was at this time, however, no notion of an individual whose identity was 'homosexual'; indeed, historians believe that it was only in the last 100 years or so that people have begun to found their personal identity upon their sexual preference. Having sex with another man, or loving another man in a sexual way, did not make a man 'gay'. When plague struck London in 1592, the theatres were closed and Shakespeare was supported by the patronage of the Earl of Southampton. Many scholars believe that his sonnets were written to this aristocrat. If they are taken as sincere (some critics have just regarded them as a merely literary exercise), they suggest he had very strong feelings for Southampton and may well have had some sort of sexual experience with him. This was a time, though, when love for another man was not regarded as strange and while having sex with another man was strictly illegal and considered sinful, if men wanted to do it they would.

theatre. Figures like Viola dressed as Cesario 'are sexually enticing *qua* [in as much as they are] transvestied [sic] boys, and that the plays encourage the audience to view them as such' (Jardine 1983: 29). Jardine means that watching the boy playing Viola as Cesario allowed men who perhaps liked looking at young men to feel they were *really* attracted to a woman, even though they knew they were actually desiring a boy.

The American critic Steven Orgel points out, however, that homosexual desire, and even homosexual acts, were not regarded as sufficiently scandalous to necessitate such an indirect and surreptitious route to these pleasures. He sees the culture's refusal to countenance women on stage as evidencing a more deep-seated fear: that of the public unleashing of female desire (Orgel 1996a: 49). The reason usually given at the time for all-male casting was that only a 'whore' (that is, a woman who behaves promiscuously, but not necessarily a prostitute) would want to display herself on stage, showing emotion freely, for all to see. Men were scared that their authority would be compromised by their wives' infidelity. Such a representation was regarded as a provocation and encouragement to women to pursue socially unacceptable desires. The free expression of female sexuality on stage might seem to many men to be the public broaching of a range of ideas and emotions whose eventual outcome would be female adultery (see Box 3.2, p. 65). They did not want to let women publicly express sexual desire because such behaviour invites a male response.

But, Orgel points out, this was not how women saw it. The theatre's popularity among women of the time may well have stemmed, in part, from the theatre's capacity to question – by means of such conventions as males playing female roles – what were held to be fixed gender divisions in society (Howard 1994: 128). Gender roles were shown to be *performed*, not God-given or natural. Women might, at the end of a play, end up back under male control, but an alternative, a liberating suggestion, was present in the very casting of a play. Women in the audience watching an actor who was *biologically* male being taken for a woman because of the particular ways in which he talked, moved and behaved *might* have seen here the suggestion that the restrictions on women's lives were actually *also* a matter of male-imposed *convention* (just as this one was on the stage). Such restrictions, then, might have no *necessary* connection to the female anatomy. If a woman could be represented convincingly by a male actor, it was possible that the way society defined women was as un-God-given as were the conventions which governed the way characters were created on stage.

Such a political reading was certainly present at some level, but the limited evidence we have of how audiences responded to boy actors on stage seems to indicate that they were often convinced by the convention and seemed to forget that the role was being played by a boy rather than a woman (Dawson 1996: 35; White 1998: 84–5). In any case there must have been considerable variety in the levels of female impersonation executed by the boys, ranging from a studied naturalism to a camp sending-up of stereotypical 'feminine qualities' (White 1998: 87–8). As with other conventions, it seems to have been the language and the action that established the dramatic effect (in this case femininity) not the appearance of the actor's body.

This is perhaps borne out by a remarkable passage in *Antony and Cleopatra*. Finally defeated in battle by Octavius Caesar, the Roman general Antony has committed suicide and his lover, the queen of Egypt, is contemplating her fate. If taken prisoner, she may be paraded in Octavius' triumph through Rome while the people perform satirical plays about her:

Cleopatra The quick* comedians
        Extemporally* will stage us, and present
        Our Alexandrian revels: Antony
        Shall be brought drunken forth, and I shall see
        Some squeaking Cleopatra boy my greatness   220
        In the posture* of a whore.

                                    (V 2 216–21)

    * [216] *quick* lively [217] *Extemporally* improvising [221] *posture* role

In 1606–7 these lines would have been spoken by a boy. The character Cleopatra is pointing out that she is too feminine and sophisticated a person to be portrayed by an adolescent male, and yet that is exactly the status of the person playing her and speaking these lines. At this point Cleopatra *imagines* the boy who will be playing her, rather than the actor imagining the character (Dusinberre 1996b: 53). In this reversal we can perhaps see that the language, the role itself, does not depend on the physical body of the actor to create the sensual, playful and powerful role which dominates the play.

The feminist critic Juliet Dusinberre points out that, in modern times, actresses who have relied too much on their physical attractiveness in the role of Cleopatra have been less successful than those, like Judi Dench at the National Theatre in 1987 (see Figure 4.2), who have allowed *others* to make as important a contribution to her irresistible aura, in the way they describe and react to her, as the actress's own performance (Dusinberre 1996b: 54). This might provide a clue to the original portrayal of Cleopatra, suggesting that physical appearance was not as significant to the role on stage as it tends to be now.

Another interesting point to emerge from Dusinberre's discussion invokes a fascinating contrast between the play today and the play then; it may also explain some of *Antony and Cleopatra*'s impact. The role of Antony is sometimes seen as a thankless task for a leading actor. Cleopatra continually upstages him, in terms both of the play's action and of the lines she speaks. She gets the fifth act, with all its energy and poetry, to herself. The famous twentieth-century Shakespearean actor Laurence Olivier said of the role of Antony: 'it's a wonderful part. But just remember, all you future Antonys, one little word of advice: Cleopatra's got you firmly by the balls' (quoted in Dusinberre 1996b: 60).

In the original production, a boy, presumably a teenage apprentice, would have upstaged and dominated the company's leading actor, the famous Richard Burbage, in the role of Antony. The youth will come across as more sexually potent and powerful within the theatre company, and the humiliation of Antony–Burbage, in thrall to the boy-Cleopatra, will be all the greater. This is a dimension to the performance obviously lost today, and it underlines yet again how the meaning of the play is tied to the specific circumstances of its production and its reception by the audience.

PERFORMANCE *NOW*

I want to illustrate this last point by looking at three twentieth-century productions. I have chosen the first two because of their obvious political engagement with issues of race, gender and sexuality at the times when they were performed. The presentation of these themes on Shakespeare's stage, in a society in which white heterosexual men enjoyed power and authority over all others, is of particular interest to contemporary critics. My third selection is one of the most successful American productions of recent years. I will look briefly at how, in each case, production choices – including the time and place of performance – underlined the political significance of these theatrical events.

Of course, the analysis of Shakespeare in performance need not be framed by an explicitly political agenda. Exciting and significant productions can produce their meanings for particular audiences without being primarily engaged with any of these issues (though I feel that they are always present in some form). Two of the three

Figure 4.2 Judi Dench as Cleopatra and Anthony Hopkins as Antony in the 1987 National Theatre production of *Antony and Cleopatra*

productions discussed below were in contexts in which race, in one case, and gender and sexuality, in the other, were certain to be in the foreground. I have chosen these productions because they allow me to illustrate how the concerns of contemporary criticism – issues of power and social justice – can intersect with close readings of 'performance texts'.

PAUL ROBESON'S OTHELLO

How relevant is skin colour to the casting of a Shakespeare play? What effect will the casting of black actors in particular roles have on the meaning the play has for its audiences? The answer seems to be that it all depends on the roles, the audience and the moment at which the performance takes place.

The casting of Othello, the black general in the service of Venice whose colour is so important to the play, is a particularly interesting issue. Othello the Moor marries the white Desdemona and is then falsely persuaded by his lieutenant, Iago, that she has been unfaithful to him (see p. 61). Othello kills her, and then himself when he discovers the truth. He is very much a black outsider in a white world. Ira Aldridge in the nineteenth century was, so far as we know, the first black actor to take the role. Aldridge, an American who came to Europe to escape the racially segregated theatres of the United States, was never engaged by either of the principal London theatres, Covent Garden and Drury Lane, though he had been acclaimed as the 'African Roscius' (Vaughan 1994: 181). The first black Othello in London's West End theatres was Paul Robeson, at the Savoy in 1930.

The son of a former slave, Robeson had made his name at Drury Lane in 1928 in the American musical *Showboat*. He remains a controversial figure. A fighter for civil rights and a socialist, he lost his US passport for 'un-American activities' during the 1950s and spent his later life in exile. The casting of Robeson as Othello was not, however, motivated by anti-racism. Racism had developed slowly throughout the nineteenth century. By the early twentieth century it was felt by many 'educated' people – particularly in the United States, where black slavery had been completely abolished only in 1865 – that blacks and whites were intellectually and emotionally so dissimilar as to belong to different species. This racist view was, of course, strenuously opposed by many others. But it came to be thought that a rational, civilized, white man who was in control of his emotions was temperamentally unsuited to the role of Othello. A theory of racial difference, then, not an egalitarian principle, underlay Robeson's casting.

Although Robeson was at first very self-conscious (Vaughan 1994: 183) about playing love scenes with a white woman (Peggy Ashcroft as Desdemona – see Figure 4.3), there was no obvious opposition from London audiences to the casting of Robeson (though Ashcroft did receive hate mail, and Robeson himself was not made welcome at the Savoy Hotel that adjoins the theatre [Vaughan 1994: 183]).

Even so, Robeson saw the project as political in his own terms. He saw the Moor not as in any sense 'primitive', but simply as having come from a different culture – and it was as a defence of that culture's dignity that Robeson intended his own performance. He later told a theatre historian:

> [Othello] is intensely proud of his colour and culture; in the end, even as he kills, his honour is at stake, not simply as a human being and as a lover, but as Othello. The honour of his whole culture is involved.
>
> (Quoted in Vaughan 1994: 196)

The production did not, however, allow him to realize this aim. The sympathy and humanity that an audience may have seen in the performance were undermined by crucial directorial decisions. The set, created by an inexperienced designer, ensured that most of the action took place right at the back of the stage, itself separated from the front of the audience by an orchestra pit. The lighting was often very dim, and Desdemona's death at Othello's hands was hidden by bed curtains. Much of the emotional impact of the playing, then, was muffled by the distance, or otherwise obscured, and the audience was unable to experience the characters' feelings at close hand. It was as if the director had been worried about exposing the audience too closely to inter-racial love. Furthermore, all reviewers seem to have agreed that Maurice Browne's Iago lacked any real wickedness, cunning or energy. His lines were cut to the extent that he had neither rapport with the audience nor presence as a demonic tempter.

Iago had been told by the director that his hatred of the Moor sprang from frustrated homosexual lust, but did not involve racial feeling. This made Othello's emotional outbursts appear all the more irrational and overblown – perhaps what was expected of what one reviewer, James Agate, called 'nigger Shakespeare' (Vaughan 1994: 188). Robeson's tight costume, European rather than Moorish, detracted from his dignity. Again Agate gave expression to gross racial stereotypes: 'his hands appeared to hang below his knees, and his whole bearing, gait, and diction were full of humility and apology: the inferiority complex in a word' (quoted in Vaughan 1994: 188). Some reviewers lamented Robeson's inability to speak the verse adequately. Others praised his performance because he fitted the stereotype of the simple, trusting, emotion-driven black man expected by the white middle-class audience. The literary critic John Dover Wilson later wrote of the performance that 'trustfulness and simplicity ... seem [Othello's] by nature when he is played by a Negro gifted with all the winning integrity of that race' (quoted in Vaughan 1994: 190).

Perhaps Robeson's political ambitions for the project would always have foundered on the prejudices of a West End audience in 1930. The point remains, however, that decisions involving casting, cutting, design and directorial approach undermined whatever chance the production had of emphasizing the humanity the black Othello shared with white people, both on and off stage.

Fear of racist opposition prevented Robeson playing Othello in America until 1943. Indeed, no financial backers could be found, and a new director, the British actor Margaret Webster, eventually got the project going by casting unknown actors in the main parts and opening the run before liberal audiences at Harvard and Princeton universities. Stars were unwilling to risk taking part and no Broadway theatre would back the project. Though Webster saw the role in academic and racial terms, this time the production allowed the power and dignity of Robeson's performance to come through. *Othello* was a great success. It transferred to Broadway and completed a national tour, becoming at that time the longest running Shakespeare production in US history (Vaughan 1994: 193). Robeson was very proud of his achievement and considered it a blow against racial prejudice in general (Vaughan 1994: 192). Wartime America, her citizens black and white fighting side-by-side

Figure 4.3 Paul Robeson as Othello and Peggy Ashcroft as Desdemona in the 1930 production at the Savoy Theatre, London

(albeit usually in different units), was clearly a more receptive audience than the London of 1930, and the production allowed sympathy to develop for the Moor.

Laurence Olivier wore black make-up as the Moor in 1964, as did Anthony Hopkins for the BBC Shakespeare video in the 1980s. Both were controversial castings. Such make-up is too redolent of the racist stereotype of the 'nigger minstrel' to be acceptable today. Moreover, there are too many black actors obviously capable of excelling in the role to justify a white Othello on the professional stage. Yet we are used now to seeing black performers in 'white' roles in Shakespeare, and even 'siblings' and 'sons' of different colours on stage, which audiences seem to accept without demur. At the time of writing, there has yet to be a black Hamlet, Macbeth or King Lear in Britain at the Royal Shakespeare Company (RSC) or National Theatre, but it can be only a matter of time, and such casting would not crucially affect audience response. Adrian Lester played the Prince in Peter Brook's 2001 *Hamlet*; David Oyelowo will play Prince Hal for the RSC in 2007. Yet a white Othello?

Othello is, for us, a play about race and colour. These are very much live issues today, though they would not have been (at least not in the same way) in 1604. Consequently, I think audiences will be more critically aware of the casting than they would be in a production of *Hamlet* or *King Henry IV*. Perhaps there is a clue here to how early modern audiences saw transvestite casting: often they ignored it, but when sexuality or gender was at issue in the text, an awareness that they were watching males dressed as females would have been very much to the fore in their minds.

CHEEK BY JOWL'S AS YOU LIKE IT

How significant is the gender of an actor to the casting of a Shakespeare play? It seems to depend upon the audience response it produces in a particular production. It also, of course, depends on the play itself.

The main action of *As You Like It* requires the heroine, Rosalind, to disguise herself as a boy, Ganymede, while she is in exile in the Forest of Arden. There she comes across her lover Orlando, who does not recognize her. As Ganymede, she tells Orlando that his love for Rosalind is 'madness' and that she can 'cure' him of it (III 2 399–405), if he pretends to court her as if Ganymede really were Rosalind. To prove his love he agrees, and engages in witty banter with the 'youth' as if he were 'her' lover (IV 1 38–196). So, in a conventional modern production the actress playing a woman pretends to be a boy pretending to be a woman. But if a *male* plays Rosalind, of course, then in this scene a male impersonates a female impersonating a male impersonating a female.

In scenes like this, the way in which *gender* is represented on stage is clearly going to be the substance of the comedy. The humour would be expected to arise from the caricature of 'male' and 'female' qualities and behaviour.

Cheek by Jowl was probably the 1990s' most imaginative and successful group of British performers of classical drama. When the company chose to stage the play at the Lyric Theatre (in Hammersmith, west London) in 1991 with an all-male cast (see Figure

Figure 4.4 Adrian Lester (Rosalind) and Patrick Toomey (Orlando) in Cheek by Jowl's *As You Like It*, Lyric Theatre, Hammersmith, London, 1995

4.4), some critics were cynical. Director Declan Donnellan and designer Nick Ormerod are gay and, in the general climate of hostility towards homosexuality which was encouraged by certain individuals in the Conservative government and the tabloid press at the time, there was some suggestion that the casting was an excuse for transvestite camping. ('Camp' is usually understood to mean, in this context, an ironically self-aware, over-theatrical parody of effeminacy, often accompanied by an acerbic wit.) This had been the case in an earlier production of the play. In the very different climate of sexual politics that followed the decriminalization of homosexuality, Clifford Williams had in 1967 produced a 'coy and camp' (Holland 1993: 128) version of the play for the National Theatre. It was a liberal ('swinging sixties') response which saw homosexuality as an amusing and harmless comic subject for a 'straight' audience. Almost twenty-five years later Benedict Nightingale, writing in *The Times* (5 December 1991), did not think Donnellan's production had moved on very far. He declared the production to be 'lively if limited'. The effect of the casting was 'no more, if no less than to give the play a strong homoerotic feel'. Tom Hollander, as Rosalind's friend Celia, affected 'the slightly camp, mincing voice only seldom to be found among gay men, let alone women'. Over three years later in the same paper (27 January 1995) Jeremy Kingston *did* admit that the production was 'marvellously funny, though the sight of men playing women is usually the source of it'.

But between these two dates the play had been enormously successful both in Britain and all over the world. *The Australian* (according to Michael Billington in the *Guardian*, 16 March 1992) called it the best Shakespeare seen in Adelaide since 1970. The production played to excited audiences on both sides of the Atlantic. They didn't see it as arch and camp; rather they found it 'marvellous' (Alan Sinfield in the *Guardian*, 27 April 1992), 'exhilarating' (Holland 1993: 128) and, indeed, 'as the audience liked it' (Bate 1996: 6). Donnellan's 'directorial conception was deeply and committedly . . . [an] unabashed celebration of gay desire' (*ibid.*).

Its success was doubtless due in part to the direct simplicity of its staging and costumes, and the energy and irreverence of its style of popular theatre. The famous speech beginning 'All the world's a stage, / And all the men and women merely players' (II 7 139–40) was put at the beginning. On the second line the cast divided into their gender roles, and at this point Adrian Lester became Rosalind merely by donning a shapeless dress and old lady's spectacles. He removed them whenever he became Ganymede. The forest was produced by clever lighting effects and some strips of green cloth. A tuba and trombone accompanied the songs and some energetic dancing.

The play did more than just provoke laughter, 'pathos and tenderness', as the *Guardian* (6 December 1991) put it. The 'exhilaration' seems to have been produced by the way the casting and the acting explored the nature of love as it is depicted in the text: 'The problem of love and desire was defined as lying beyond gender, simply coming into being, irresistibly and unaccountably' (Holland 1993: 128). Homosexual desire between men playing men in the text wasn't hidden but clearly depicted (Jaques, Le Beau and Orlando); there were also different representations of female desire as played by men, or by men pretending to be women pretending to be men. But instead of being caricatured or mannered, these representations were seen to be at once *conventional* and yet *still* moving. The audience heard the words and saw the gestures of these different lovers, but the play was performed to suggest that love is something *different* from the gender or sexuality of those who have that feeling. When, at the end, Rosalind revealed to Orlando that she was Ganymede all the time, there was no glib, conventional, smiling acceptance. It took time for Orlando to overcome his shock and shame to come downstage to claim her, his love having overcome all. The production had a commitment to lived experience and emotion despite its play with the sign language, theatrical and otherwise, of love and gender.

Two academics, Jonathan Bate and Peter Holland, were among those who saw the production. Bate (1996: 6–7) said this:

> The extraordinary thing about Adrian Lester was that, with his beautiful voice and grace of movement, when he played the female Rosalind playing at being the male Ganymede he seemed more like a woman playing a man than a man playing a woman. And when he played at Rosalind playing Ganymede playing Rosalind, one simply gave up trying to work out in one's mind whether one thought he was a woman playing a man playing a woman or a man playing a woman playing a man playing a woman.

Holland (1993: 128) observed that the

> play-acting of Rosalind–Ganymede was both more intriguing and simpler than it usually is when a woman plays Rosalind but the tremendous erotic charge between Rosalind and Orlando had nothing glibly homoerotic about it. Instead one enjoyed the gaps of gender action as when Orlando playfully punched Ganymede's arm and Rosalind awkwardly and tentatively returned the male gesture, though the actor could clearly have made the gesture with ease.

As literature professors, Jonathan Bate and Peter Holland are very aware of the debates about whether gender is something we are born with or something that is socially constructed (see pp. 230ff.). They located the play's power, in this production, in its ability to lay bare the common human emotion love, which is beyond how we talk, how we dress, what we do in bed (or even with which sex organs we are equipped). The production's distinctive celebration of love accounted for its extraordinary impact. University English departments are not, I am sure, usually centres of overt discrimination against homosexuality. These two academics brought with them to the performances they watched an attitude towards sexuality that, in either case, proved receptive to what Donnellan was doing.

I am not arguing that the play teaches a universal and 'timeless' message about love. But I am arguing that this production found in the text a meaning which in performance had a particular impact at a time of shifting attitudes towards love and sexuality.

At the same time, there were women who objected to the portrayal of Audrey, the 'lascivious goat-girl', as the female stereotype of sexiness and intelligence never going together, and did find it a homosexual romp. More conservative reviewers, confident that Shakespeare's original audience 'cannot have thought of the Rosalinds, Violas and Portias as male at all' (*The Times*, 5 December 1991), seemed to have similar opinions. But what Cheek by Jowl demonstrated – at least to those who at that time were disposed to see the production *both* in and out of its gay context – was that the all-male casting did change the meaning of the play and in doing so took it to a more profound level. Such a reading, whether the director intended it or not, was not available in 1967, when acceptance of the 'naturalness' of homosexuality was much less wide-spread. The political-social outlook on sexuality was at that time far more restricted in its scope and sophistication. Productions of Shakespeare's plays are the products of times in which they are conceived and performed. But they also act on those times to change the people who see them. Cheek by Jowl's *As You Like It* did not, I am sure, make very many of its audience more narrow-minded about love and sexuality.

SHAKESPEARE IN NEW YORK: KEVIN KLINE'S FALSTAFF

In the mid-nineteenth century Shakespeare was a central part of popular entertainment in the United States. Indeed, the Astor Place riots in New York in 1849 were the result of a clash between US nationalists championing their own star Shakespearean, Edwin Forrest, against a perceived assertion of English cultural superiority in the figure of the actor William Charles Macready (Foulkes 2002: 19–20). In the twentieth century, however, two home-grown art forms – the cinema and the stage musical – became dominant in popular culture both in the USA and, when exported, in much of the rest of the world.

A production of *Henry IV* opened at the Vivian Beaumont Theatre in New York City's Lincoln Center on 20 November 2003. The dramaturge Dakin Matthews had adapted the two texts of Part I and Part II, moving the order of some scenes and adding some of his own linking dialogue. This particular production was praised as a genuine piece of American Shakespeare. One critic wrote that this *Henry IV* 'lays to rest all the talk about Americans being unable to match Shakespeare's countrymen in capturing the soul of his characters and doing justice to his language' (Sommer 2003: 1), and another that it 'restores faith in the notion that high-caliber Shakespeare in New York need not be spoken with British accents' (Peter Marks in the *Washington Post*, 23 December 2003). In the role of Falstaff, the fat old drunken knight who is the dissolute companion of Prince Hal (see above, p. 32, and below, pp. 193ff.), was the Oscar-winning Kevin Kline, regarded by some as the 'American Olivier'. The acclaim which the production won from both critics and audience can be considered in the light of its appeal to particularly American sensibilities.

In Britain, actors who become film stars often begin their careers performing Shakespeare in the National Theatre or the Royal Shakespeare Company. Obvious examples are Judi Dench, Ian McKellen and Patrick Stewart. In America it seems more common for established film stars to demonstrate their mastery of the craft by acting in Shakespeare, whose cultural status remains high in the USA despite his eclipse as popular entertainment. This production featured not only Kline, but also Ethan Hawke as Hotspur and the Broadway musical star Audra McDonald as his wife Lady Percy. Both Hawke and McDonald explicitly drew upon their association with these other art forms as part of their performance. Hotspur is a fiery and heroic rebel nobleman, a rival whom the prince must overcome in order to demonstrate his martial prowess and fitness as heir to the throne (see above, p. 66). Hawke expertly spoke the lines in his familiar persona, in a style which made them seem like modern American English, 'a contemporary inflection . . . which works remarkably well' (Byrne 2003: 3), in a performance 'which crackles with desperate vigor', as Christopher Rawson in the *Pittsburgh Post-Gazette* put it (27 November 2003). Ben Brantley in the *New York Times* (21 November 2003) felt that Hawke 'may be too contemporary for some tastes' – and indeed his performance was not well received by all; *USA Today* (21 November 2003) called it 'shrill and mannered'. As Brantley noted, 'it's hard to credit him as the embodiment of an older order of chivalry'. But, as Rawson suggested, this was a piece of irony. Hawke's interpretation boldly claimed the role for contemporary America, and in doing so not only made it speak directly to its audience outside the alienating envelope of conventional Shakespearean delivery, but also suggested that self-justifying martial violence may have a modern resonance, rather than just being what Rawson called 'a rearguard drag on the centralizing monarchy of the Lancastrian kings'. McDonald as his wife, an actress famed in musical theatre, delivered the line 'I will not sing' (III 1 258), when invited to compete with Mortimer's Welsh wife, 'as something of a consciously planted joke' (Sommer 2003: 3). According to one reviewer, she nevertheless gave 'a highly musical performance' of the role (Murray 2003: 2). Thus the appeal and impact of the production were aided by the explicit acknowledgement of the personae of these two actors from film and stage musical. The production did not aim at some authentic, but ultimately bogus, Englishness in what is recognized as *the* English epic, but consciously acknowledged its American context.

The production's director, Jack O'Brien, is well known for his work on musicals. The set, 'a latticework of constantly reconfiguring and lumbering wooden beams and staircases', made Matthew Murray swear 'that if it wasn't for the almost total lack of songs . . . that *Henry IV* was a musical' (Murray 2003: 2). Yet it was the production's cinematic qualities which earned it praise, 'filmic' being interestingly used as a term of commendation by US reviewers. *USA Today* thought that 'the macho carousing and dueling are staged with the cunning vibrancy of a thinking man's action / adventure flick'. The *Washington Post* observed that the production used the cinematic convention of illuminating frozen major characters at the beginning 'in short flashes, as if they've been startled by a camera' (Byrne 2003: 2). The battle of Shrewsbury is also staged in a manner reminiscent of film technique, where different shots are intercut with each other; as the same review continues: 'the skirmishes seem to be taking place in multidimensional montage'. Byrne (2003: 2) remarks that the fight director 'sets a new, almost cinematic, standard for what can be done and what is believable on stage'. The play's striking final tableau was described as an 'unforgettable split screen image of Hal being crowned at one side of the stage, while the melancholy Falstaff kneels front and center' (Sommer 2003: 3). Film and, to a lesser extent, the musical are the touchstones by which the *theatrical* success of the play is measured.

Distinctly American concerns were also obvious in the production's treatment of the play's politics. Several reviewers commented on possible allusions to President George W. Bush, whose own younger days and succession to his father's eminence might have some analogy with Prince Hal's own journey. But there was no attempt to make any contemporary reference in the play's design or direction. 'That's the kind of thing which I as director am immensely leery of,' said O'Brien in an interview. '*Henry IV* is about fathers and sons' (*Washington Post*, 4 January 2004). In a country which has always been assertively republican and which, unlike Britain, has no feudal past, it should not be surprising that the play's politics (see below, pp. 193ff.) should find no contemporary political resonance. The conflict between father and son, on the other hand, is a central theme in much US culture (consider, for example, Arthur Miller's classic *Death of a Salesman*), and this conflict is a natural concern in a country where emigration and naturalization are central experiences. 'The political events' in this production, wrote Murray, are 'a backdrop', since the interpretation is 'focusing primarily on the personal relationships between Henry IV (Richard Easton), his eldest son Hal (Michael Hayden) and the jolly knight whom Hal sees as a surrogate father, Sir John Falstaff (Kevin Kline)'.

To many critics and audiences Falstaff remains an engaging enigma. To David Scott Kastan he is:

> a fully developed and autonomous creature ... a coherent and complex personality that erupts into the play's world, and a personality that it cannot easily contain. Moreover, neither sentimentalizing Falstaff nor moralizing about him quite do. What one must say is that he is unquestionably unreliable and self-indulgent, but also that his behaviour marks a commitment to life (at least his own) over a set of thin abstractions that too often deny it.
>
> (Scott Kastan 2002: 44, 51)

Yet Kline's Falstaff, though beautifully acted and extremely entertaining, *was* contained and invited straightforward moral judgement. He did not dominate the play. Brantley remarked (*New York Times*, 21 November 2003) that his 'oft-quoted speeches on the suicidal nature of heroism [Part I: V 1 126–41] and the saving graces of alcohol [Part II: IV 3 86–125] are persuasive, amusing and slightly chilling. Falstaff knows the price of staying alive in a brutal universe.' He is 'an inherently cynical character, a man who hides his craven self-interest under a dissembling outward demeanor' (Byrne 2003: 2). John Lahr in the *New Yorker* (1 December 2003) noted that 'what we get from this Falstaff is the irony of his well-spoken words, not the infectiousness of his high spirits'. In the *Village Voice* (26 November 2003) Michael Feingold felt that Kline's solution to the paradoxical nature of Falstaff, a character at once both loveable and despicable, 'is to sidestep the challenge by toning everything down about the character'. The audience still pitied him at the moment of his rejection (Part II: V 5 47), but Hal's moral choice was, to many critics of the show, obviously one with which the audience sympathized.

In a radio interview Kline said he could not begin to define his Falstaff (Brown 2003: 4). But it may have been that, in the context of a production which owed much to the aesthetic of mainstream US cinema, it was inevitable that Falstaff would be a character about whom it would be possible to make a clear moral decision within the world of the play.

SUMMARY

- This chapter has emphasized an approach that regards the plays as blueprints for stage performances.

- When we read them, we must always be aware that any realization on stage will produce a fuller meaning than will mere reading. The conditions at time and place of staging can also be powerful factors in the production of meaning.

FURTHER READING

A good reconstruction of how an original performance may have gone can be found in Thomson (1983: Part II) and in White (1998: Chapters 4 and 5). Stern (2004) traces in lucid detail the whole process by which a script became realized on the early modern stage. Gurr (1992) presents the evidence for playhouse practices very thoroughly. Bate and Jackson (1996) provide very interesting illustrated summaries of the many ways in which Shakespeare has been performed and understood in performance over the centuries. Wells (1997) has published a very useful anthology of performance reviews from 1700 to 1996, as well as incisive comment on homo-eroticism in the plays (2004).There has been recently published a large literature dealing with the performance histories of many plays in detail. The Cambridge University Press series *Shakespeare in Production* includes volumes on *Hamlet* by Hapgood (1999), *King Henry V* by Smith (2002), *A Midsummer Night's Dream* by Griffiths (1996), *The Taming of the Shrew* by Schafer (2003) and *The Tempest* by Dymkowski (2000). These volumes look at the performance history of the plays not just in Britain. The Arden

Shakespeare at Stratford series includes accounts of Royal Shakespeare Company productions of *The Merchant of Venice* by Gilbert (2001) and *The Winter's Tale* by Tatspaugh (2002). The Manchester University Press *Shakespeare in Performance* series includes volumes on *King Henry IV Part I* by McMillin (1991) and *Macbeth* by Kliman (1995). Finally, there a good introduction to performance theory with regard to Shakespeare in Bulman (1996: Chapter 1).

FURTHER THINKING

- Is it possible to say that performance criticism is actually more valid than traditional text-based criticism because it is based on something concrete, not abstract?
- Is there a problem that performance criticism can narrowly become just criticism of individual performances of the plays?

SHAKESPEARE ON FILM

The rest of this book discusses the plays as they are read or seen in
the theatre. In fact many more people encounter Shakespeare's
plays in the cinema or on television, or in video or DVD versions of
Shakespeare films. Yet film drama represents the world in a totally
different way from the theatre of early modern London. It is an art
form whose very nature requires words to be subordinate to the
visual image. This is the exact opposite of the nature of theatre in
1600. This chapter looks at how the challenge of turning the play-
text into a successful film can reveal much about the nature of both
Shakespeare's theatre and about the medium of film. It will look in
detail at four different ways of putting Shakespeare on screen,
ranging from a 'faithful' rendering of an entire text of *Hamlet* to a
playful modern reworking of *The Taming of the Shrew*.

HOW *DO* YOU FILM SHAKESPEARE?

One important function of film and video for Shakespeare studies is
that such technologies have been able to act as a permanent record,
of a kind, of notable stage productions. The simplest answer to the
question 'how do you film Shakespeare?', then, might be simply to

film a play in the theatre. However, if you have ever sat through a recording of an uninterrupted live stage production, even one edited from the footage of three or four different cameras, you will know how dull and unaffecting the whole experience usually is. The inappropriateness of this method of turning a play into a film is even more notable in the case of Shakespeare (or early modern theatre in general).

There are several important reasons for this. First, location is absolutely crucial in film; the actors and what they do and say are secondary to the way the medium works. The critic Anthony Davies quotes the French theorist André Bazin in pointing out that 'in the theatre . . . the drama proceeds from the actor; in the cinema it goes from the décor to the man. This reversal of flow is of decisive importance' (Davies 1988: 8). In the cinema we believe that there is a world continuing beyond the edge of the screen which gives meaning and function to the characters which we see inside the frame. In the theatre, as Davies points out, we know that beyond the margins of the acting space is only the theatre building (Davies 1988: 5–7). On stage, the drama is located in the interactions of people; the representational realization of those people's imaginary location is of very little importance to the success of the play. This is clearly the opposite with cinema.

Second, the member of a theatre audience remains in control of what they choose to look at on stage. They can focus on one actor, or on the reactions of all the actors on stage at once (something which film finds very difficult to achieve). Their spatial position in relation to the actors on stage remains constant. In the cinema that spatial relationship is dynamic and is manipulated by the director as the camera zooms, tracks or offers low or high-angle shots, or magically shifts ground as the editing cuts between different shots and locations. The rhythm, pace and emotional temperature of the scene on stage are created by the relationship between the actors and between the actors and audience, but in the cinema it is usually the rhythm of the cutting and, very often, the accompanying music which dictate rhythm, pace and emotion. With film, 'the normal frontiers between the spectator and the work of art are broken down', writes Davies; 'the spectator is invaded by, and participates in the laws of the existing structure' (Davies 1988: 8).

Third, it follows from this that if early modern theatre, even in modern stagings, is a public event, a live communion of minds and feelings in a common space, cinema is an art form which takes place inside the heads of individual spectators as they sit in the dark. The American critic Jack A. Jorgens quotes the psychologist Hugo Munsterberg to point out that film tells a story 'by overcoming the forms of the outer world, namely space, time, and causality, and by adjusting the events to the forms of the inner world, namely attention, memory, imagination and emotion' (Jorgens 1998: 21). To this extent, film closes down the plurality of meaning and response in a public context which the Shakespeare play had in its original performance conditions and can still achieve today. Film, like traditional pre-theory literary criticism (see above, p. 1), writes the left-wing critic Catherine Belsey, tends to see 'the analysis of subjectivity as the origin of thought and action, dwelling on the personal and experiential at the expense of the public, abstract and political issues also raised in the play' (Belsey 1998b: 67).

Finally, the on-stage actor in Shakespeare acknowledges the presence of the audience, not only directly in soliloquies and asides (a perennial problem for film directors), but also in the general interactions with the audience which are required by many parts (see above, pp. 58ff.). On the other hand, mainstream film convention requires a closed, psychologically consistent, 'realistic' characterization so that people with whom the audience can sympathize as if they were authentic individuals can be created. In film, 'attractive, interesting people will encounter difficulties and overcome them . . . and take something less than two hours to do so' (Jackson 2000b: 6). Shakespearean characters on stage do not offer such an easy division between art and life, nor such a reductively simplistic view of human personality in its necessarily social context. Bridget Escolme puts it this way:

a good reason for continuing to produce four-hundred-year-old plays is their potential for permitting us, albeit in a fleeting and fragmentary way . . . to stand outside our own ways of being, embodying, performing the human, brought up sharp by other efforts at performance, performance from the past.

(Escolme 2005: 17)

There are, then, fundamental differences between the early modern theatre and the modern cinema which make it very difficult indeed simply to film a stage performance and expect it to work. There are some exceptions: the 1969 film of *Hamlet* directed by Tony Richardson uses the cavernous darknesses, on and off stage, of its original setting, London's Round House (an ex-engine turntable shed), to great effect. Trevor Nunn's video version of his 1990 RSC *Othello* works well because it focuses tightly on the performers' faces, a requirement of productions made for the small screen (Willems 2000: 38–9; 42). But successful films of Shakespeare must generally be *films* first and Shakespeare texts some way second.

Such films, however, often find effective cinematic means for expressing the original script. It is almost always necessary to make major reductions to the number of lines spoken. Most films use between 25 and 30 per cent of the original text (Jackson 2000b: 17). It will also be necessary to re-order speeches and whole scenes in order to produce a narrative which will work according to the rhythm of a medium where extended scenes in one location, let alone long speeches by individual characters, are rare. The *mise-en-scène* (whether naturalistic or symbolic), lighting, editing and music all work to express the mood and concerns of a particular scene (or a whole play) which the original expresses in actors' words. Visual images used as backgrounds to, or set in juxtaposition to, the words spoken can work powerfully in an analogous way to the functioning of imagery in stage poetry. Recurring symbols in the play can be literally and insistently presented on the screen. Changes of viewpoint and use of montage in the film can operate on a cinema audience in a manner similar to the way in which the plays' polyvocal language and often unstable characterization can unsettle in the theatre. Though soliloquy cannot be communication with the audience, if spoken as voice-over with the speaker in a specific public or private context the speech can be illustrated, commented on or rendered ironic by that visual setting. Much in cinema is conveyed by the close-up of the human face, especially through the use of reaction shots. These can stand in for much stage dialogue. On film not only can the use of foreground and background express relationship between characters, and between characters and their setting, but the camera can also reduce a human figure to an insignificant size on the screen or make them dominate the audience's view. Visual images can efficiently show those elements of the narrative which need to be told on stage. By all these means, verbally dense poetic theatre can be successfully transformed into film which is true to the original script, providing, it seems, that there is a coherent vision at work.

The need for such a coherent vision and what can happen when two very different film-makers address the issue of how to transform poetic theatre into moving pictures are evident in two contrasting films of *Hamlet* which I discuss next. Subsequently, I turn to a version of *Twelfth Night* which, in showing great integrity in itself as a film, produces a brilliant insight into that comedy and into the nature of the Shakespeare film itself. Finally, I consider a prime example of Shakespeare's continuing importance in mainstream popular cinema by considering a modern reworking of *The Taming of the Shrew*.

HAMLET IN CONTEXTS: KENNETH BRANAGH (1996) AND MICHAEL ALMEREYDA (2000)

Kenneth Branagh is probably the major figure in contemporary Shakespeare film. He has now directed and starred in five features (*Henry V, Much Ado About Nothing, Hamlet, Love's Labours' Lost* and *As You Like It*), at least two of which have crossed over into the mainstream and achieved box office success. His 1996 *Hamlet* is the most ambitious and remarkable in many ways. Although a shorter, edited version was later released, the original film presents a 'full' text of the play, with the lines (with some minor exceptions) in the order in which they would appear in a 'collated' edition of the text. This means that the film runs for very nearly four hours, 'the longest commercial film released since Joseph Mankiewicz's *Cleopatra* (1964) and certainly takes top honours for the film with the most dialogue' (Crowl 2000: 232). Both these aspects are central to the work's impact.

Mankiewicz's *Cleopatra* was a Hollywood epic on a vast scale. Its cast list was packed with stars, and every scene was a spectacle. Branagh chose to use 70mm film for his *Hamlet*, a film stock associated with the epic genre, and which gives a rich density to the on-screen image. His cast list is a remarkable collection of classical British and Hollywood actors across many generations, including Julie Christie, Billy Crystal, Gerard Depardieu, Judi Dench, Colin

Figure 5.1 Kenneth Branagh (Hamlet) in his 1996 film of *Hamlet*

Firth, John Gielgud, Charlton Heston, Derek Jacobi, Jack Lemmon, Michael Maloney, John Mills, Timothy Spall, Robin Williams and Kate Winslett. Many of the famous faces appear briefly in minor roles. The recognition of the famous face by the audience is in a sense alienating, but Branagh draws on the star's 'persona' to give the character a specific meaning, as is normal in mainstream cinema. Importantly, however, the presence of these actors gives the film a monumental quality. The gathering together of so many illustrious faces marks the historical significance of the film. This is a gala production, a unique celebration of the great play. The film is shot at a famous English monument, Blenheim Palace, a grandiose eighteenth-century mansion in Oxfordshire built as a present from the nation to one of Britain's great generals, the Duke of Marlborough. The film's opening shot is of the word 'Hamlet' being chiselled in bold Roman capitals onto a stone plinth. This is intended to be a monumental *Hamlet*, an authoritative, enduring landmark in film history.

The single setting makes the work's major challenge even more urgent: how to make the full text work on film ('almost an oxymoron', remarks one critic [Kliman 2001: 152]). Branagh is working in a medium which 'as the years of silent cinema proved . . . is *not* based on spoken language' (Davies 1988: 2). The problem is particularly evident during the play's long speeches, which, if shot in a single take, are very uncinematic. The soliloquies in fact work surprisingly well, spoken not as voice-overs but aloud. Hamlet's determination henceforth to be a man of action and finally avenge his father's murder (IV 4 31–66) is roared into the air, as we see Fortinbras's army steadily advancing over a snowy plain. Hamlet is shot speaking the 'To be or not to be' soliloquy (III 1 55–89) by a camera positioned behind his right shoulder as he talks into a two-way mirrored wall (see Figure 5.1). Behind the mirror lurk Derek Jacobi as Claudius the king (who was his father's murderer) and Richard Briers as Polonius (the king's chief minister), concealed in order to overhear the prince. Other mirrored doors reflect the image into infinity. As Samuel Crowl writes, this evokes Hamlet's situation:

> Hamlet is fragmented and fractured; his psyche is troubled by the way in which he not only opposes, but reflects Claudius; and while he keeps trying to hold the mirror up to both Gertrude's [his mother] and Claudius's natures it keeps throwing back more images of his turmoil than of their transgression.
>
> (Crowl 2000: 234)

Other long speeches are treated with less assurance. Sometimes the camera dizzily circles around the actors to no discernible purpose.

Most notably, Branagh chose to intercut speeches either with flashbacks or with dramatizations of what the speech is describing. Thus during the ghost's account of his murder (I 5 42–91) we see the poison being poured into the king's ear and Claudius's reaction to his deed, as well as Claudius flirting with Gertrude (Julie Christie) during a game of indoor bowls. The Player's performance of the speech about the death of Priam (II 2 468–518) is intercut with a perfunctory illustration of the scene. When Hamlet recollects the jester Yorick as he holds his skull (V 1 184–95), we see a youthful prince at play with the comedian. Most controversially, we see Hamlet and Ophelia (Kate Winslett) in bed together. As Polonius warns his daughter to have no more to do with the prince, the speech is intercut with images of Hamlet making love to her. That this is not merely a fantasy of hers is confirmed by another flashback of Hamlet reading the love letter to her as Polonius addresses the king and queen (II 2 115–22). While all this can be justified as the 'subtle translation of the multiple layers of Shakespeare's text into film vocabulary' (Crowl 2000: 234), it can also be seen to damage the film's impact. Instead of using visuals to substitute for words, as is often the case in Shakespeare films, Branagh gives us both. Not only is there potential confusion because there is no clear distinction in film language about whether the 'flash-cut' is to be taken as 'illustration' or 'flashback', but their very use also implies that there is a kind of 'omniscient narrator' (Kliman 2001: 159) who can clear up all the text's ambiguities, thus diminishing its overall dramatic impact. There remains a possibility that the ghost may be a devil sent to deceive the prince (II 2 598–603) right up to Claudius's confession to the audience (III 3 36–8). For some critics, the possibility that the ghost is unreliable remains throughout the play (see Hawkes 1986: 101ff.). But Branagh's flashback immediately establishes the ghost's veracity and reduces the dramatic doubt and tension: this is the meaning of flashback in film language. The flashback of Hamlet and Ophelia in bed actively diminishes both the prince and her. Hamlet becomes precisely the seducer and abandoner of young women whom both her brother and father warned her about (I 3 5–45, 115–35), especially since in this film he cruelly rebuffs her after he has murdered her father. It also makes her a liar to her brother (I 3 45–6) and father (I 3 110–11). This is a possible interpretation, of course, but it produces a far less admirable protagonist. However, 'if [Ophelia] is willing to lie to her brother and father to protect their relationship, it seems inconceivable that she would lie to Hamlet or help others spy on him [III 1 89ff.]. The two parts of her characterization do not mesh' (Kliman 2001: 161). Perhaps not inconceivable, but strange within the overall framework of psychological realism which the film proposes. In any case, the nature and history of their relationship is dramatically best expressed in their delivery of the lines. The flashback single-mindedly destroys ambiguity. Thus in attempting to provide visual variety in this wordiest of all films, the technique can be seen to undermine the film's dramatic qualities. Gertrude's account of Ophelia's drowning (IV 7 166–83) is only illustrated by a brief image of her body in the stream at the end, and works all the more powerfully for that.

A lack of clarity, on the other hand, seems to be an issue in the film's setting and overall conception. The costumes make it clear that we are in the late nineteenth century, but not much use is made of this. The film's concerns are much more contemporary. The critic Julie Sanders puts Branagh's *Hamlet* in the context of the crisis in the British royal family in the 1990s. Branagh himself suggested that he wanted to 'look at the very private lives of very public individuals. If you like, these people could be stepping out the pages of a nineteenth-century *Hello!* magazine' (quoted in Sanders 2000: 153). Unprecedented media coverage, especially in such celebrity magazines, exposed to the world every detail of the collapse of the marriages of two British princes, turning them and their wives into figures of public fascination, sympathy or contempt. Ophelia in the film seems to Sanders reminiscent of Princess Diana, as her love letters are read aloud to others and her mental disintegration is turned into a spectacle for spectators (Sanders 2000: 153). Not only is there a dark secret at the heart of Denmark's royal family, but the affection between Ophelia and her brother Laertes (Michael Maloney) seems more physical than is usual. Their father Polonius is seen dismissing a prostitute from his bed at the very time he is setting a spy on his son to find out whether he also goes 'drabbing' (II 1 26). The play's protagonists are all part of dysfunctional, morally compromised families. This is 'an unsustainable world, which has eaten itself apart with corruption and betrayal, yet it is also one that Branagh's film seems inexplicably nostalgic for and sentimental towards' (Sanders 2000: 154). The film condemns the very figures for whom it creates the most sympathy. Sanders thinks that this may reflect contemporary British attitudes to the monarchy and its authority.

The most resonant piece of late-twentieth-century iconography in the film occurs in its closing moments, when we see the statue of Old Hamlet, which earlier walked as his ghost, being felled by the hammers of the new king Fortinbras's soldiers. This clearly recalls the sight of statues of Stalin and Lenin being toppled in the former Soviet-dominated states of Eastern Europe in 1989 and 1990. Is this supposed to suggest that Old Hamlet was some sort of tyrant, the loving father for whom the film has developed such sympathy? Once again, 'Branagh seems at turns appalled and enticed by the power invested in a figure such as Old Hamlet' (Sanders 2000: 156). The image is iconic but seems to be used for its iconicity alone, without a clear idea of how it fits into the overall political concept of the film. This lack of clear focus stands out even more at a time when stage productions of *Hamlet* have consistently taken a great interest in the political dimensions of the play (see, for example, the director Steven Pimlott's rationale for his pro-Claudius production for the RSC in 2000–1 in McEvoy 2006: 100–1).

Branagh's film contains many brilliant performances, not least from Branagh himself and from Christie, Jacobi and Winslett. Its boldness may well ensure the historical stature it aims for. But it also underlines the problems of translating a verbal act of live communication into the dead visual medium of film, especially if the director does not possess a clear concept of a crucial dimension of the text.

In comparison to Branagh's epic, the American director Michael Almereyda's film of *Hamlet* (2000) is a relatively low-budget, abbreviated version of the play, running at only 106 minutes and shot entirely on location in Manhattan. Almereyda's interpretation of the tragedy is resolutely conventional, yet the work is clearly focused and tautly directed. In this way it might be argued to be a more convincing realization of the tragedy, even if it lacks the grandeur and beauty of the Branagh film (whose actors also speak the text with more assurance).

In his introduction to his own screenplay, Almereyda suggests that at 'the core of Hamlet's anguish' is 'the frailty of spiritual values in a material world' (Almereyda 2000: xi). This Hamlet is the son of the recently deceased Chief Executive of the Denmark Corporation in contemporary New York. In this film Claudius (Kyle MacLachlan) and Gertrude (Diane Venora) are glamorous and powerful figures in the business world, whose habitat is the limousine and high-rise penthouse. Hamlet (Ethan Hawke) is a rather shabby figure in a woollen hat and greatcoat, ill at ease in these surroundings. He is clearly artistic, with a talent for film-making. The *Mousetrap*, originally the play which Hamlet stages to make his uncle face a re-enactment of the murder, is here a film collage of animation and archive footage. Hamlet's film pointedly underlines his grief for his lost father and expresses his disgust for his mother's and uncle's conduct. Its première in a private cinema has the desired effect on the king. Ophelia, the chief minister's daughter and Hamlet's lover (Julia Stiles), is artistic, too; she is a photographer, who hands out polaroids rather than flowers when mad (IV 5). A key idea in the film seems to be that the sensitive, creative young people are trapped in a prison which frustrates that creativity and individuality. Almereyda notes Hamlet's opinion that 'Denmark's a prison' (II 2 243) and sees 'contemporary consumer culture' as a powerful restraint upon us all: 'the bars of the cage are defined by advertising, by all the hectic distractions, brand names, announcements and ads that crowd our waking hours' (Almereyda 2000: xi). Video monitors and electronic displays are everywhere in the film. Hamlet's 'To be or not to be' soliloquy (III 1 55–88) is delivered in the aisle of the 'Action' section of a Blockbusters video store, as Hamlet seems to measure himself against the screen avengers playing on the monitors behind him. The prince also stands in front of the wittily placed advertising banner exhorting the shopper to 'go home happy'. The ghost (Sam Shepard) disappears into a Pepsi machine. After his soliloquy confessing his guilt for his brother's murder (III 3 36–72) Claudius emerges into a lobby where the stock-market prices are streaming past on a huge electronic display behind him, and, in the words of the screenplay, 'he's back in his element, confident, self-possessed' (Almereyda 2000: 77).

In apparent contrast to Branagh, Almereyda sees his function as director to 'imagine a parallel visual language that might hold a candle to Shakespeare's poetry. There was no wish to illustrate the text, but to focus it, building a visual structure to accommodate

Shakespeare's imagery and ideas' (Almereyda 2000: x). To this end, much of the action takes place in narrow, confined locations, or in restless, transitional spaces that are neither one place nor another: corridors, aisles, canyon-like streets flanked by huge office blocks, balconies many stories up in the air. Lobbies and hallways feature a great deal; characters are often seen getting in and out of taxis and limousines, or entering or leaving airport terminal buildings. In this way, both the idea of modern materialism as a prison, epitomized by the ubiquitous transnational corporation, and the rootless anxiety which that materialism brings to all are expressed. The film's setting is a bleak cityscape of cold concrete, steel and glass, with much of the action shot in night-time gloom. The most memorable splash of colour is made by Ophelia's red clothes; and indeed Stiles plays her as passionate rather than passive.

Modern communications technology in the film provides the means both for surveillance and for personal reflection and expression. The ghost is first seen on CCTV security monitors at the 'Hotel Elsinore'; Polonius (Bill Murray) 'wires up' his daughter so that the king can overhear the conversation between Ophelia and Hamlet (III 1 88–149). Hamlet has a 'pixelvision' portable television on which he can play back his thoughts himself. The 'player' whose capacity for tears he wonders at in the soliloquy beginning 'O what a rogue and peasant slave am I' (II 2 550–605) is a recording of James Dean in the film *Rebel without a Cause*, an iconic figure of youthful rebellion in American culture. The recorded image has power in this film, as the power of Hamlet's own *Mousetrap* demonstrates. The film is also introspectively self-aware of its own position in the history of this most-produced of the world's plays. Hamlet pores over footage of the great British actor John Gielgud playing the prince of the 1940s. When Hamlet gets out of a taxi having failed to shoot his uncle (III 3), the Disney reworking of the tragedy, *The Lion King*, is playing at the theatre in the background.

Hawke's Hamlet is not murderously inclined. His intention is rather to make Claudius 'face his own guilt' (Almereyda 2000: ix). When, in the final duel scene, the prince finds himself dying, with Laertes' gun in hand, facing his uncle, he seems surprised to find himself shooting the king. His mother knowingly drinks the poison which Claudius had prepared for her son, apparently acknowledging her own complicity. Claudius's culpability seems to stem from the fact that he is not willing to reach the same self-knowledge. Thus the film takes what might be regarded as a thoroughly Romantic interpretation of Shakespeare's play: the prince is an artistic and vulnerable soul struggling to cope in a harsh materialist environment. As the nineteenth-century critic William Hazlitt put it, 'the very excess of intellectual refinement in the character . . . makes the common rules of life, as well as his own purposes, sit loose upon him . . . His habitual principles of action are un-hinged and out of joint with the time' (Hazlitt 1906: 84). To that it marries a modern American ideal, the importance of self-realization and total honesty about one's 'inner self'. In this way, the film strives to achieve its director's aim, 'to see how thoroughly Shakespeare can speak to the present moment' and how the present moment informs our understanding of Shakespeare (Almereyda 2000: ix). Despite its star-filled cast and *film noir*-like *mise-en-scène*, the film never becomes totally absorbed into the familiar genre of a thriller set in a world of corporate corruption. Its coherence and energy come from the Shakespeare text, not its filmic mode.

REWORKING THE TEXT ON FILM: *TWELFTH NIGHT* (2003) AND *TEN THINGS I HATE ABOUT YOU* (1999)

In 2003 the British director Tim Supple produced a film of *Twelfth Night* for use in schools and colleges. Supple edited and reorganized Shakespeare's text so that it ran for only 102 minutes. So powerful and insightful was this version that it was also shown on prime-time television. Supple brilliantly confronted two major problems any director will meet when transforming early modern comedy into film and in doing so discovered a powerful and surprising reading of the play.

Although he was famous for his magical retelling of folk tales and mythology when he worked at London's Young Vic theatre in the 1990s, Supple's Illyria is recognizably contemporary. Only at one moment, when Viola and Sebastian disappear into twinkling stars as they climb through a window to escape their persecutors and go into exile, does Supple employ the technology of film for magical purposes. In his film the twins are political refugees from the Indian subcontinent, who at times speak in subtitled Hindi (as does Antonio, the sea captain who loves Sebastian). As we see in a flash-cut, their father was an assassinated general (his uniformed corpse is shown lying face down in a pool of blood). Before the shipwreck Viola and Sebastian are stowaways in a cargo container together with other refugees. Their eventual destination is a modern, multicultural London, where Sebastian and Antonio walk through a street market consulting an A to Z street guide. Our sympathies in the film are with the persecuted heroine and her brother, so Supple clearly takes sides in the controversy concerning asylum and illegal immigration which was current in the UK at the time. But Supple goes further in making a sultry summer London Illyria. He stays faithful to the text, which does contain several correspondences with Shakespeare's own adopted home (III 1 134, III 3 39–40), but more significantly suggests that this hot, bustling, violent city is also a welcoming place of transformation where race and culture are irrelevant to love and desire, where identity itself is fluid and where new homes and lives can be made. Duke Orsino (Chiwetel Ejiofor) and his stylish court are all black; Olivia (Claire Price), whom Orsino loves, is white, Catholic and upper class (the costume designer, Jemma Cotton, based Olivia's clothes on those of the late Princes Diana, and those of Orsino on the footballer David Beckham). The fisherman who rescues Olivia is from Eastern Europe. The film thus acquires authority and authenticity not only through its contemporaneity, and through its association with the genre of romantic thriller, but also through its ability to portray a city with insight and truth.

The most remarkable transformation, however, occurs when Supple accepts that film cannot accommodate the subtle distancing of the audience from the play's inherent sorrow, violence and cruelty which the text in theatrical performance can achieve. Lacking the facility of direct-audience address, which the text calls for on a dozen occasions, not to mention the many times when an actor's 'performance objective' (see above, p. 58) is to address the audience, the passions of Olivia, Viola and Olivia's steward Malvolio and the practical jokes of her kinsman Sir Toby and maid Maria are unmediated by either the complicity produced by confessional soliloquy and dramatic irony or the explicit awareness of the fictionality of the situation. There are some asides, and other lines, spoken as 'voice-overs' to represent thought (such as Viola at II 4 41–2), but this is merely in line with film convention.

Consequently, the anguish of the lovers comes across as all the more disturbing, and the actions of Sir Toby and his friends as cruel and violent. *Twelfth Night* in Supple's film is a dark and fiery text, rarely funny and often moving.

In the theatre an actor in soliloquy can confide directly to an audience the discovery that he or she is falling in love, or convey his or her feelings about being loved by someone else (as Olivia does at I 5 289–98 and Viola does at II 2 17–41). When this happens, the audience are being addressed as someone who will listen sympathetically. The audience are aware of that strange duality of actor and character which constitutes the moment of soliloquy or aside, and know that the words are spoken to convey a feeling; we are not getting direct access to the internal consciousness of a *real* person. Both these factors work to distance the audience from the less complex and unambiguous intensity of emotion which film can communicate. Thus the film audience know exactly the moment when Olivia falls in love with Viola in male disguise as Orsino's servant 'Cesario' in I 5, because they see two flashes of light framing an image of Viola which they understand by film convention to be taking place 'inside' Olivia's mind. The audience also hear romantic guitar music playing to signal when her feelings are aroused, and the point is reinforced by the camera playing over the pictures of soft-fleshed young women on the walls of Olivia's chapel, the shot ending unambiguously on a naked breast. Dramatic irony is thus achieved visually: this is not the sort of body which Olivia is thinking about, as we know. The film strives to give us a direct expression of Olivia's feelings unmediated by words or the fact of personal communication.

In stage performance Viola's surprise at the ring which Olivia sends her as an obvious token of her love is expressed as a soliloquy in which the audience are directly asked four questions as Viola struggles to understand her predicament (II 1 17–41). In Supple's film, Parminder Nagra as Viola addresses this speech to a mirror, making it clear that we are hearing her true *inner* reflections, again unmediated by the ambiguities of theatrical representation or of two-way communication. As she ponders the consequences of the fact that she really is a female, she unbuttons her nightshirt suggestively in close-up, reminding the audience of the earlier close-up shot where the naked Orsino ran his fingers down the front of

Viola's shirt, having just emerged from his bath (I 4 30–5 in the text). In this bed-time scene in the film (II 1 17–41) Viola is not dressed as a male. There is no ambiguity about gender in this moment. The impact of the earliest performance of Viola would of course have depended quite significantly on the fact that in this scene a boy was playing a woman who was impersonating a boy (see above, p. 84f). On film, emotion and sexuality are simply and powerfully expressed, but from *one* point of view and *for* that point of view, and without any of the *simultaneous* ambiguities which theatre can deliver. Thus what the critic Penny Gay takes to be the dominant late-twentieth-century reading of the play, which sees love in *Twelfth Night* as 'the apparently infinite variations of *eros*, [as] physical and spiritual attraction between two people in any gender combination' (Gay 2003a: 35), gives way to a simpler, more individual, internalized heterosexual desire: the shirt unbuttoned for the film audience positions us as Orsino, as well as being an act of narcissism as Viola looks into the mirror, seeing what she wants Orsino to see. Desire in the film is not various, or even immediately about 'combination': it is a picture in the darkened cinema of the mind, as is made evident in Orsino's opening speech, which is flash-cut with an image of Olivia, or when we hear Olivia's imagined voice reading the fake letter in Malvolio's mind. A film of *Twelfth Night* which has integrity as a film will not have any ironic playful examination of love and gender, but will reveal powerful individual emotions: this is the great insight of Supple's work. The alternative would be a film of rather less assurance, such as the vaguely camp *Twelfth Night* directed by Trevor Nunn in 1996. Film by its very nature does not rely on the audience being happy to ignore the evidence of their own eyes. This is why the obvious difference in the physical appearances of Viola and Sebastian (Ronny Jhutti) grates in a way which does not happen in a good stage production of the play.

In the scene where Malvolio opens the letter (II 5) the theatre audience are placed in a similar position to the hidden Sir Toby Belch and his friends Sir Andrew Aguecheek and Fabian, observing Malvolio's behaviour and, probably, laughing at him. The staging thus makes the theatre audience complicit by association. On stage there is at least the fictional possibility that Sir Toby's and Sir Andrew's exclamations will give the game away, and both have to be told to be quiet, principally by Fabian (II 5 30–76). In Supple's film the three jokers watch Malvolio (Michael Maloney) on a black and white closed-circuit television monitor which is part of the security system for Olivia's house. The safe distance from which they observe renders their actions even more cruel. Malvolio talks to himself (which always appears strange on film), not to an audience. He does not treat the audience as fools who would believe his misplaced fantasies. We have no reason to side with Sir Toby and the others or to be associated with their eavesdropping. Our feelings as a film audience are much less compromised. There is something cold about the way Malvolio becomes an object of surveillance in the film, like a street criminal, and about how Sir Toby and the others are placed in the role of security officials possessed of state or private power. The coarse and unrestrained delight of David Troughton as Sir Toby only makes the scene even less funny and seem more like bullying.

When locked up, after being hooded and noosed like a condemned man, Malvolio kicks and struggles violently in his cell. Later, when Sir Toby sets up the duel between Viola and Sir Andrew, the fight is not played for laughs but for real, with slashing knives wielded by genuinely frightened combatants, using the swirling camera techniques employed to depict fights in action films. We are invited to be excited, not to laugh. The officers who arrest Antonio, who intervenes to stop the fight, do so violently, one holding a gun to his head. There is finally plenty of blood shed in the film's closing moments, after Sebastian has beaten both the knights. Violence, like desire, is a serious matter in this version of *Twelfth Night*.

Supple's primary audience was school students of Shakespeare. But those who go to the cinema solely for 'entertainment' cannot escape the influence of the plays either. As the British academic Tony Howard writes, '"Shakespeare" permeates our culture iconographically . . . so in mainstream film culture the plays have functioned as myths and sources; they materialize repeatedly and often unnoticed on cinema screens through allusions and variations, remakes, adaptations and parodies' (Howard 2000: 295). He means that the idea of 'Shakespeare' as a marker of cultural worth and traditional values is very powerful in English-speaking cultures (and beyond), and this makes him surprisingly central to mainstream popular culture. Such centrality seemed to be especially evident in the last decade of the twentieth century, when Hollywood was responsible for a number of Shakespeare films of one sort of another, including Branagh's *Hamlet* (1996) and Luhrmann's *Romeo + Juliet* (1996), but also the pseudo-biographical *Shakespeare in Love* (1998). *The Lion King* (1994) and *Last Action Hero* (1991) were both reworkings of *Hamlet*. *O* (1999) was a modern *Othello* with a high-school setting. Gil Junger's *10 Things I Hate about You* (1999) was a version of *The Taming of the Shrew* also set in an American school. It is the last film which I discuss in this chapter.

Perhaps, as Howard considers, this plethora of Shakespeare films reflected 'Hollywood's globalization of film culture – the recycling of certain internationally recognizable cultural icons – and the targeting of high school and college audiences familiar with canonical great books' (Howard 2000: 309). Indeed, the final decade of the last century, following the fall of the communist regimes from 1989 onwards, was a time when American power seemed more than ever a truly global force. The American cultural critic Denise Albanese has argued that Hollywood's embrace of Shakespeare at this time was an attempt to appropriate him for triumphant US capitalism, seeing 'literature as a regressive formation exempt from direct market instrumentality'(Albanese 2001: 209). It was finally time to rescue Shakespeare from those who would see him as immune from market values.

Junger's decision to turn *The Taming of the Shrew* into an example of a popular film genre, high-school comedy romance, might be surprising. But the wise-cracking dialogue of the script lends itself well to the satirical tone of Shakespeare's comedy. In *The Taming of the Shrew* all the more or less foolish principal figures are held up for the audience's amused scrutiny. At 'Padua High' to be spectacularly sarcastic, rude and offensive is the normal mode of conversation for both students and staff. Much of the film's humour resides in this. All the high-school students are very wealthy and privileged, just like Shakespeare's aristocrats and merchants.

Junger stays ingeniously faithful to Shakespeare's plot in the first part of the film. The beautiful Bianca Stratford (Larisa Oleynik) is sought both by the vain and predatory male model Joey (Andrew Keegan) and by a new boy from a military family, Cameron (Joseph Gordon-Levitt). Cameron and Joey correspond to Lucentio and

Hortensio respectively. Bianca's father is a paranoid obstetrician (Larry Miller) who will not allow Bianca to go out with boys until her elder sister Kat (Julia Stiles) does, echoing Baptista's actions in the play. Kat, however, shows only sarcastic and savage contempt for all male attempts to win her favours, and indeed for her fellow students and their social habits. Prompted by Cameron's friend Michael (David Krumholtz), Joey pays a mysterious newcomer with a wild reputation, Patrick Verona (Heath Ledger), to win Kat over so that both of Bianca's suitors have a chance to ask her out. Just like Petruchio and Katherina, Patrick is motivated to woo Kat for the sake of money (I 2 75–6). Cameron, just like Lucentio, becomes Bianca's tutor in an attempt to get closer to her (III 1), but not in disguise. Early in the film he even uses one of Lucentio's lines to express his feelings about Bianca ('I burn, I pine, I perish' [I 1 155]).

But the similarities are not enlighteningly sustained. In *The Taming of the Shrew* Katherina's bad behaviour seems to be a general fault in her personality, perhaps inspired by jealousy of her younger sister (II 1 31–6). Modern critics have read her hostility as an unconscious reaction to the injustice of her social position as a mere male possession (see below, pp. 146ff.). In Junger's film Kat's contempt for those around her does seem to have some validity. In an amusingly satirical opening sequence, Michael shows Cameron the different and mutually hostile student groups with their different 'lifestyles': white Rastafarians, cowboys, 'future MBAs' and so on. Bianca tells her friend that she knows the difference between love and lust because she 'likes her Skechers [shoes], but loves her Prada Backpack'. There is comic exaggeration happening here, but the bookish and politically engaged Kat has a point when she points out the shallowness of their 'meaningless, consumer-driven lives'. But Kat's political views are themselves revealed to be shallow: after her ideas are mocked sarcastically by Bianca and her friend Chastity (Gabrielle Union), she starts to satirize herself. It then turns out that her bitterness towards others has psychological, not political origins: her guilt at having had under-age sex with the unworthy Joey years earlier, and her resentment for the mother who abandoned her family. The absent mother turns out to be the real villain of the film. No feminist reading can be sustained of this *Shrew*.

Katherina's behaviour gets better as Petruchio 'tames' her. As Kat grows to love Patrick, she demonstrates her abandonment of her 'shrewishness' by drunkenly dancing on a table at a party, and by exposing her breasts to her football coach in order to distract his attention during a detention session. Petruchio achieves Katherina's submission by humiliating her. Patrick wins Kat, and grows to love her himself, by taking an interest in her favourite things and looking after her kindly when she is drunk. Romantic love triumphs over everything in this film. In Junger's climax Kat's love for Patrick even makes her forget that he originally only sought to date her for financial advantage, as she tearfully confesses in a maudlin poem she recites to her English class: ten things she hates about him, a recital which acts as an equivalent to Katherina's submission speech (V 2 136–79; see below, pp. 143–4). Patrick seals their reconciliation by using the money he was given to take her to the prom to buy her an explicitly featured Fender Stratocaster electric guitar, so that she can start a rock band. Some might see this as a kind of continued rebellion, but there is no doubt that Kat has joined the consumerist society.

Kat's poem was written in response to her teacher's request to write a version of Shakespeare's sonnet 141 ('In faith I do not love thee with mine eyes, / For they in thee a thousand errors note'). Michael wins the love of Kat's Shakespeare-mad friend by dressing up in a distant approximation of early modern dress and using lots of 'thees' and 'thous' to her. Thus the film wears its Shakespearean origins knowingly but subsumes them in its enormous energy, wit and romantic sentiment. To be in love and to have fun, to enjoy yourself now, is all that matters. This is the truth which Kat needs to discover. In the film's final shot we see a triumphant rock band playing, perhaps appropriately, a song called 'Cruel To Be Kind' high up on the school roof over a sunlit Seattle. There is no challenging moral or social conclusion as in Shakespeare's play: *The Taming of the Shrew*'s 'regressive' literary qualities have been appropriated into a 'feel-good' product.

SHAKESPEARE VIDEOS AND DVDS

There follows a necessarily selective list of important or remarkable film versions of the plays which are currently available and not discussed in this chapter. I have also included 'offshoots', films closely based on the original scripts. These are marked with an asterisk.

AS YOU LIKE IT

(1992) Dir. Christine Ezard (UK). The Forest of Arden as inner-city London.
(2006) Dir. Kenneth Branagh (UK/US).

HAMLET

(1948) Dir. Laurence Olivier (UK). Olivier's dark, brooding Oedipal prince.
(1966) Dir. Grigori Kozintsev (USSR). Denmark is a prison, infested by spies and oppressed by a corrupt political system.
(1969) Dir. Tony Richardson (UK). Nicol Williamson as a cynical, intellectual prince in a decadent and sensual court.
(1990) Dir. Franco Zeffirelli (USA). Mel Gibson as the all-action prince shares the billing with his glamorous mother, Glenn Close.

KING HENRY IV PARTS I AND II

Chimes at Midnight (1966) Dir. Orson Welles (USA). Falstaff's story collated from the two plays and *The Merry Wives of Windsor*.
*My Own Private Idaho (1991) Dir. Gus Van Sant (USA). Hal is a politician's son who drops out and becomes a rent boy in Bob's underclass gang.

KING HENRY V

(1944) Dir. Laurence Olivier (UK). A multi-layered patriotic celebration of English arms and civilization.
(1989) Dir. Kenneth Branagh (UK). A relatively gritty exploration of the pressures on the king at war.

KING LEAR

(1969) Dir. Grigori Kozintsev (USSR). Set in a cruel and bleak dark-age, in this *Lear* only fools and madmen have any moral worth.
(1971) Dir. Peter Brook (UK). Against a wintry and desolate medieval landscape, an alienated and brutal society tears itself apart.

Ran (1985) Dir. Akiro Kurosawa (Japan). The Lear story spectacularly transposed to feudal Japan.

KING RICHARD II

(1997) Dir. Deborah Warner (UK). A TV version of Fiona Shaw's passionate, trapped Richard.

KING RICHARD III

(1955) Dir. Laurence Olivier (UK). A fast-paced and energetic version which is overtly theatrical and melodramatic.

(1995) Dir. Richard Loncraine (UK/USA). Ian McKellen is fascist ruler in 1930s Britain.

(2004) Dir. Max Day (UK). An award-winning, jagged cut of the text set amongst criminals on a Brighton housing estate (available from redfilm.co.uk).

MACBETH

Throne of Blood (1957) Dir. Akiro Kurosawa (Japan). A brooding Samurai *Macbeth*.

(1971) Dir. Roman Polanski (USA). An epic and bloody medieval version which retains the feel of the 1960s.

(2003) Dir. Greg Doran (UK). Anthony Sher's powerful and intelligent Macbeth; a film of the RSC production.

THE MERCHANT OF VENICE

(2001) Dir. Trevor Nunn (UK). A film of the National Theatre production set in 1930s Italy, with Henry Goodman and Derbhle Crotty.

(2004) Dir. Michael Radford (USA). Al Pacino is Shylock in a sumptuously shot Venice.

A MIDSUMMER NIGHT'S DREAM

(1935) Dir. William Dierterle and Max Reinhardt (USA). 1930s Hollywood blockbuster with James Cagney and Mickey Rooney.

(1996) Dir. Adrian Noble (UK). A film of the colourful RSC stage romp.

The Children's Midsummer Night's Dream (2001) (UK). Dir. Christine Ezard. All the parts are taken by children.

(1999) Dir. Michael Hoffman (USA/Italy). Kevin Kline is Bottom and Michelle Pfeiffer Titania.

OTHELLO

(1952) Dir. Orson Welles (USA). Shot over many years, Welles' film is a highly cinematic and psychological version of the tragedy.

(1991) Dir. Trevor Nunn (UK). A film of the National Theatre production set in a US Cavalry stockade, with a brilliantly psychotic Iago in Ian McKellen.

ROMEO AND JULIET

West Side Story (1961) Dir. Jerome Robbins and Robert Wise (USA). Leonard Bernstein's musical about New York street gangs.

(1968) Franco Zeffirelli (UK/Italy). Two young actors play the passionate leads in a brightly coloured Renaissance Italy.

(1996) Dir. Baz Luhrmann (USA). The lovers are doomed by the violent feuding of their decadent, super-rich families. The film is manically shot in 'contemporary' Verona Beach, USA.

THE TAMING OF THE SHREW

Kiss Me Kate (1953) Dir. George Sidney (USA). The Hollywood backstage musical of the *Shrew*.

(1967) Dir. Franco Zeffirelli (USA/Italy). A vehicle for the tempestuous off-screen lovers Richard Burton and Elizabeth Taylor.

THE TEMPEST

Forbidden Planet (1956) Dir. Fred M. Wilcox (USA). A Cold War sci-fi 'updating'.

(1979) Dir. Derek Jarman (UK). A discordant but striking version.

Prospero's Books (1991) Dir. Peter Greenaway (UK). John Gielgud speaks the text in a dream-like journey through the play.

TITUS ANDRONICUS

(1999) Dir. Julie Taymor (USA). Anthony Hopkins is Titus in an unflinching depiction of masculine brutality.

TWELFTH NIGHT

(1995) Dir. Trevor Nunn (UK). A jolly late Victorian comedy.

THE WINTER'S TALE

(1998) Dir. Greg Doran (UK). A version of the RSC production, including interviews with director, designer and cast.

FURTHER READING

Two excellent collections of essays are those edited by Jackson (2000a) and Shaughnessy (1998). Both books focus on the issues involved in filming the plays and deal in detail with notable productions. Davies and Wells (1994) is also a very useful collection. Davies (1988) contrasts cinematic and theatrical use of space in the work of four classic directors of Shakespeare on film. Burnett and Wray (2000) is a study of Shakespeare films at the end of the twentieth century, while Boose and Burt (1997 and 2003) examine the process by which the medium has popularized the plays. For reference, McKernan and Terris (1994) is a full list of all the film and television versions of the plays and their spin-offs which are held in the UK National Film and Television Archive.

FURTHER THINKING

- Are Shakespeare films primarily to be studied as films or as examples of Shakespeare in performance?
- Are Shakespeare films a separate genre of film in their own right?

PART II
THE GENRES

6

WHAT IS GENRE?

A legacy of Romantic thinking is the belief that when a writer sits down to create, he or she is free to go wherever the imagination may lead. If this were ever true, it is certainly not true of writing that seeks to succeed commercially. Shakespeare and his fellow writers depended for their livelihood on writing plays that they knew a theatre company would buy; and they were aware that what a theatre company looked for was a play that built on the elements of other successful popular plays. I am not denying the brilliance and originality of many of Shakespeare's plays, but the plays were generally written to please a paying audience whose tastes were known.

One of the most popular plays throughout this period was Thomas Kyd's *The Spanish Tragedy*, first produced in its original form around 1582, just as the theatre was becoming a commercial and professional venture. In this play Kyd had drawn upon elements of Roman tragedy, but the parts of his play which were most popular with audiences included the appearance of a ghost, the actions of a character who pretends to be mad in order to conceal his plans for revenge, and a conclusion in which a public spectacle turns to vengeful murder and mayhem. These and other elements are to be found in *Hamlet* (1600–1) and also in a large number of similar plays of the period. Middleton's *Women Beware Women* (c. 1623) and Webster's *The Duchess of Malfi* (1614), for example, share many of the same conventions, as also does *The Atheist's*

BOX 6.1 THEATRE COMPANIES

The appearance of the first professional secular theatres in Elizabethan London was a remarkable feature of the age. Key figures in this respect were Philip Henslowe and James Burbage, entrepreneurs who put up the capital and managed the companies of actors.

Each company was named after its aristocratic or royal patron. A company's core comprised eight to ten 'sharers': performers, and sometimes writers, who bought into the company and shared its profits. Another ten or so actors, musicians, costume managers, a prompter, front-of-house staff and so on were hired on contract, and paid very little. Some of the hired backstage staff were female. Companies were rather unstable, with actors moving from one to another, and back again. When Burbage built The Globe in 1599, Shakespeare became a shareholder, making the sharers of his company – the Lord Chamberlain's (subsequently The King's Men) – majority owners of their own playhouse. Clearly this was a more stable arrangement, and it was copied by other companies. With up to 2,500 playgoers a day at The Globe, there was much money to be made. The company was later able to expand into the Blackfriars Theatre.

Companies performed six days a week in the public playhouses, putting on a different play each day. A new play would be added every two weeks or so, with more popular plays repeated and others abandoned. Henslowe's company offered thirty-eight plays in its 1594–5 season, of which twenty-one were new. The demand for new plays was high and playwrights often collaborated in teams or reworked others' material.

Playwrights sold individual plays to company managers. Additional payment seems to have come from 'benefit days', when the dramatist took all profits from a performance. The plays were usually considered the property of the company which bought them, but Shakespeare seems to have kept ownership of his early plays and to have taken them with him when he changed companies in 1594. A few established writers were put under contract to produce a certain number of plays in a specified time, receiving a 'salary' on top of the usual payments.

Shakespeare's 1594 contract with the Lord Chamberlain's Company, probably for one 'serious' and one 'light' play during the year, was, so far as we know, the first of these rare arrangements.

When King James came to power in 1603, he and his family became patrons of London's three main companies. The Lord Chamberlain's Company became The King's Men, alongside the Queen Anne's Men and Prince Henry's Men. For the companies this meant regular and lucrative performances in the royal palaces, but it also gave the court influence over the theatre.

Tragedy (1607, attributed to Cyril Tourneur). They all belong to the genre of *revenge tragedy*.

A genre, then, is a type of play, book, film and so on, each example of which has certain characteristic features or *conventions*. The stories in Shakespeare's plays had, by and large, set paths on which to run, and along which the audience expected them to run. Any deviation from those paths would be measured in terms of the effectiveness of the difference from the expected path taken.

CLASSIFICATION BY GENRE

John Hemmings and Henry Condell, editors of the First Folio of 1623 (see Box 1.2, p. 23), divided up Shakespeare's plays into comedies, histories and tragedies. There has been considerable critical debate over the years about these terms and their use as classifications for particular plays. The 1997 *Riverside Shakespeare* uses a fourth category: romance. The conventions can be crudely summed up as follows.

The conventions of comedy include disguise (often involving cross-dressing), thwarted love, mistaken identity and marital and romantic misunderstandings. Comedies end in multiple marriage. Among the conventions of history are conspiracy, fighting, prominent sub-plots involving non-noble characters, a large number of characters and a decisive on-stage battle. The conventions of tragedy include a single heroic main character (the protagonist), some dreadful dilemma or wrong decision, conspiracy, fighting, (often) madness and many deaths at the end. Romance conventions include natural disasters, remarkable adventures, unlikely coincidences, conflict between generations and within families, and an unforeseen conclusion in which forgiveness and reconciliation are achieved against all the odds.

This fourfold division seems to make sense, but it also has limits as a useful means of classification. There are many plays which do not neatly fit *one* of these four categories because, for particular effects, they combine elements characteristic of one or more of the other three genres. In these texts, some of which used often to be called 'problem' plays, conventions from several genres sit together more or less uneasily. *Measure for Measure*, for example, features disguise and ends with a multiple marriage. The darkness of its mood and grimness of its plot, however, make it hard to classify it as a comedy. *The Merchant of Venice* is generically a comedy, but the character of the Jewish moneylender Shylock, who dominates the play, has often been seen as a tragic figure of some sort. The second half of what would seem a typical history, *King Henry V*, features several comedic conventions (disguise, a practical joke and a comic wooing ending in marriage).

Part II discusses each of the genres in turn. I provide an approach to understanding the nature of each, according to the interests and ideas of contemporary critics. In the process, I aim to show the limitations of criticism that is based predominantly on character, theme and plot. The critical approach employed here, it is important to add, is not the only way of reading Shakespeare. What follows is a sample of modern critical ideas for you to use as a springboard in your own work. Influential though these ideas are, they are not rigid principles that cannot be challenged or developed.

I tackle the genres roughly in the order in which the plays were written. Broadly speaking, Shakespeare started with comedies, and moved on to histories and then tragedies. He concluded his career as a writer of romances.

BOX 6.2: SHAKESPEARE'S PLAYS

There are thirty-seven surviving plays which seem to have been written by Shakespeare, either on his own or in collaboration with another dramatist. One play, *Cardenio*, which he wrote with John Fletcher in 1612–13, is now lost. He may well also have contributed to two other plays which partially survive, *Edward III* (1592–5) and *Sir Thomas More* (1594–5). There is still some dispute as to the dating of some plays. My source for dates here is the second edition of the *Riverside Shakespeare* (Blakemore Evans 1997: 78–87), and for some of the playhouses and companies Andrew Gurr's *The Shakespearean Stage* (Gurr 1992: 233–43). It is also controversial to ascribe a play to a particular genre in some cases, and my classifications are therefore to be taken provisionally in these cases. The theatre given is the place of recorded first performance.

Play	Date	Genre	Playhouse	Company
Henry VI Part One	1589–90	History	Rose?	Admiral's/Strange's
Henry VI Part Two	1590–1	History	Theatre?	Pembroke's
Henry VI Part Three	1590–1	History	Theatre?	Pembroke's
Richard III	1592–3	History/Tragedy	Theatre?	Pembroke's
The Comedy of Errors	1592–4	Comedy	Gray's Inn	Pembroke's?
Titus Andronicus	1593–4	Tragedy	Rose/Theatre?	Pembroke's/Strange's/Sussex's
The Taming of the Shrew	1593–4	Comedy	Theatre?	Chamberlain's

(continued on next page)

Play	Date	Genre	Playhouse	Company
The Two Gentlemen of Verona	1594	Comedy	Theatre?	Chamberlain's
King John	1594–6	History	Theatre?	Chamberlain's
Richard II	1595	History/ Tragedy	Theatre?	Chamberlain's
Romeo and Juliet	1595–6	Tragedy	Theatre?	Chamberlain's
A Mid-summer Night's Dream	1595–6	Comedy	Theatre	Chamberlain's
The Merchant of Venice	1596–7	Comedy?	Theatre	Chamberlain's
Henry IV Part One	1596–7	History	Theatre?	Chamberlain's
The Merry Wives of Windsor	1597	Comedy	Westminster / Theatre	Chamberlain's
Henry IV Part Two	1598	History	Theatre?	Chamberlain's
Much Ado About Nothing	1598–9	Comedy	Curtain?	Chamberlain's
Henry V	1599	History	Curtain	Chamberlain's
Julius Caesar	1599	History/ Tragedy	Globe	Chamberlain's

(continued on next page)

Play	Date	Genre	Playhouse	Company
As You Like It	1599	Comedy	Globe	Chamberlain's
Hamlet	1600–1	Tragedy	Globe	Chamberlain's
Twelfth Night	1601–2	Comedy	Globe	Chamberlain's
Troilus and Cressida	1601–2	Comedy?	Globe? But may well not have been performed	King's Men, if performed (i.e. after 1603)
All's Well That Ends Well	1602–3	Comedy?	Globe	Chamberlain's
Measure for Measure	1604	Comedy?	Whitehall Palace/ Globe	King's Men
Othello	1604	Tragedy	Globe	King's Men
King Lear	1605	Tragedy	Globe	King's Men
Macbeth	1606	Tragedy	Globe	King's Men
Antony and Cleopatra	1606–7	Tragedy/ History	Globe	King's Men
Coriolanus	1607–8	Tragedy/ History	Globe	King's Men
Timon of Athens	1607–8	Tragedy/ History	Globe? But may well not have been performed	King's Men, if performed

(continued on next page)

Play	Date	Genre	Playhouse	Company
Pericles (with George Wilkins?)	1607–8	Romance	Globe	King's Men
Cymbeline	1609–10	Romance	Globe	King's Men
The Winter's Tale	1611	Romance/ Tragi-comedy	Globe	King's Men
The Tempest	1611	Romance/ Tragi-comedy	Blackfriars	King's Men
Henry VIII (with John Fletcher)	1612–13	History?	Globe	King's Men
The Two Noble Kinsmen (with John Fletcher)	1613	Tragi-comedy	Blackfriars	King's Men

7

UNDERSTANDING COMEDY

The Taming of the Shrew,
A Midsummer Night's Dream,
Measure for Measure,
The Merchant of Venice and
Twelfth Night

Comedy might simply be defined as a dramatic presentation which makes us laugh. Literary and cultural critics, however, tend to regard something as a comedy because a certain set of conventions is being followed. Laughter may also be evoked in other genres, including tragedy. The conventions of comedy include disguise (often involving cross-dressing), thwarted love, mistaken identity and marital and romantic misunderstandings. Comedies end in multiple marriage. Even if these 'rules' are deliberately broken, they remain an unspoken presence against which the play is reacting.

What all the comedies seem to have in common is their preoccupation with the journey of young women (and sometimes men) from the state of virginity to that of marriage. Whereas tragedy works towards death, that moment which gives a particular meaning to the actions of the protagonists, comedy traces the passage of young people out of their parents' control and into marriage. Thus Portia in *The Merchant of Venice* has to endure the ritual of the caskets prescribed by her father and simply hope that it will produce a man she can love; Hermia in *A Midsummer Night's Dream* has to run away into the woods with her lover Lysander in order to avoid marriage to Demetrius, the husband chosen for her by her father. It is, of course, clear why death in a tragedy is regarded as the end of the story (though it isn't for the survivors). It is less obvious why marriage should be regarded as an end. If anything, it is the beginning of a totally new story. It is the point, however, where sexual desire becomes legitimized (approved of by those in power), socialized (accepted by society at large) and channelled in a particular direction. In other words, comedy is often about one or more young persons whose love meets an obstacle of some sort.

Often some sort of resistance to this obstacle, be it parental disapproval or the apparent refusal of the loved one to return that feeling, is shown. The central plot of a comedy often requires the young people to disguise themselves (usually with women crossdressed as men, like Portia in *The Merchant of Venice*, Viola in *Twelfth Night* or Rosalind in *As You Like It*), or to abscond into the woods (like Hermia and Helena and their lovers in *A Midsummer Night's Dream* or Rosalind in *As You Like It*), or to undertake a journey (like Petruchio and Katherina in *The Taming of the Shrew*). When they emerge on the other side of the experience, something will have happened to make their love a social reality in some way, and the play ends with an apparently happy union. This journey may involve a different and strange world, where the rules of 'everyday' life do not apply, such as the wood in *A Midsummer Night's Dream* or the chaotic confusions of Illyria in *Twelfth Night*.

It should be borne in mind that a woman was not supposed to have the right to choose for herself a suitor or spouse. That was the male's prerogative. Comedy can therefore be seen as a challenge to the authority of fathers or husbands-to-be, which is played out in some imaginary world such as the magic wood, or a place where women in male disguise are never recognized until they wish to be. The whole play is itself, of course, a make-believe world, too.

Many contemporary critics seem very concerned about the question of prerogative when it comes to comedy. Two alternatives seem possible:

1   Are these plays to be seen as acting out a fantasy of female independence through some kind of symbolic revolt against the power and authority of fathers? And is this revolt shown only to demonstrate in the end the rightness of the inevitable progression from youthful desire to the socially approved institution of marriage? In other words, Hermia may think she is choosing for herself and going against her father's wishes, but she still ends up *married*, and with the approval of the Duke of Athens himself. She learns that it is best for a woman to control her desires and obey someone; if not her father, then her husband and the duke.

2   Might they, on the other hand, show that the world need not be as it is? Do they show women escaping the descriptions and identities which society imposes on them so dynamically that when the ending of the play comes, they do *not* become fully reabsorbed into society? Does the ending suggest that in fact after the wedding ceremony there is another story to be told – one of the kind of male–female relationship in which there is the potential for power to be more evenly distributed?

The first position tends to be associated, very broadly speaking, with the *new historicist* critics, the second with the *cultural materialists* (see pp. 229–30). Any question of the possible subjugation or liberation of women in these plays is naturally a matter of concern to feminist critics.

There is considerable disagreement among historians and critics about the position of women in English society in Shakespeare's time. Some writers stress the utter oppression of women in all domains of life: economic, domestic, sexual, familial and personal. Others point out that while it is certainly true that women were in no way regarded as the equals of men in official aspects of life, the Puritan doctrine of 'companionate marriage', which stressed the spiritual equality of man and wife in a loving relationship, was related to a kind of feminist flowering in this period among the middle-class women who would have attended the London theatres; that is, women whose Protestant beliefs encouraged them to consider themselves the spiritual equals of their husbands, but who did not hold anti-theatrical views. There is also considerable evidence that women were far more active in economic life as skilled workers, managers of large domestic organizations and small businesses than has often been assumed (Orgel 1996a: 73–4). Of the Puritans, the critic Juliet Dusinberre has written:

> Their reforms were aimed at men and women equally, but their effect was greater for women because they alleviated the exploitation made possible by the economic dependence of the woman. Thus the agitation for women's rights and for changed attitudes to women which was a vital aspect of the society for which Shakespeare wrote was to a large extent set in motion and furthered by the most powerful pressure group, both numerically and morally, of the time, and one which had the moral support of the most talented and creative of Shakespeare's contemporaries. This was the climate ... in which Shakespeare took root as a dramatist. The drama from 1590 to 1625 is feminist in sympathy.
>
> (Dusinberre 1996a: 5)

After this period writers were more committed to writing for the indoor theatre and the court rather than for the public playhouse. The way women were then presented, she argues, changed for the worse.

Other critics see this period as one of male backlash against the freedoms which, they say, women had in fact enjoyed in the late medieval period (Davies 1995: 14). Since Dusinberre first published her views in 1979, they have been challenged and qualified by other feminist writers. Whether this was a period of relative freedom for women or one of an oppression totally unacceptable by modern standards remains a moot point. For example, the novelist and critic Stevie Davies has pointed out the legal realities of life for a married woman in Shakespeare's time:

> Possessing no civil or civic functions, she was debarred from office in camp [the army], council [government], bench or jury-box [the courts]. She could neither vote nor be a candidate, nor (generally) give evidence in a lawcourt. She could not make a contract, sue or be sued. The reason for this was that a married woman did not, in law, exist. . . . Furthermore she could not own property because she was property. She owned neither the dowry she brought with her, nor the roof over her head, neither the jewels, if any, round her neck, nor the very clothes in which she stood up.
>
> (Davies 1995: 10)

Whatever the true situation may have been, it remains the case that in this debate the plays themselves stand as important pieces of evidence about the status of women in this period. They are not separate from their background, but part of our understanding of women's lives at this point in history.

COMEDY AND GENDER: *THE TAMING OF THE SHREW*

If there is a play from this period that seems unequivocally misogynistic (expressing a dislike of women), it is surely *The Taming of the Shrew*. Katherina is a young woman who always speaks her mind and is not afraid to be rude and aggressive when she needs to be. She wants a husband, but not the one approved of by her father. She is courted against her will by Petruchio, who openly admits that he has come to Padua in search of a wife with a rich dowry, no matter what she is like (I 2 5–76). Katherina's father is very happy to get her off his hands, even though she positively refuses the match. In this comedy, the desire of a woman to reject all suitors who are not to her liking is the female need which is to be brought under male control. It is done in the most domineering way possible, short of actual violence. That act of control might be seen either as exposing the injustice of male definitions of what a woman should be, or as simply reinforcing those definitions. That seems to be a central issue for critical study of the play.

Petruchio's courtship and marriage seem designed to humiliate Katherina and break her spirit. His behaviour is calculated to embarrass and degrade her as much as possible. After the wedding he takes her off to his house where he refuses to let her eat or sleep, pretending that he is doing it for her own good (IV 1 197–211). Eventually she seems to accept that his authority over her is complete, even to the point where she will agree that the sun is the moon if he says it is (IV 5 18–22), or that an old man is a young woman (IV 5 37–41). In the final scene Katherina wins for her husband a dinner-party wager. She demonstrates that she is the most obedient of those wives present by stooping in a gesture of submission and placing her hand beneath Petruchio's foot. In the longest speech of the play she offers the other wives a series of well-worn traditionalist reasons why man should have authority over woman:

Katherina　Thy husband is thy lord, thy life, thy keeper,
　　　　　Thy head, thy sovereign, one that cares for thee,
　　　　　And for thy maintenance; commits his body
　　　　　To painful labour, both by sea and land;
　　　　　To watch the night in storms, in day the cold,　　　　150
　　　　　Whilst thou liest warm at home, secure and safe;
　　　　　And craves* no other tribute at thy hands
　　　　　But love, fair looks and true obedience –
　　　　　Too little payment for so great a debt.
　　　　　Such duty as the subject owes the prince,*　　　　155
　　　　　Even such a woman oweth to her husband;
　　　　　And when she is froward, peevish,* sullen, sour,
　　　　　And not obedient to his honest will,
　　　　　What is she but a foul contending rebel,
　　　　　And graceless traitor to her loving lord?　　　　160
　　　　　I am ashamed that women are so simple*
　　　　　To offer war when they should kneel for peace,
　　　　　Or seek for rule, supremacy and sway,*
　　　　　When they are bound to serve, love and obey.

　　　　　　　　　　　　　　　　　　　　　(V 2 146–64)

* [152] *craves* asks for [155] *prince* monarch [157] *froward, peevish* pushy,
obstinate [161] *simple* foolish [163] *sway* power

This speech is so unambiguous a statement of women's subservience that feminist critics who wish to argue that the play is no simple story of just male triumph over a foolishly rebellious woman have much work to do. The *Guardian's* theatre critic, Michael Billington, famously asked 'whether there's any reason to revive a play which seems totally offensive to our age and society' (6 May 1978). Looking at the way the play ends, his question seems perfectly reasonable.

Many critics and directors have sought to interpret the play as ironic, making its suggested deeper meaning (an implicit rejection of the way Katherina is treated) much more significant than its surface meaning (women must learn to obey men in all circumstances). This may stem from a refusal to admit that Shakespeare could write a play as sexist as this appears to be. After all, other outspoken female characters are treated with far more sympathy: Emilia in *Othello* (see pp. 233ff.) and Paulina in *The Winter's Tale* (see p. 249), not to mention Beatrice in *Much Ado about Nothing*.

At the same time, however, if the portrayal of Katherina seems so 'out of character', it could be argued that this is one of his earlier plays (1593–4). Shakespeare's immaturity about sexual politics might explain the lack of sophistication.

Some of the arguments which have been advanced in order to recuperate this text emphasize the play's subtlety. What is unusual about *The Taming of the Shrew* is the framing – or, actually, half-framing – of the action by the Christopher Sly plot. The play begins with an 'Induction', in which a drunken tinker, Christopher Sly, is thrown out of a pub and falls asleep outside. Found by a lord who is out hunting, Sly is taken back to the lord's house and, as a practical joke, treated as if he were its owner. His 'previous life', he is told, was just a dream. The household members even provide him with a 'wife', who is actually a page dressed as a woman (Induction I 1 105–35). The play *The Taming of the Shrew* is staged by a group of players for the entertainment of Sly, the lord and his household. It is a play within a play and so is not presented to its audience as a 'reality' in which they are to believe. It is not just self-confessedly fictional, but actually presented as part of a conscious deceit. (In fact, the other side of the frame is missing: the Folio text forgets about Sly and the lord, and the play ends without their reappearance. Modern directors often add on the conclusion of the Sly framing plot from a play called *A Shrew*, a Quarto text which seems to be an earlier version, of some sort, of Shakespeare's play. For an explanation of 'Folio' and 'Quarto' see Box 1.2, p. 23.)

The point is that the play itself does not invite us to take seriously Petruchio's actions and Kate's submission: the play becomes a kind of fantasy of male wish-fulfilment, while consciously admitting that this view of the male–female relationship exists only in fiction. We are, then, free to see it as a demonstration that the gender roles played by men and women in society are in fact 'constructed' (see pp. 230–1) and do not form part of their essential natures. The comic swapping of identities among the other characters also underlines the idea that all of what we observe on stage is only role play. None of those we see has any 'fixed' nature: Tranio pretends to be Lucentio; the pedant pretends to be Vincentio; and Lucentio is in disguise as Cambio. What we are seeing in this part of the plot is not real, even within the context of the fiction in which it is set. That so many of the characters seem drawn from the stock types of the Italian *commedia dell'arte* (Davies 1995: 50) also undermines any confidence the audience might have that they are supposed to regard these characters as a representation of the world as it is. Consequently, Katherina's submission is very much an *imaginary* resolution of the conflict with her husband. Her final speech holds up the conventional reasons for male supremacy, as advanced by Renaissance writers, as fictions that are no more to be believed than the reality of Tranio or Lucentio's characterization, whether as *themselves* or as someone else. The speech's doctrines are so at odds with the experienced needs of men and women, then and now, that it is only in a make-believe world that they could bring domestic harmony. The ending, argues Juliet Dusinberre (1996a: 108), is, to say the least, ambiguous and equivocal. The clinching last line of the play expresses the incredulity of the other characters that Katherina really has been 'tamed' at all (V 2 189).

In what may be a clue to how the play was understood at the time, Dusinberre (1996a: 105–6) points to John Fletcher's sequel about Petruchio's second wife, *The Woman's Prize, Or The Tamer Tam'd*. Katherina, now dead, is reported to have remained resistant to taming until the end of her life. Fletcher was Shakespeare's successor as principal dramatist of The King's Men. The play was written some time between 1604 and 1617.

The American critic Karen Newman has suggested that when gender relations on stage are shown to be 'natural' in a fantasy play such as this, the artificiality of those relations is exposed by the drama (Newman 1986: 46). This is especially true in a theatre where boys play women. She sees Katherina's behaviour, right up to the end of the play, as a refusal to be categorized and controlled by the power structures by which men subordinate women. She refuses either to be silent or to submit herself as a passive public object for the male gaze. In this period obedient women were praised for their appearance. Disobedient women, especially those who 'talked too much', were publicly shamed by being ducked in rivers or ponds. In some cases a vicious metal gag, called 'the branks', was clamped around the mouth. Katherina, according to Newman, refuses to be seen and not heard. She takes on the male language and undermines it in two ways.

The first is her riddling word-play with Petruchio, through which she refuses to accept that he has a right to decide on the meaning of his own words. In fact, her puns expose marriage as an (unequal) sexual exchange in which women are exploited to produce offspring for men with no benefits (such as respect or affection) for themselves. Her word-play emphasizes the transparency of Petruchio's interest in her as a mother to his children, irrespective of whether she wants him or not. Her language emphasizes his unworthiness to be her partner:

Petruchio	Myself am moved* to woo thee for my wife.
Katherina	Moved! In good time!* Let him that moved you hither
	Remove you hence. I knew you at the first
	You were a moveable.
Petruchio	Why, what's a moveable?*
Katherina	A join'd-stool.*
Petruchio	Thou has hit it; come sit on me.*
Katherina	Asses are made to bear, and so are you.
Petruchio	Women are made to bear,* and so are you.
Katherina	No such jade* as you, if me you mean.
Petruchio	Alas, good Kate, I will not burden* thee,
	For knowing* thee to be but young and light.*
Katherina	Too light* for such a swain* as you to catch,
	And yet as heavy* as my weight should be.

     195

     200

     205

(II 1 194–205)

* [194] *am moved* desire [195] *In good time!* Indeed! [197] *a moveable* a piece of furniture; she means a dumb object, but also a mere household item (which he would make her). It also means fickle, unreliable emotionally [198] *A join'd-stool* a low stool that was proverbially easy to overlook; Petruchio's inferiority to her as a potential partner is the focus of her punning in what follows [198] *sit on me* a crudely sexual proposition [200] *bear* i.e. 'have me on top of you', but also 'bear my children' [201] *jade* a horse that soon tires; Petruchio wouldn't be able to satisfy her in bed,

perhaps [202] *burden* 'bother', but also 'accompany' (in a song) and a reference back to 'bear' [203] *For knowing* 'Because I know you are'; *light* 'delicate', but also in the sense of 'promiscuous' [204] *light* quick, elusive; *swain* country bumpkin [205] *heavy* serious, worthy of respect. There is also the sense that she is *true* coinage, not a coin that has been clipped or is counterfeit: she means what she says.

She may be the object of his sexual innuendo, but she retains her dignity and has the last word about what the language of the exchange actually means.

Throughout the trials of her wedding day and night, Katherina insists on her right to have her voice heard (III 2 207–21; IV 3 73–80). Petruchio deliberately mishears her, distorting what she says to suit his meaning. Female speech in the play is associated with female independence. It is not to be listened to.

Newman (1986) reads Katherina's apparent capitulation in the final scene as too knowing and blatant to be accepted at face value. After all, the only language available for a public statement like her final speech is male language. The only rhetoric she is allowed to deploy is male rhetoric. As a woman capable of 'miming' the male role to such effect, she exposes its internal contradiction: that she speaks at all goes against the content of what she is saying. She has *not* in the end been silenced. The comedy genre's resolution requires a 'happy' union. This is the speech to which the plot has been leading; it is the only way in which the comedy can end. But it is not Petruchio who speaks it. If she is tamed, how is it she holds the stage at the end, unsilenced? Newman says that the effect is to put the speech 'in italics' (Newman 1986: 51). Katherina is quoting someone else in order to bring to attention that person's mistake. Newman sums up the argument like this:

> Kate's having the last word contradicts the very sentiments she speaks; rather than resolve the play's action, her monologue displays the fundamental contradiction presented by a female protagonist, between women as sexually desirable, silent objects and women of words, women with power over language who disrupt, or at least italicize, women's place and part in culture.
>
> (Newman 1986: 51)

Petruchio's actions produce not a mute beauty, the object of his taming, but a female version of himself.

For some feminist critics, this is all too much. 'Manifest evasion', Stevie Davies (1995: 62) calls it. The play is a blatant and offensive metaphor for man as the tamer of an unruly horse or a wayward hawk. Men are masters and women are their animals to be tamed. If at the end two shrews (Bianca and the Widow) remain, that just shows how never-ending the task is.

When Petruchio describes his wife as 'My household stuff, my field, my barn, / My horse, my ox, my ass, my anything' (III 2 231–2), it is not intended to shock; it is a simple statement of the legal realities of marriage (see p. 142). Katherina's language doesn't quite escape Petruchio's control through its wit and word-play. Instead he often makes it appear as if she is only repeating what he wants her to say (see, for example, the exchange with the tailor in IV 3 103–5). It is not that he wilfully mishears her throughout the play, either. If she will not be silent and speak only at his bidding, then her language is not worth listening to. He knows what she really means, even if she is saying the opposite (see, for example, the scenes at his house in IV 1 and IV 3). She must learn this. When Katherina at his bidding calls the sun the moon (IV 5 2–22), it is not exposing the absurdity of Petruchio's demand for total domination. Rather it shows her realization that nature itself is turned upside down, if she insists on turning the equally natural social order of male supremacy upside down (Davies 1995: 11).

At the end Katherina is allowed the play's longest speech, even though a woman, because it is her husband speaking through her at last. Her voice, too, is now fully his, and there is no irony intended. No other evidence within the play suggests that the speech is not sincerely meant. Indeed, the idea that Katherina will have some sort of power by publicly going along with Petruchio's wishes while getting her own way at home is, as Davies argues, 'demeaning to both parties' (Davies 1995: 55).

The play can also be seen, then, to be a plain statement of the right of men to control and dominate their wives. It can be argued, moreover, that the play itself has actually operated over the years to reinforce that domination, no matter what Shakespeare may or may not have said in other plays.

COMEDY AND POWER: *A MIDSUMMER NIGHT'S DREAM* AND *MEASURE FOR MEASURE*

If Davies is right, *The Taming of the Shrew* is a crude but theatrically energetic statement in support of the rights of the powerful. Other critics have found Shakespeare's comedies to be more subtle reinforcements of ruling-class values.

In the Athens of *A Midsummer Night's Dream* the rule of the father over a daughter is enforced in a savage way. Duke Theseus is about to marry the Amazon queen Hippolyta, whom he wooed, he boasts, 'with my sword' (I 1 16). A nobleman, Egeus, insists that his daughter Hermia marries Demetrius, rather than Lysander, the man she wants. By the law of the state her refusal will be punished either by death or banishment to a convent. Theseus gives Hermia until his own wedding day to make up her mind. Once alone, the lovers plan to elope to stay with a favourable aunt outside the city, where they can marry. They arrange to meet that night in a wood. They tell Hermia's friend Helena, who is in love with Demetrius, of their plans. She tells the audience that she will inform Demetrius of their escape. He will then pursue them, and she him, into the magic wood. There the four undergo various transformations at the playful hands of the woodland fairies, led by their quarrelling monarchs Queen Titania and King Oberon. When their nocturnal adventures are over, Hermia and Lysander and Helena and Demetrius will be happy together and will marry with the blessing of Theseus himself, overruling the wishes of Egeus (IV 1 179–81).

Their experiences in the wood not only untangle the knot of their conflicting desires, but Demetrius's account of his transformation from 'sickness' to 'health' (IV 1 160–76) seems to win over Theseus to the cause of true love and all is resolved happily for the young people.

Once in the wood the lovers seem to think that they can choose for themselves, free from state and patriarchal authority. But, argues the American Marxist critic Elliott Krieger, this is an illusion. What the play demonstrates is that state and patriarchal power is enforced not only physically, by law and punishment, but also by aesthetic means (*aesthetic* means concerned with art and beauty). In this play sexual passion and the need for individual liberty in defiance of Duke Theseus' power are always transformed to an imaginary artistic level on which violence can be glossed over in beautiful language, and in a purely make-believe world rebellion can be played out to the satisfaction of the players inside that world, but never actually challenges those who hold power in the real world.

The Amazons were a race of warrior-women who rejected men altogether from their lives. Theseus' defeat of Hippolyta is firmly reinforced by her marriage to him – a marriage for which, in the first scene, she notably expresses no desire. (In some productions she is made to be obviously hostile; and in a famous 1966 production she was even brought on stage in a cage [Holland 1994: 51].) But the violence of his conquest is to be turned into beauty, aestheticized, by its representation as public spectacle:

Theseus   Hippolyta, I wooed thee with my sword,
          And won thy love doing thee injuries;
          But I will love thee in another key,
          With pomp, with triumph and with revelling.

(I 1 16–19)

The festivities of the wedding are only a shift in musical 'key'. Violence is swiftly transformed into art. In the same way, Theseus relishes the musical sound of his hunting hounds' baying (IV 1 105, 110, 124–5) and their physical appearance (IV 1 119–23), rather than any actual ability they have to perform their proper function: the capture and killing of gentler creatures (Krieger 1979: 48–9). The court performance of *Pyramus and Thisbe* by Bottom and the other craftsmen is another example of how tragedy and thwarted desire are turned into a safe aesthetic experience to be enjoyed by an aristocratic audience. Normally the weaver, the carpenter and the tailor transform nature into something useful. In Theseus' court they can transform only themselves into useless *representations* of nature for aristocratic approval.

The wood appears to the lovers to be a place of pastoral escape, safe from the power of Theseus and Egeus; that is why they agree to meet there. It was, after all, the place wherein the two women used to feel free to tell each other their youthful dreams (I 1 214–16). But it is actually full of Theseus' power. Quince calls his rehearsal at the 'duke's oak' (I 2 110) in the 'palace wood' (I 2 101). The fairies who rule there are a kind of aristocratic fantasy, blessed with magic powers and enjoying the happy service of a crowd of retainers, in a parallel power structure to that which obtains in Athens. Titania's dispute with her husband over possession of the Indian Boy is resolved happily through Oberon's magic powers (IV 1 71ff.). Oberon wants the child to enter his service; Titania had promised a close female friend, now dead, that she would not part from him (II 1 119–37). Meanwhile in Athens the desire of women to express solidarity with one another without the intervention of male power is crushed through military action in Theseus' victory over the Amazons. In the wood, on the other hand, male art-magic resolves conflict in ways that please and amuse.

The fairies themselves are a literary creation, a transformation of the actual world. As a fantasy expression of a ruler's power, they can control nature itself through their actions. The fiction of the magic potion is a metaphorical expression of the power of society to make people love in a way approved by the state. In the fairy world, the world of the wood, the love of the four young people is in fact confirmed as love expressed via the literary conventions of courtly and pastoral poetry. In this kind of poetry, often written by aristocrats, the young man writes of his unfulfilled desire in elaborate language full of mythological reference. The sought-after woman is said to possess a physical beauty way beyond that of any real woman; the man's love has a power and intensity which can be expressed only in powerful and often dense metaphor. Thinking and speaking in this literary language, the lovers in the wood cease to communicate directly with each other, for they are living in a world whose language is the creation of an external literary-aristocratic authority, and not an expression of their own authentic subjective desires: 'while in the forest', writes Krieger, 'they reiterate, in a different form, the authoritarian social system that controls Athenian love' (1979: 43). In Athens, sexual desire is controlled through the conventional language in which it is expressed. Before they went into the wood, Lysander had talked of love in terms of a right justified through social status (I 1 99–102), or as a process following certain literary expectations (I 1 132–5). Hermia's promise of true love to him is in accordance with mythic and literary notions of what love is (I 1 169–74).

But in the wood the language of the lovers doesn't actually change. When Lysander wakes up from his sleep, affected by the potion, he sees Helena and falls in love with her. It's not her beauty he loves, says Krieger (1979: 45), but the *story* of beauty in a love-fiction:

Lysander   Reason becomes the marshal to my will,   120
             And leads me to your eyes, where I o'erlook
             Love's stories written in Love's richest book.

                                                        (II 2 120–2)

When Demetrius falls in love with Helena, his feelings for her are expressed in the language of the most conventional love poetry. These are clichés, not sincere words. That is why they often get a laugh in the theatre:

Demetrius   O Helen, goddess, lymph, perfect, divine!
              To what, my love, shall I compare thyne eyne?*
              Crystal is muddy. O, how ripe in show
              Thy lips, those kissing cherries, tempting grow!   140
              That pure congeal'd white, high Taurus'* snow,
              Fann'd with the eastern wind, turns to a crow
              When thou holds't up thy hand.

                                                        (III 2 137–43)

* [138] *eyne* eyes – an old-fashioned, literary form [141] *Taurus* a mountain
                 range in Turkey often referred to in classical poetry

Even the violence threatened between them is literary rather than real: Lysander wishes to stab the word 'Demetrius' with his sword, not Demetrius himself (II 2 106–7). Passion and desire are social-ized, not freed from constraint. No matter what they themselves think, the untangling of the lovers' relationships has happened in a space and in a language under the control of Theseus. He licenses their desire and makes it part of his own wedding celebrations. Egeus doesn't get his way; but Theseus' own patriarchal power is enhanced, not diminished. It should also be noted that, during the rule of the Tudors and Stuarts, state and church control over marriage and the family increased. The controlling power of indi-vidual men over their families, particularly among the aristocracy, correspondingly decreased.

The threat to established power of youthful sexuality, which tends to disregard authority and social convention, is, Krieger argues, defused by giving it literary rather than authentic expression. But *A Midsummer Night's Dream* is itself both a literary expression of certain desires and anxieties and an attempt to tell its audience that these desires and anxieties can be satisfyingly resolved. The American critic Louis Adrian Montrose, for example, suggested (1996) that the play represented, and itself influenced, certain Elizabethan social anxieties about the relations between men and women. Here was a country in which men had a near-monopoly on power, but whose symbolic and political head was a woman. Whether looking at Hermia or Hippolyta or Titania, the play shows again and again women's disruption of male bonds; but ultimately male power regains ascendancy. Montrose, in one particularly subtle reading (1996: 127), gives an explanation of Oberon's story about Cupid's dart. Cupid aimed his love-dart at a beautiful virgin, but it was deflected on to a 'flower / Before milk-white, now purple with love's wound' (II 1 166–7). Montrose says that this story can be seen to represent Queen Elizabeth's own virginity paradoxically keeping in place a social system in which men had power over the virginities of all other women. The Queen is the 'fair vestal throned by the west' (II 1 158); other women are the 'little western flower' (II 1 166). This flower's juice is, of course, used by Oberon's servant Puck to control who loves whom in the wood (II 2 26 sd; II 2 78–9; III 2 453 sd).

Comedy for critics like Montrose, then, is about the containment of challenges to the symbolic and actual power of men over women. But, as we have seen, it can also be read as a manifestation of women's potential to burst the bounds of that power. Thus the play's problematic nature actually reveals political and social contradictions inherent in society's view of itself in Shakespeare's time. In particular it reveals that the power *inscribed in* male love comes into conflict with the actual nature of human sexual desire, as well as showing its own contradictory nature. 'Inscribed in' means that male love cannot exist in this society without containing and being shaped by the inequalities of power between men and women which existed then. This inequality of power is 'written into' all the stories of love that are told, because it is built into the very language of those narratives.

The same exploration of sexual inequality and conflict inherent in a society's language and thinking is found in the later, darker comedy *Measure for Measure* (1604). The Duke of Vienna, worried that sexual licence has grown out of control, pretends to go away from the city, leaving in charge his strict deputy Angelo. The duke expects Angelo to enforce the cruel law that makes sex outside of marriage a capital offence. It is a law which he himself has been too lenient to enforce. Meanwhile, disguised as a friar, the duke watches what develops. Angelo decides to make an example of Claudio, a gentleman whose fiancée Juliet is pregnant. Claudio's sister Isabella, herself about to enter a convent, goes to Angelo to plead for her brother's life.

Their debate is carried out initially at the level of abstract discussion (II 2 25–136). But it is not her reasoning that has the most impact on Angelo. Claudio's friend Lucio had told her that she was the right person to sue for his life, because when a young virgin kneels before authority and asks for mercy, all tradition says that she will be granted it (I 4 80–3). In a society where virginity stands for moral purity, a pleading virgin must be impartial; to deny her mercy would be to deny 'fairness' itself, in both senses of the word (look at how Lucio greets her at first meeting [I 4 24]) (Piesse 1996: 61). Yet a virgin's moral power rests on the unstated premiss of her desirability: she is female beauty unsullied by the potent threat of awakened female sexuality. She is, in theory, outside the sexual struggle. Men are attracted to the unthreatening moral purity of the virgin, but they want her, obviously, in order to take that purity from her. The whole contradictory construction is based on fear of female sexuality and the power it has over men. But in this play men speak a language about love that controls and neutralizes that sexuality.

Men want their sexual desire to be dominant. Yet women have a crucial and obvious advantage in this struggle. Males require females in order to reproduce themselves. Husbands need to control their wives' sexuality if they are to have sons whose paternity is beyond question. The fear of this real power that women have recurs in the imagery of so many of the exchanges in this play.

It is when Isabella moves the discussion away from the abstract and asks Angelo to consider his own feelings that he sees her as an individual, and therefore as a particular woman, rather than a symbol of virginity. Has he not wanted to do the very thing for which he now condemns her brother?

> *Isabella*　Go to your bosom,
> 　　　　Knock there, and ask your heart what it doth know
> 　　　　That's like my brother's fault. If it confess
> 　　　　A natural guiltiness, such as is his,
> 　　　　Let it not sound a thought upon your tongue　　　　140
> 　　　　Against my brother's life.
> *Angelo (Aside)*　She speaks, and 'tis
> 　　　　such sense* that my sense* breeds with it.
>
> 　　　　　　　　　　　　　　　　　　　　(II 2 136–42)
>
> 　　　* [142] *such sense* reason; *my sense* my sensuality

Angelo suddenly finds himself sexually attracted to her. Isabella's ability to plead, Angelo's language makes clear, is not actually a function of her power of reason, but of her sexual attractiveness. An obscene pun, which Angelo unconsciously makes once she has gone, reinforces this: 'Is this her fault, or mine?', he says, at the beginning of his soliloquy (II 2 162). 'Fault' was used as a term for the vagina. His 'fault', however, as a man, can only be in reasoning or behaviour. Once she has gone, he finds that he 'loves' her (II 2 176), but what sort of love it can be remains open to question. It may be a subconscious recognition that, since he has power over this individual woman, he can get sex from her and father his child on her. This would be his definition of 'love'.

Sexual attraction is common to all societies and eras but is always constructed by the political and economic power structures of those particular societies and eras. Given the stories this society tells about female desire and virginity, sexual relations must inevitably be distorted. Angelo has the power, and therefore control over the meaning of words. Because Isabella, the novice-nun, talks about sex in the same religious language that Angelo uses to justify the law, her own words make her a subject of male power, as well as the contradictions within that power. Men want women to be pure but at the same time want to take that purity from them.

Isabella is quite unaware of how her words will be interpreted once her language is thought of in sexual terms, as it inevitably will be in the world of the play. She continues to use the religious language, unaware that it carries within it that denial of normal sexuality which is at the root of Vienna's problems. That form of Christian morality which regards all non-procreative sex as wrong simply does not fit with the facts of human life. When Pompey the pimp is arrested, he puts the matter to the magistrate very succinctly: 'Does your worship mean to geld [castrate a male] and splay [sterilize a female] all the youth of the city?' (II 1 230–1). The law must accept the fact of human sexuality, not impose a religious rigour which serves the interests of the powerful, who are in this case men, since it is women who 'tempt'.

Isabella herself applauds the law and hates fornication (II 2 29–30). But her own language is full of suppressed sexuality, even when she uses religious ideas. When she returns to Angelo to plead once more for her brother's life, she says she would rather die than yield up her virginity to save his life. Yet the language she uses is startling. He asks what she would do if a judge said he would pardon her brother, if she slept with him:

Angelo   What would you do?
Isabella   As much for my poor brother as myself;
That is, were I under the terms* of death,   100
Th' impression of keen whips I'ld wear as rubies,
And strip myself for death, as to a bed
That longing have been sick for, ere* I'ld yield
My body up to shame.

(II 4 98–104)

* [100] *terms* sentence [103] *ere* before

She is unaware of the impact of her words. She gives an image of herself as receiving blows from a whip with pride and pleasure, and of herself undressing for a bed which she had desired so much that it had made her sick. The discourse of Christian asceticism contains a repressed sexuality which makes her all the more attractive to Angelo. He sees her as a woman and tells her that she must stop teasing him and become what she must be, a sexual partner to a superior man who desires her. But he also despises her *because* he desires her. She is attractive because chaste; but that attraction tempts a man to sin.

In a crucial speech she admits that women are frail, as men sometimes are, in the context of their powers of reasoning (II 4 117–23). But she goes on to pick up Angelo's promptings about the specific frailty of women. She agrees that women are inferior, and thinks she is talking about their natural susceptibility to male reasoning and power. But Angelo is alert to the sexual possibilities in her speech and tells her she must take up the role allotted to her by the language she is speaking.

Angelo	Nay, women are frail too.	
Isabella	Ay, as the glasses* where they view themselves,	125
	Which are as easy broke as they make forms.*	
	Women? Help, heaven! Men their creation mar	
	In profiting by them.* Nay, call us ten times frail,	
	For we are soft as our complexions are,	
	And credulous to false prints.*	
Angelo	I think it well;	130
	And from this testimony of your own sex	
	(Since I suppose we are made to be no stronger	
	Than faults may shake our frames), let me be bold.	
	I do arrest* your words. Be that you are,	
	That is, a woman; if you be more, you're none;*	135
	If you be one (as you are well expressed	
	By all external warrants*), show it now,	
	By putting on the destined livery*.	

(II 4 124–38)

* [125] *glasses* mirrors [126] *Which are as easy broke as they make forms* which break as easily as they reflect images; but also (of women) 'who conceive a child as easily as their virginity is broken' [127–8] *Men their creation mar in profiting by them* 'Men spoil their creation in God's image by taking advantage of women' [130] *credulous to false prints* easily persuaded of untruths; but also 'willing to conceive an illegitimate child' [134] *arrest* stop; but also 'take into my custody and control' [135] *if you be more, you're none* if you are more chaste than a woman really is, you are not a woman at all [137] *external warrants* outward signs (Angelo is using legal language to describe her female attributes) [138] *livery* a servant's uniform – so *destined* livery has the sense here of 'the badge of the role which, as a woman, you were always bound to assume sexually with a man'

Women's ability to conceive is actually the same thing, in this story, as their weakness and inferiority to men. Her own words contain this admission, so she should accept that she is destined to be his mistress. She finally understands what he is saying and appreciates the sexual subtext. She pleads for a return to a plain, non-sexual, discourse which cannot implicate her. But how can they return to what wasn't there in the first place? He defines what love is, not her:

Isabella	I have no tongue but one;* gentle my lord,	
	Let me entreat you speak the former language.	140
Angelo	Plainly conceive,* I love you.	
Isabella	My brother did love Juliet,	
	And you tell me that he shall die for't.*	
Angelo	He shall not, Isabel, if you give me love.	

(II 4 139–44)

> * [139] *no tongue but one* 'one level only of meaning to my words' [141] *conceive* understand; but yet another parallel between men making women understand them, and men fathering children on them [143] *for't* for it

Meaning in the play is actually a function of power. Those with power have the final judgement on what words mean. This is made explicit soon afterwards. If Isabella goes out and proclaims Angelo's actions to the world, his good name and political position will mean that people will interpret her accusations as baseless slander (II 4 154–9).

The strange ending of *Measure for Measure* plays with the generic ending of comedy, multiple marriage. But it uses marriage as a punishment. Angelo must marry his ex-betrothed, Mariana, a death sentence – which he thought his rightful punishment (V 1 370) – being waived. This what Mariana wants, for it gives the jilted woman the social status she thought she would never have. Whether either will be happy in the union is another matter. Lucio, Claudio's witty and insolent friend who slanders the Duke, regards his sentence of marriage to Kate Keepdown, the prostitute whom he impregnated, as equivalent to 'pressing to death, / Whipping and hanging' (V 1 522–3). Claudio and Juliet are happy, but they were happy in their love and prospective parenthood before the state intervened. It is not really surprising that the text gives Isabella no response to the Duke's surprise proposal of marriage (V 1 534–7).

BOX 7.1: LONDON

In 1600 nine-tenths of England's population lived in the countryside and its small market towns. Farmland, forest and moorland were punctuated by enclosed parks kept by noblemen for hunting deer and boar. Norwich, Bristol, York, Salisbury, Newcastle, Exeter and Coventry were the only towns with populations in excess of 5,000, and there was only one city by European standards, London. It was here that Shakespeare spent most of his working life, and aspects of the city are revealed in many of his plays.

Between 1550 and 1600 the population of the capital city trebled to around 150,000. In Europe, only Paris and Naples were larger. Maybe 15 per cent of Londoners were wealthy: the court, the aristocrats and important merchants. The vast majority of England's trade passed through London and here the merchants increased their wealth and power. Merchants had to be members of the livery companies which regulated the market against new competition. The senior officers of these companies governed the City of London and made its laws. Junior members – craftsmen, clerks, shopkeepers, apprentices – represented the typical 'citizenry' of London. They tended to be Puritan in their religious observance and very proud of their status. Below them were the great mass of servants and, beneath, the genuinely poor who eked out a living one way or another.

London's 150,000 inhabitants were crammed into an area from the Tower in the east to Westminster in the west. The old city walls still stood, and the gates were locked at night, but increasingly new buildings were being erected outside the walls. London's great public buildings, the Tower and Whitehall Palace (sites of royal power), Westminster Abbey and old St Paul's Cathedral (symbols of the Church's importance), the Guildhall (the site of City government) and the Royal Exchange (the site of trade) were spread across the city. They were surrounded by the parish churches, houses, shops, taverns, inns, schools, prisons and workshops of the rest of the population. The mansions of the rich, mostly along the Strand, were surrounded by the hovels of the poor in a warren of narrow, mostly unpaved, streets. The administration of the City of London did not extend fully north of the walls or south of the river. These areas were former monastic territories known as the 'liberties', and it was on the South Bank, beyond the control of the Puritan councillors, that The Swan, The Rose and The Globe theatres stood, alongside pits for bear-baiting and cock-fighting and a large number of brothels. There was only one bridge, 'London Bridge', situated near the Tower in the east. Houses and shops lined its sides, and the heads of executed felons stood on pikes over its southern gateway. The Thames was the main artery of transport, with watermen rowing passengers among the ships and barges of merchants and traders.

London was a crowded, dirty and dangerous place, with a high mortality rate. Each 'ward' of the city had its 'scavengers' who were supposed to deal with sanitation, but most sewage just went down a gutter in the middle of the street, towards the Thames or one of the other London rivers. Plague was a constant bringer of sudden death, with bad outbreaks in 1593, 1597 and 1625, when 40,000 died. Clean water was not easily available, and it may have been typhoid from infected water that killed Shakespeare (Honan 1998: 407). Beer was safer than water to drink, and most people drank beer from an early age. Some historians have remarked that the violence of early modern city life may have been connected to the general low level of sobriety.

It was easy to get away with criminal activity in London, and many homeless and unemployed people, supporting themselves by begging, trickery and prostitution, drifted towards the capital. Many men went about armed, and fatal brawls were common. Shakespeare is very satirical about the inefficient police system of watchmen in *Measure for Measure* and *Much Ado About Nothing*. As well as the sight of violent street brawls, Londoners would have been used to public executions, the carcasses of slaughtered animals and, not so very rarely, corpses in the street.

London was nevertheless the most exciting and energetic place in the country. Money and power flowed through its streets alongside its stench and ever-present danger. Its merchant class, which was to defeat the forces of absolute monarchy later in the seventeenth century, were the most progressive and dynamic group in the country, even if they usually opposed the theatre.

Shakespeare's probable first play, *King Henry VI Part I*, is known to have been performed in London in March 1592. His long poem *Venus and Adonis* was registered with the government censor and literature licensee, the Stationer's Office, in April 1593. We know that until 1585 he was in Warwickshire. What he was up to between 1585 and 1592 and how it was that he should suddenly have appeared in London as a writer have been subjects of considerable speculation. There are tales of deer-poaching, fighting against the Spanish in Holland and of visiting Italy, but there is no firm evidence for these stories. Evidence that he was a tutor to a Catholic family in Lancashire (Honan 1998: 65; Wilson 2004, ch. 2) is plausible but inconclusive. We know little, in fact, other than that he made his name in London. The world of its taverns, brothels and palaces is represented in many plays, vividly so in *King Henry IV Part I* and less explicitly in *Measure for Measure*.

Marriage in this scene is used to punish and control. Isabella perhaps now realizes that once you speak the language of the powerful, you will be implicated in their system.

Measure for Measure shows how the imposition of patriarchal law distorts sexual desire. This *may* reveal the resourcefulness of the powerful; or it may indicate a community's need to control the destabilizing force of lust outside marriage. Alternatively, it may point forward to a utopian sexuality wherein desire and procreation find their own level free from legal constraint.

What I have argued in this section, it should be noted, is not that Shakespeare wrote *Measure for Measure* as an attack on marriage. Instead I have followed that contemporary critical approach which finds the source of the 'problems' of the plays not in the writer's design or dramatic skill but in the contradictions that, from our perspective, are evident in the ideas about sexual love current in Jacobean London. In the comedies written in the 1590s love and marriage, while never simple, were not interrogated so darkly.

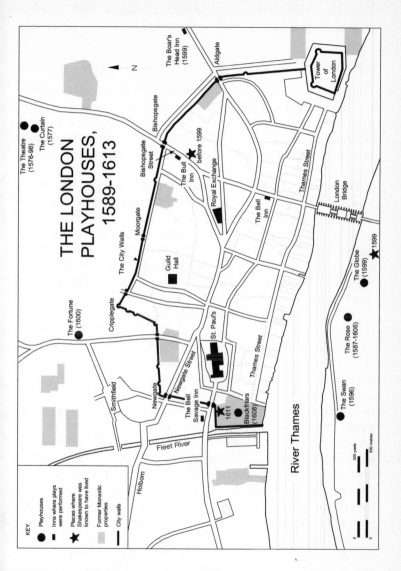

Figure 7.1 The London playhouses, 1589–1613

There does seem to have been a shift in outlook with regard to these issues in the plays written after 1600.

COMEDY AND UTOPIA: *THE MERCHANT OF VENICE*

The story of the defeat and humiliation of Shylock, the vengeful and 'inhuman' Jew, would seem an unlikely place to look for egalitarian sentiments about the rights of those who are denied full expression of their humanity. But some contemporary critics have argued persuasively that it is precisely here that such sentiments are to be found.

The heroine of this play, the wealthy Portia, has two obstacles to overcome before she can marry the man whom she loves, Bassanio. The first is her father's will, a legally binding document which requires her to marry the man who solves the riddle of the three caskets. He who correctly interprets the words inscribed on the gold, silver and lead boxes, and consequently chooses aright, will become her husband, whether she wants it or not. The second is that Bassanio's friend Antonio has managed to acquire the money for Bassanio's wooing of Portia only by borrowing from Shylock the Jew (Antonio loves Bassanio and will do literally anything for him; it seems to be a same-sex love which is not returned [III 2 318–22]). Apparently as a joke, for 'merry sport' (I 3 145), at first, Shylock requires Antonio to forfeit a pound of his flesh, if he fails to repay the 3,000 ducats on time. Antonio's ships are supposedly lost at sea, and Shylock, now enraged at his daughter Jessica's elopement with Lorenzo, a Christian, demands his 'bond' in full. Refusing all pleas for mercy, and even three times the original sum in compensation, Shylock knows that the laws of Venice cannot deny him the forfeit, which he demands. He is about to make the fatal cut, when Portia, appearing in disguise as a young (male) lawyer, points out that while the law will allow him to take his pound of flesh, any Jew who sheds Christian blood will, by another law, forfeit all his goods to the state. Furthermore, there is another law decreeing that any 'alien' who seeks to take the life of a Venetian will lose all his property and have his life put at the mercy of the duke. Dispossessed and forced to convert to Christianity, Shylock leaves in despair. The disguised Portia then tests Bassanio's loyalty by demanding a ring he wears as payment for her work as his lawyer – she had previously given Bassanio this ring, telling him that it would be the end of their love, were he ever to give it away (III 2 171–4; see below). The reluctant Bassanio is eventually persuaded and gives her the ring. It is possible that she feels prompted to put Bassanio to this test, having heard him say during the trial that he would rather his wife were dead than that Antonio should lose his life (IV 1 282–7).

The play's final scene was seen by some earlier critics as a light-heartedly romantic resolution of the comic plot in the aristocratic surroundings of Portia's Belmont, away from the commercial values of Venice. But this is to gloss over the uncomfortable atmosphere of the play's ending. Shylock, though clearly having sought savage revenge on a man who had long despised him for his race and religion (I 3 106–13), has just left the stage to vicious Christian abuse. Shylock's daughter Jessica and her husband Lorenzo begin the scene by saying that the night reminds them of many other famous love affairs: Troilus and Cressida, Dido and Aeneas, Medea and Jason – all of which, though they do not mention it, ended disastrously. A large part of the scene (V 1 142–270) is taken up with Portia and Nerissa berating their husbands for giving away their rings; they suggest that it was a kind of symbolic giving of their own wives to other 'men' (258–65) (see below). Though Nerissa promises faithfulness (282–3), Portia does not address her husband with real affection at the end. And it is Portia who remains in charge, inviting all the others to leave the stage. It can be argued that this is a play that ends with a woman very much empowered, while the men have been embarrassed and outwitted.

Karen Newman (1998) has argued that the exchange of goods (including women) between men characterizes the play's action. In a patriarchal society men have rights over women that are not reciprocated. In the world of the play, Portia's father has the right to choose her husband. The women, however, cannot propose to the men. In fact, Newman argues, anthropologists have noted that men establish their relationships and their pecking order by the granting of gifts. But, Newman says, in this play Portia's rhetoric makes it clear that *she* is making a gift of herself to Bassanio, and one which *she* can withdraw. When Bassanio chooses the right casket and claims her as his wife, she talks of herself impersonally, in the passive voice (III 2 166–7), acknowledging herself as a property which at a particular moment is 'converted' to another's legal possession:

Portia   Happiest of all, is that her gentle spirit
          Commits itself to yours to be directed,
          As from her lord, her governor, her king.   165
          Myself, and what is mine, to you and yours
          Is now converted.

(III 2 163–7)

This material transaction is not represented as 'naturally' binding, however: it may be undone again. Its material and arbitrary nature is symbolized by a token, her ring, the significance of which can change just as any representational token, be it a word or a picture or a coin, may have its reference altered. You own me now, she says; but lose my ring and you lose me.

Portia   This house, these servants, and this same myself   170
          Are yours – my lord's! – I give them with this ring,
          Which when you part from, lose, or give away,
          Let it presage* the ruin of your love,
          And be my vantage* to exclaim* on you.

(III 2 170–4)

* [173] presage foretell [174] vantage opportunity; exclaim on denounce

Bassanio's response to such a bold assertion, so untypical of a woman's love-pledge in romantic comedy, is to liken the confusion in his head to the experience of one who has just heard a 'beloved prince' (179) speak. He acknowledges that she has made him a gift of herself and her wealth, which is so great that he is effectively in her power (she seems like *his* lord) because he can never repay it (Newman 1998: 124–5). Maybe it is her wealth, vastly superior to his own, that gives her the right to assign meaning to the ring, now and in the future, if he betrays her love. There is, however, another source of power in the text.

Once Bassanio has given the ring to a woman dressed as a man, it ceases to be the token of the husband's possession of the wife and instead becomes associated with an unruly woman who wears men's clothes. Cross-dressing was a subversive breaking of the rules. Fashionable, or adventurous, poor, young women who did it in Shakespeare's time found it both empowering and sexually liberating, which made it all the more condemned by moralists. Some were pilloried or whipped for it (Orgel 1996a: 119; see also Howard 1994: 96). (It is interesting to note that men taking part in acts of violence against their employers or lords would sometimes adopt female dress; cross-dressing was a mark of subversion [Howard 1994: 105]). Portia also triumphs in the male profession of lawyer, a profession founded on the very qualities of reason and skill at public speaking that women were supposed to lack. Bassanio thinks he is engaging in a bond with another man, but Portia's identity, as both woman and man, as both his 'prince' and yet his possession, changes the meaning of the ring as a token. The ring comes to mean female self-expression, female sexuality (V 1 307), changeability and unruliness. The symbol of male possession of women is transformed into a symbol of women slipping out of male power. Portia's successful refusal to be bound by the rigid category of femaleness exposes the truth that women are more than commodities to be exchanged.

It is characteristic that the means by which Portia defeats Shylock is the riddle, or quibble. Shylock can have his pound of flesh only if he does not shed a drop of Antonio's blood (IV 1 305–12). The same kind of riddling word-play is used by Portia and Nerissa to baffle their husbands in the final scene, when they assert that they have slept with the lawyers to whom the rings were given (V 1 258–62). To understand the riddle is to grasp that women can be taken for men. If women can thus escape their 'nature', they can escape the definitions and restrictions which men and their language place upon them.

Some critics have felt that Portia surrenders to her husband's power at the end of the play. That this is highly debatable, even on the surface of the text, I have argued above. In fact she can be seen to become a person who has escaped male control through her slippery and riddling disguise and language. 'Unruly' women who can be taken for men don't ever actually become men. They are neither men nor women, but both at the same time. They become something that slips out of the control of male language and control, like the ring that no longer fits the category of symbol which it was assumed to have done when first given. Because a riddling language can't be pinned down, nor its implications refuted, it is a challenge to those who seek to exert power. As Catherine Belsey puts it:

> Riddles demonstrate that meaning is neither single nor transparent, that words can be used to conceal it. They show that language itself seduces and betrays those who believe themselves to be in command of it . . .
>
> (Belsey 1998a: 144)

In the final scene Portia and Nerissa, like the audience, know the answers to their riddles. But there is another meaning which is at work here, once this language gets to be spoken. The riddle asserts a kind of equality between men and women. Portia's teasing of Bassanio in the fifth act (for example V 1 224–34), like the sexual pun of the last line of the play, asserts the difference between men and women (or does it?). But the riddles suggest that the women are *both* the 'other' that inspires desire in the men *and* the equal of the men, in as much as they were treated as men by the men. As Portia says: 'If you had known . . . / . . . half her worthiness that gave the ring' (V 1 199–200) – 'The lawyer Balthazar was your equal, at least because he saved Antonio and you'. Women are very different from men but actually the same. Perhaps this ending hints at a utopian sort of marriage, when husband and wife treat each other as equals. At that historical moment of Puritan ascendancy, writes Belsey, 'the meaning of marriage is unstable, contested, and open to radical reconstruction' (1998a: 149). Could a woman be the sort of friend (/lover?) to a man that Antonio was to Bassanio? That is the possibility posed by the riddle at this moment.

I have focused here on two feminist critics' readings of the play. It is interesting to note that the same arguments about the need for equality of treatment between men and women could be applied to the even more obvious issue of anti-Semitism, as it is displayed by many of the Christians in the play. Shylock famously asserts his own right to equal treatment, after all: 'Hath not a Jew eyes? Hath not a Jew hands, organs, dimensions, senses, affections, passions . . . ' (III 1 59–73). Because the two feminist readings focus on questions of sexual equality, they are clearly *partial* readings of the play. It is, however, in the nature of Shakespeare's plays that the very richness of the material often makes it hard to provide a critical reading which can comprehensively discuss a whole play.

In *The Taming of the Shrew*, then, Katherina is 'tamed', but perhaps this 'taming' exposes the injustice of the social system that regards women as objects of exchange; in *A Midsummer Night's Dream* Hermia's and Helena's experience in the wood, on the other hand, may be seen to demonstrate the complex system of ideas which keeps social inequality in place. Portia concludes *The Merchant of Venice*, however, with a demonstration that women can and should be the social equals of men.

COMEDY AND PERFORMANCE: *TWELFTH NIGHT*

Much of the criticism in this book tries to understand the plays by reading the texts as literary documents from two particular points in history: from the historical moment in which they were produced, and from the time in which we read them now. But this is not the kind of encounter with the text which most people have with a Shakespeare play in the theatre. At its most basic, an audience encounter 'a particular succession of sights, sounds and events that create a unique theatrical experience with its own tempo, rhythm, and pauses, its own moments of engagement and detachment, and its own natural points of emphasis' (Howard 1984: 178–9). Here Jean Howard is writing about *Twelfth Night*, which of all the comedies is perhaps most self-consciously concerned with the sounds and sights which comprise its own performance and the way in which those sounds and sights produce meaning.

In *Twelfth Night* two twins, Viola and her twin brother Sebastian, have been separated in a shipwreck and cast ashore apart in the kingdom of Illyria. Viola, disguised as a young man, becomes the servant of Duke Orsino ('Cesario'), who employs her as his messenger in his vain attempt to woo the Countess Olivia. Olivia falls in love with the disguised Viola, who in turn is in love with her master Orsino. All is not resolved until Sebastian's arrival. Olivia marries Viola's twin, thinking him to be Cesario. When the twins are reunited, Viola can reveal her identity to Orsino, who marries her. Even such a minimal summary of the play's main plot throws up its obvious concern with questions of identity, with how we can tell who is who, and with how words and names connect with the real world.

Also evident here is the playful slipperiness of language itself: the names of the two women in the love triangle are near anagrams of each other: Olivia and Viola. The Australian critic Penny Gay has proposed that 'its seductive musicality, its wit, its linguistic games . . . seem ultimately part of the *meaning* of the play' (Gay 2003b: 430).

Rather than see the play as a romantic comedy about psychologically credible characters, Gay suggests that if we pay attention to the delightful experience of attending to the drama, what we get is a fantasy-world in which language itself seems to be playing with the inhabitants of Illyria (Gay 2003b: 443; see also the discussion of Tim Supple's 2003 film of *Twelfth Night*, pp. 117–21 above). Feste, the play's jester, spends much of his time undermining his social superiors with his slippery wit. He demonstrates Olivia to be a fool for mourning her brother, for example (V 1 57–72). In a scene which is literally central to the play he also tells Viola, in disguise as Cesario, how words simply cannot be trusted:

Feste   To see this age! A sentence*
             is but a chev'ril glove* to a good wit. How
             quickly the wrong side may be turn'd outward!
Viola   Nay, that's certain. They that dally* nicely
             with words may quickly make them wanton.*   15
Feste   I would therefore my sister had no
             name, sir.
Viola   Why, man?
Feste   Why, sir, her name's a word, and to dally
             with that word might make my sister wanton . . .   20
             Troth, sir, I can yield you none without
             words, and words are grown so false, I am loath to
             prove reason* with them.

                                                            (III 1 11–20; 23–5)

* [11] *sentence* any statement [12] *chev'ril glove* a soft leather glove that can easily be turned inside out [14] *dally* play flirtatiously [15] *wanton* have whatever meaning you want; but the word also means 'unchaste' (line 20) [25] *prove reason* demonstrate truth through reasoning

The play is full of puns and plays on words of the kind Feste deploys here, using two meanings of 'wanton'. Puns are like the near-identical twins of the comedy, apparently the same but different. Just as time will untie the knot of the play's plot and of Viola's fate for the audience (II 2 40–1), the amusing confusion of meaning when we first hear the pun will be resolved when the pun is explained. Time will also resolve the riddle of who Viola is (her name is not revealed to an audience until V 1 241), and this is a play packed with questions and riddles. Olivia's vain puritanical steward Malvolio is tricked into believing that his mistress loves him by means of a crude riddle in a letter which purports to be in Olivia's hand (II 5 103–7). Viola talks in riddles to Orsino (II 4 120–1) and to Olivia (I 5 27–8), and also in this passage, where the play's dense playfulness with language, including its fondness for rhyme, comes across strongly:

Olivia   I prithee tell me what thou think'st of me.
Viola   That you do think you are not what you are.
Olivia   If I think so, I think the same of you.   140
Viola   Then think you right: I am not what I am.
Olivia   I would you were as I would have you be.
. . .
Viola   By innocence I swear, and by my youth,
       I have one heart, one bosom and one truth,
       And that no woman has, nor ever none
       Shall mistress be of it, save I alone.   160
                      (III 1 138–42; 157–60)

The audience understand Viola. Olivia cannot at this point. Knowing the answer to a riddle, just as being able to explain the pun, or answer questions about the identity of characters on stage, is to exercise a power, writes Gay. Being subject to that power as well as wielding it form part of the pleasure of the audience's experience of engaging with the play.

But some of the characters in *Twelfth Night* revel in the enclosed self-referentiality of the play's language and yet remain in cahoots with the audience. Feste's linguistic playfulness is spoken with at least one eye on the audience, and his language positions him half-inside and half-outside the world of the play in comparison to the upper-class main plot characters (Olivia and Orsino). But it is not only Feste who makes great use of this *platea* space at the front of stage (see above, p. 82). Viola speaks witty, riddling blank verse, not prose (see above, p. 31), to the audience, and in so doing undermines the high-status, fixed-gender figures of Olivia and Orsino. And indeed, despite their power and status these two figures do seem cumbersome and unimaginative compared to Viola, the 'self-aware, self-delighting performer (boy/girl/boy) chatting wittily to the audience about "her" situation' (Gay 2003b: 442). Materialist critics such as Catherine Belsey have demonstrated how the *text* of *Twelfth Night* can be seen to disrupt, albeit momentarily, the stable system of sexual difference on which sexual stereotyping depends (Belsey 1985b: 185–90). Gay also finds a progressive reading by considering the experience of witnessing a *performance* of the play.

Terence Hawkes has found in these qualities of the play 'a model for, and emblem of, a "good", participating, creating society [which shares a common oral culture], in the face of a "bad", passive, inert society of consumer-spectators' (Hawkes 1991: 172). Comedy which, for a laugh, reverses the priorities and hierarchies of the 'everyday' reveals the possibility of a better world; but it also relies on a double vision where we can see both the comic-inverted and the 'normal' at the same time. It also requires the audience to participate in the action by listening and laughing. The Puritan Malvolio's *single* vision of the world must be punished in the comedy, and he is consequently required to dress absurdly and be subject to ridicule by both the audience and other characters (III 4 13–125). This play, writes Hawkes, is an example of a comedy which is a 'structured . . . confusion between holiday and everyday', and

> in the versions of that [confusion] which the art of an oral society raises to great heights, such as the duplicity of meanings celebrated by the pun, the *double entendre* or the confusion between male and female, stage and auditorium . . . is the good society constituted.
>
> (Hawkes 1991: 174)

In the performance of just such a confusing, riddling comedy we participate in a model of a more humane, co-operative and life-enhancing society.

SUMMARY

- In comedy, young people, and women in particular, are commonly seeking union with a lover, often against the wishes of their fathers. In the end they do marry those they sought.
- Given that Shakespeare was writing in a very male-dominated society, some critics read these plays as a kind of playful rebellion in sexual matters by young people against the authority of parents. That rebellion is, however, always absorbed by those in authority. At the end passionate love is transformed into safe, socially sanctioned, marriage.
- Other critics argue that although a kind of social order is imposed by the event of marriage at the end, the subversive comic energy of the 'rebellion' is such that it demonstrates that a more equal kind of relationship between men and women is possible, and indeed desirable.
- The playful, riddling language of some of the comedies in performance not only delights the audience but draws attention to itself, sometimes to radical effect.

FURTHER THINKING

- How could you apply these ideas about successful or unsuccessful female subversion of male authority to the women who marry in *Much Ado About Nothing* and *As You Like It*? Are they applicable at all to, say, Viola in *Twelfth Night* or Luciana in *The Comedy of Errors*?
- Are comedy audiences more involved in the meaning of a performance than silent spectators at a tragedy? If so, does this reveal anything about the nature of the genre?

FURTHER READING

A good place to start is Ryan (2002), which gives a reading of the comedies that is both accessible and radical. There are good introductions to the genre and useful collections of essays in Waller

(1991) and Smith (2004). The latter gives a clear presentation of different possible critical approaches. Dutton and Howard (2003) is compendious and wide-ranging. Davies (1995) is both readable and well written, and clarifies some complex matters of theory. The Macmillan 'New Casebooks', edited by Dutton (1996) and Coyle (1998), are valuable resources for the student, particularly in their summaries of a wide range of important criticism. Finally, the Routledge 'Sourcebooks' on *Twelfth Night* (Massai 2006) and *The Merchant of Venice* (Ceresano 2004) are superb guides to the text, contexts and critical history of these plays.

8

UNDERSTANDING HISTORY

King Richard II, King Henry IV Part I and *King Henry V*

During the early part of Shakespeare's career (roughly until about 1600) many plays about English history in the fourteenth and fifteenth centuries were being staged. Some were popular romps, mixing comic working-class characters with idealized portraits of jovial monarchs who were at one with their subjects. An example of this is Dekker's *The Shoemaker's Holiday* (1600). Shakespeare's plays were, however, much more closely based on serious records like the Tudor chronicles. Even so, they did not deal solely with kings, queens and lords. They generally gave some sort of portrait of the nation as a whole, with peasants, workers and soldiers having roles to play, often in a comic sub-plot of some sort.

It was during this period that the idea of England as a *nation* was gaining strength. The history books and the plays themselves were part of a process by which people came to see themselves as belonging first and foremost to 'England' rather than to family, household, village community or lord's retinue.

When discussing Shakespeare's history plays, scholars generally talk about two *tetralogies* (a tetralogy is a group of four works). The plays that comprise the first tetralogy were written in the earlier years of his career. They tell the stories of the civil wars between the two noble houses of York and Lancaster in the mid-fifteenth century, known as the Wars of the Roses. The first tetralogy comprises the three parts of *King Henry VI* and *King Richard III*. The second tetralogy, which is the concern of this chapter, comprises *King Richard II*, *King Henry IV Part I*, *King Henry IV Part II* and *King Henry V*. Three of these plays are discussed in this chapter. The three plays cover a period of roughly twenty-five years, from the late 1390s through to Henry V's peace treaty with France in 1420.

Richard II (reigned 1377–99) was a weak and vain king, deposed by his cousin Henry Bolingbroke, Duke of Lancaster, who became King Henry IV. Once in power Henry quarrelled with the noblemen who had helped to put him on the throne, and his reign (1399–1413) was marked by civil war and factional fighting. The two parts of *King Henry IV* tell the story of those years. Henry V (reigned 1413–22), Bolingbroke's son, achieved some measure of national stability, uniting the English nobility to wage a war against France that culminated, at the Battle of Agincourt (1415), in an unlikely victory against great odds. In so doing, Henry V became a national hero. After his death in 1422, at the age of 35, the peace with France broke down as the French fought to reconquer territory possessed by the English king. England meanwhile was plunged into a long and bloody civil war between two aristocratic factions, each seeking control of a weakened throne.

In the England of the 1590s, it was the period covering the deposition of Richard II and the wars which followed that interested people greatly. The reasons for this particular fascination in Shakespeare's time are discussed in what follows.

HISTORY AND HISTORY

We are constantly aware that the society in which people lived centuries ago was very different from that of today. Similarly, we expect that society in a couple of hundred years' time will not much resemble the one we know today. But throughout the medieval period people would not have thought along such lines. In a period when the population was growing very slowly (or, in some areas, even declining) and technological progress was minimal, the past was thought to have been very similar to the present. The future was expected to be little different.

The economy was based on agriculture, and often at not much more than a *subsistence* level. This term means that people grew what they needed and did not usually work to produce a surplus with which to trade. Society was organized in a rigid hierarchy. It was very difficult in practice (and, in theory, impossible) to rise above the class or 'estate' into which an individual was born. Indeed, it was quite rare for people to move from the village where they were born. Society was held together by bonds of loyalty (*fealty*) between individuals. The lords owed loyalty to the king, and were in turn owed allegiance by their knights. The knights were supported by their yeomen, who were the lords of the peasants. People's identities were defined largely by these bonds of loyalty, rather than by their occupation, gender, political feelings and aspirations. The theory, as it applied to the ordinary people (the 'peasantry'), was that the lord of the locality would offer protection and grant the right to hold land in return for military service in his army. Notice that women, who were not soldiers, could fit into this picture only as the possessions of the men. The lords ruled by birth, but their right to rule had been originally established by their ancestors' prowess as mounted warriors. Consequently the values of the warrior were taken very seriously by the rulers. This society valued loyalty to the lord's family as a central virtue. Bravery and skill in battle were similarly important. To simplify a little, these two values together became generally known as 'chivalry'. Chivalric loyalty towards the king often came into conflict with loyalty to the family and one's own honour (see the discussion of *Macbeth* below, p. 217). These conflicting loyalties contributed significantly to the constant state of war there seems to have been between the medieval barons. This system, known as 'feudalism', had long seemed unchangeable, but by the fourteenth century it was already in transition.

The universal Catholic Church (see Box 8.1, p. 178) was organized in a hierarchy parallel to the social one, and belief in its authority in all matters of religion was widespread. Culture tended to be based around the calendar and rituals of Catholicism.

By 1600, however, people could recognize that feudalism was clearly a thing of the past; but they missed it. They were uncertain about the new society which had evolved from it: 'modernity' or 'capitalism'. There is much debate about how and when the transition

BOX 8.1: RELIGION

In 1600 religion continued to provide the focus by which people in England saw the world. The two poles of belief were Catholicism and Protestantism.

Roman Catholicism was officially banished from England by Henry VIII's Reformation in the 1530s, only to be restored when Mary took the throne (1553–8) and then banished again under her sister Elizabeth's rule (1558–1603). English monarchs became Supreme Head of the Church of England, the state-run Protestant Church.

The Catholic faith had dominated western Europe since the time of the late Roman Empire. Authority and obedience were the key ideas, reflected by the hierarchy of deacons and priests, bishops and archbishops, and the cardinals who were subordinate to the Pope. The Church had the ultimate right to interpret scripture and throughout the Middle Ages most believers had no access to the Bible, which was available only in Latin. Its stories were revealed, but the sacred text was never read to Catholic congregations in their own language. The Mass was conducted behind a perforated screen, in Latin, with the celebrant priests facing away from the congregation. At the moment when they believed that the bread and wine became Christ's body and blood, the church's bells would ring and the congregation would kneel down in prayer. Salvation was offered to all who took the sacraments of baptism, confession, communion, confirmation, marriage and the last rites, conferred only by priests. All people were born in a state of sin, but baptism took that sin away. After that, offences could be forgiven through confession, provided that the sinner was truly sorry. 'Good works' were also required. The Church became closely linked to mystery, magic and ritual.

By the late Middle Ages many felt that its accumulated power and wealth had corrupted the hierarchy of the Church. The incumbent Pope was a major prince; he had his own army and often sired children. Monasteries were seen as places of ease rather than havens devoted to the contemplative life. All this had been true for some time, but in the fourteenth century a new way of thinking was beginning to make its mark. A new class of essentially secular-minded intellectuals celebrated the application of reason rather than simple obedience to authority. One of the key ideas of these 'humanists' was that through careful reading of Greek and Roman texts they could recover the understanding of the world which, they thought, made ancient times superior to their own. It soon became apparent that critical reasoning should be applied to the Bible itself. And if reading the Bible was the route to Christian knowledge and virtue, then it should be made available in the languages people actually spoke. In these ideas lay the beginning of the Protestant Reformation.

Protestantism is usually traced back to the teachings of the German monk Martin Luther in the early sixteenth century, although similar ideas had been circulating for roughly 200 years. Luther taught that the individual had a personal relationship with God and found his or her own truth through close study of the Bible, without priestly intervention. Furthermore, an individual could go to heaven 'through faith alone', or simply by believing that he or she was saved. Sacraments were unnecessary, and 'good works' were a sign of being saved rather than the means of achieving salvation.

By stressing the importance of revelations of divine truth to individuals, Protestantism fostered the splitting of the Church into different sects, each convinced of the authenticity of its own version of Christianity's message. In a country with one state-established Church, headed by the monarch, such diversity could not be tolerated. The more 'extreme' of these sects would not tolerate any ministers at all, and it was a short step from denying religious authority to denying royal authority. The Church of England kept its hierarchy of priests and bishops and defended its position.

The most influential form of Protestantism in England in 1600 was Calvinism, named after Jean Calvin (1509–64), who had set up a model Protestant community in the Swiss city of Geneva. While Mary, a Catholic, ruled England, leading religious opponents of Protestantism were under threat of imprisonment and execution. Many Protestant clergymen fled to Geneva. There they produced the Geneva translation of the Bible into

English, which was the version Shakespeare used. When these Protestants returned at Elizabeth's accession, they were very influential in the settlement which brought limited religious tolerance to England (although this did not extend to Catholics).

A key to Calvinism is the doctrine of predestination. If God is all-knowing and all-powerful, he must know from the beginning of time who will go to heaven and who to hell. Our fate is already decided and cannot be changed. If we look into our souls and find a calm confidence in our own salvation, then we are members of God's 'elect'. If we find there doubt, then we are probably 'reprobate' and destined for damnation. Good deeds will not save the damned, but the most apparently wicked individual could, through divine grace, become one of the saved.

The terrors and contradictions of this belief system were such that by the 1620s predestination was giving way to the idea of free will. However, at the time Shakespeare was writing Calvinism was the settled belief of a great number of people in London. As many Protestants held that wealth and power on earth were signs of God's favour and proof of election, Calvinism proved attractive to the merchant class. Poverty, by the same token, could be proof of reprobation.

Because the Calvinists and other serious Protestants regarded their teachings as a pure version of the original form of Christianity, they came to be known as *Puritans*. Today the word is associated with a disapproval of sex, drinking and taking pleasure in general. This was not the attitude of all Calvinists, but some did regard this life solely as a place of contemplation of the joys to come. It was a mark of the elect not to value the pleasures of the flesh. Many traditional festivities that involved drinking, dance, laughter and indeed fornication were regarded as expressions of superstition or else as 'Popish', and the Puritans sought to stamp out such diversions. The theatre became a target, and some London preachers regularly denounced the playhouses in their public sermons. The playwrights retaliated by satirizing Puritans as hypocrites, like Angelo in *Measure for Measure* and Malvolio in *Twelfth Night*.

Between leaving Warwickshire and arriving in London, Shakespeare may have been in the service of a Roman Catholic family in Lancashire, completing his education – or perhaps teaching (Honan 1998: 60–5; Wilson 2004: 44–70). Evidence existed that his father was a Catholic, and gossip soon after Shakespeare's death asserted that he 'died a papist' (Williams 1933: 232). We cannot know what Shakespeare actually 'believed'. Perhaps he did not know himself. In such a time of changing beliefs, many held a mixture of Catholic and Protestant beliefs. Still, the endings of *The Winter's Tale* and *The Tempest* might be seen to reflect a particularly Catholic attitude towards the Christian doctrine of sincere repentance.

began, but by Shakespeare's time social mobility (the movement of individuals from humble status to power and rank) was an obvious fact. Merchants and industrialists were already building up wealth, power and influence which were not based on the possession of land. The absolutist Tudor monarchy, with its centralizing tendencies, succeeded in doing away with the private armies of individual lords and in concentrating taxation and legal powers in a government bureaucracy based in London. In other words, kings no longer ruled with the co-operation of their armed fellow lords, but claimed the God-given right to rule exactly as they pleased. They relied on the law and an emerging civil service to see that their will was carried out all over the country. The capital grew very rapidly into a recognizably modern city, based on trade and commerce, where rich and poor existed side-by-side. Professional infantryman (pikemen and musketeers in combination) made the heavily armoured noble knight obsolete on the battlefield. Explorers opened up a world way beyond the traditional maps of Greek and Roman writers and exposed Europe to new continents and new ways of living. The universal authority of the Catholic Church was challenged by Protestantism (see Box 8.1, pp. 178–81). Powerful nation-states arose and fought wars for overtly religious and economic reasons, not just for the honour and rights of the monarch. That monarch, however, increasingly aimed at absolute power in the state and argued for his or her 'divine right' to rule as God's representative on earth.

In a world of rapid social and technological change, early modern writers tended to look back at an idealized version of the Middle Ages in which everyone knew their place and the future was secure and certain. Those same men of influence whose wealth and power depended on the destruction of feudalism looked back on it with nostalgia, insecure as they felt in the world of the emerging modern, market-based, capital-led economy. This is a world where a speculator can be rich today and ruined tomorrow, and profit is regarded as more important than personal loyalty. To many, the reign of King Richard II seemed to have been the last time when the old world order was completely present.

There was no doubt that Richard's was a true claim to the throne by descent from the great warrior-king Edward III. When Henry Bolingbroke usurped the throne, he introduced kingship based on political effectiveness rather than birth, even if not explicitly. Furthermore, as Queen Elizabeth grew older and the question of who would succeed her grew more vexed, many feared the arrival of a cunning and unprincipled Bolingbroke-like figure – perhaps the Earl of Essex – who would take advantage of her physical infirmity and seize power. A supporter of the Earl of Essex, Sir John Hayward, published a history of the reign of King Henry IV only to have it banned by Elizabeth's government. 'I am Richard II, know ye not that?' she is believed to have once exclaimed. Like the idealized Richard, Elizabeth encouraged her people to see her reign as a golden age of stability and national glory. She had always known her weakness as a woman in a turbulent political situation otherwise dominated by men. She feared threats from all quarters, but particularly from men of political and military cunning.

Shakespeare was, it appears, acutely aware that the world he described in his history plays was one that had passed away; yet he seems sometimes to write as if his characters were actually living in the England of the 1590s not the 1390s. The plays contain many anachronisms (references to items that were not available in the time the play was supposed to be set). Douglas has a pistol (*King Henry IV Part I*, II 4 345–6), even though pistols had not been invented in Henry IV's day; Falstaff drinks 'sack', a sweet wine popular in the 1590s but unknown in England 200 years earlier.

Falstaff's soldiers at the Battle of Shrewsbury are decimated by musketfire (V 3 29–39), not the arrows and crossbow bolts of the actual battle. The presence of anachronism is not, as some early critics thought, explained by supposing Shakespeare to have been ignorant. In fact these anachronisms work to ensure we have a kind of double perspective on the action. We are reminded that we are watching a play whose ideas and concerns are relevant to the present day, yet they also depict a past which has really gone and can be reproduced only by representing it as a product today, upon the stage. That this is a retrospective view on the world from the perspective of the 1590s and not a timeless commentary on human affairs is constantly signalled by the contemporary language of the working-class characters and the up-to-date weapons, artefacts and information which litter the plays (Rackin 1990: 95).

Medieval paintings in lavishly illustrated ('illuminated') books will often show historically successive events on one page as if they were happening simultaneously, with the same characters repeated next to one another. This is because, to the medieval mind, all events seem to happen at once as far as God is concerned; God sees everything from the perspective of eternity. The ways of the past are the ways of now. Society and history are static. When we see a Shakespeare history play, however, we are made aware that the text self-consciously demonstrates an awareness that these events are over and cannot come back again, except in the counterfeit form of today's actors impersonating figures of the past. A *secular* (i.e. non-religious) modern idea of time is emerging in these plays, moving forward from the past to the future in a progressive way. Tomorrow will be different from today; the world can be changed. When we watch a history play in the theatre today, of course, we need to add a further perspective, that of the contemporary present. Any reading or interpretation of these plays will have to operate at these different levels.

King Richard II is the play which is most explicit in its demonstration that feudalism has passed away. Indeed, the drama seems to concentrate very carefully on the internal forces which destroyed it. It begins with a ritual of justice long outdated by the time Shakespeare was writing: trial by combat. In the fourteenth century a man accused of treason could prove his innocence by challenging his accuser to ritual combat. God, in the form of 'divine Providence', it was believed, would ensure that justice was done (see p. 212). Henry Bolingbroke, at this time Duke of Hereford, has accused Thomas Mowbray, Duke of Norfolk, of treason and of involvement in the murder of the Duke of Gloucester, who was uncle to both the king and Bolingbroke. He accuses him also of embezzling the king's money (I 1 87–100).

That we are in a distant world where feudalism applies is apparent even in the play's opening lines; and yet there is still a subtle emphasis on the fact that Shakespeare's audience were seeing the action from a time in the future:

King Richard Old John of Gaunt, time-honoured Lancaster,
             Hast thou, according to thy oath and band,*
             Brought hither Henry Herford thy bold son,
             Here to make good the boist'rous late appeal,*
             Which then our leisure* would not let us hear,   5
             Against the Duke of Norfolk, Thomas Mowbray?
Gaunt I have, my liege.*

(I 1 1–7)

* [2] band duty owing to your superior [4] make good the boist'rous late appeal justify the shocking recent accusation [5] leisure or, rather, the lack of it [7] liege the term used to address the superior to whom you owe feudal loyalty

This is an old-fashioned formal language, with its explicit emphasis on the bonds of loyalty which held feudal society together. Respect for the chivalric virtue of bravery is made apparent by the king calling Henry Hereford 'bold' (line 3), a word which by Shakespeare's day had begun to acquire some of the connotations of rudeness and rashness which it has today. In the fourteenth century 'bold' was a term simply of praise. But notice also that John of Gaunt, a hero of English history for his valour and virtue, is both 'old' and 'time-honoured' (line 1). 'Old' in the sense of 'aged' he literally is; and he is 'time-honoured' in the sense that he is respected for his acquired wisdom. But he is old also in as much as he is an historical character, and 'time-honoured' because future generations still hold him in esteem. The double-time perspective of the text is immediately made apparent.

The contradictions within feudalism and the new forces which will destroy it are similarly made quickly apparent. Each participant in this ritual combat prefaces his challenge by protesting loyalty to the king (I 1 20–4, 31–2, 54); but it soon becomes clear that the sense of personal honour and loyalty of each to his family is more important still. After long speeches full of the archaic terms and concerns of chivalry, the king asks them both to forgive and to forget in a 'modern' semi-humorous sort of speech which draws on the distinctly unknightly trade of surgery. Here Mowbray is admitting that he once set an ambush for Bolingbroke:

Mowbray	But ere* I last received the sacrament*	
	I did confess it, and exactly begg'd	140
	Your Grace's pardon, and I hope I had it.	
	This is my fault. As for the rest appeal'd,*	
	It issues from the rancour of a villain,	
	A recreant* and most degenerate* traitor,	
	Which in myself I boldly will defend,	145
	And interchangeably* hurl down my gage*	
	Upon this overweening* traitor's foot,	
	To prove myself a loyal gentleman	
	Even in the best blood chamber'd in his bosom,	
	In haste whereof, most heartily I pray	150
	Your Highness to assign our trial day.	
King Richard	Wrath-kindled* gentlemen, be rul'd by me,	
	Let's purge this choler without letting blood.*	
	This we prescribe, though no physician;	
	Deep malice makes too deep incision.	155
	Forget, forgive, conclude and be agreed,	
	Our doctors say this is no month to bleed.	

(I 1 139–57)

* [139] *ere* before; *sacrament* the Catholic rite of the Mass. This, like the mention of confession (1 140) is an obvious reminder of the pre-Reformation setting [142] *appeal'd* charged against me [144] *recreant* faithless – by Shakespeare's time, already an archaic term; *degenerate* having declined from a once noble family – a typically feudal insult [146] *interchangeably* in turn; *hurl down my gage* throw my glove down, the

traditional chivalric gesture of challenge [147] *overweening* impertinent, going dangerously beyond the bounds of what a subject owes a king [152] *Wrath-kindled* literally, set ablaze by anger [153] *purge this choler without letting blood* it was believed that an angry disposition or fit was caused by an excess of a 'humour', or fluid, called 'choler'. The natural balance of one's body and disposition could be re-created by bleeding: letting blood and draining off some of this excess fluid

Richard doesn't seem to realize that the feudal notion of 'fealty' is a two-way thing. He has to respect *their* honours, not cast them aside so lightly. His attitude does not prove persuasive. They will not obey his command, so he gives in to them and ordains their trial day at Coventry.

In Act I Scene 3 there is a grand heraldic spectacle, and plenty more archaic feudal language and ritual. But just as they are about to fight, both on-stage and off-stage audiences are denied that dramatic spectacle by Richard intervening to prevent the combat. He sentences both challengers to exile: Mowbray for life, Bolingbroke for ten years, though this is immediately commuted to six – almost, it seems, at the king's whim. Soon after, Bolingbroke's father, Gaunt, dies, and Richard acts in the most unfeudal and tyrannical way. He seizes all of Gaunt's possessions in order to finance his Irish war, rather than let them be inherited by Bolingbroke.

In this he behaves like a divine-right monarch rather than a feudal lord. The 'absolutist' monarch of Shakespeare's day and later recognized no controls over his power from anyone else in the country, because he saw his authority coming directly from God ('divine right') and therefore not to be opposed. Richard's behaviour here exposes the contradictions within the feudal system and lays the foundations of the process which will destroy both himself and the feudal kingship itself.

In theory a feudal king was both God's anointed representative on earth – who must therefore be obeyed in all points – *and* himself a warrior-lord who must respect the honour of the other warrior-lords of the kingdom. Richard's motive for depriving Bolingbroke of his incomes and titles is to provide resources for his own personal war, as Lord of England, against Ireland. He thinks he is behaving in a way appropriate to his honour and position; but a feudal monarch cannot actually behave like an absolutist monarch of Renaissance times, demanding absolute obedience from all. After all, as Richard's uncle, the Duke of York, points out to him, it is only the principle of inheritance through birth which gives him his right to the throne:

York   Take Herford's rights away, and take from Time   195
         His charters and his customary rights;
         Let not tomorrow then ensue today;
         Be not thyself; for how art thou a king
         But by fair sequence and succession?

(II 1 195–9)

York thinks that the right of succession from father to son is so central to nature itself that Time itself cannot move from tomorrow to today without it. But it is not *natural*; and, once it has been violated, that violation both absolves everyone of their duty of allegiance to Richard as hereditary monarch and reveals the true principle that justifies the possession of absolute power: force.

Richard believes that power, both natural and supernatural, resides within himself simply because he is the king:

King Richard   Not all the water in the rough rude sea
         Can wash the balm* off from an anointed king;   55
         The breath of worldly men cannot depose
         The deputy elected by the Lord;
         For every man which Bolingbroke hath pressed
         To lift shrewd steel* against our golden crown,
         God for his Richard hath in heavenly pay   60
         A glorious angel: then if angels fight,
         Weak men must fall, for heaven still guards the right.

(III 2 562)

* [55] *balm* the sacred ointment used in the coronation ritual [59] *shrewd steel* a dangerous sword

He soon discovers that this a fantasy. Power resides in the material, in troops and weapons. The ceremonies and rituals are not the granters of power, but merely its markers. A king is really no more than a man (see III 2 173–7).

The early modern notion of absolute monarchy can be seen, then, in this play as emerging out of feudalism, and destroying it. Richard may be defeated, but the principle of absolute monarchy, already one of the forces threatening to destroy feudal society, is seen being unleashed by him. His successors waged constant civil war to secure the final victory of that principle over the feudal notion of mutual loyalty owed between king and lords. It is only at the end of the Wars of the Roses that the first Tudor monarch, Henry VII, establishes peace through absolute monarchy. *King Richard II* dramatizes the death of feudalism as its internal contradictions burst it open. At this moment we see the emergence of the early modern principle of absolute monarchy.

The way in which money operates to destroy feudalism is clear, too. In medieval society loyalty between social unequals is the glue which holds society together. Richard replaces it with a modern financial relationship between king and subjects. Richard sells to individuals the rights of tax-gathering in his kingdom in order to finance his wars, rather than relying on the military support of his own nobles. In this way he imposes on his problem the solutions of the free market, rather than co-operating in the traditional way with those warrior-lords whose chivalric gallantry in battle had always secured the sacred fame and glory of Old England – or so the dying John of Gaunt says:

Gaunt   This blessed plot, this earth, this realm, this England,   50
      This nurse, this teeming womb of royal kings,
      Feared by their breed,* and famous by their birth,
      Renowned for their deeds as far from home,
      For Christian service and true chivalry,
      As is the sepulchre* in stubborn Jewry*   55
      Of the world's ransom, blessed Mary's son;*
      This land of such dear souls, this dear dear land,
      Dear for her reputation through the world,
      Is now leas'd out – I die pronouncing it –
      Like to a tenement* or pelting* farm.   60
      England, bound in with the triumphant sea,
      Whose rocky shore beats back the envious siege
      Of wat'ry Neptune, is now bound in with shame,
      With inky blots and rotten parchment bonds;*

That England, that was wont to conquer others,   65
Hath made a shameful conquest of itself.

(II 1 50–66)

---

* [52] *by their breed* because of their war-like qualities over the generations
[55] *sepulchre* the tomb of Jesus; *Jewry* Palestine [56] *blessed Mary's son*
notice again the explicitly Catholic and pre-Reformation devotion to the
Virgin Mary [60] *tenement* farm let to a tenant; *pelting* petty, paltry [64]
bonds legal documents

Both the breeding and the acts of violence of the knights and kings
of England had made it a country as famous as the very tomb in
which Jesus was laid, and for which the crusaders fought. Even
nature itself, in the form of the sea-god Neptune, cannot capture
this stronghold of valour. Yet this king has sold the country for
money, a filthy ('inky' and 'rotten') paper transaction that has abolished the sacred glory of yesteryear. Money can do this alone; the
old, chivalric England is gone because it is no match for the values
of the marketplace.

In the second half of the play chivalry and feudal loyalty are
actually parodied – copied in a mocking way. As the old system is
breaking down, what was once admirable now seems absurd. The
noble and heraldic challenges to combat we saw delivered by
Bolingbroke and Mowbray in the first scene, with their ritual
throwing down of gloves ('gages') in an act of challenge, are turned
into an absurd spectacle in Act IV Scene 1 (Rackin 1990: 132). In the
space of fifty lines (IV 1 25–76), Aumerle, Fitzwater, Percy, Surrey
and 'Another Lord' have thrown down their gloves in challenges,
one after the other. Bolingbroke is not interested in all this
nonsense and curtly puts them all off until his old opponent is
forgiven and returned (IV 1 86–9). In Act V there is a farcical scene
where Aumerle, who has been discovered by his father, the Duke of
York, to be in possession of a document implicating him in a
conspiracy against the king, pleads for forgiveness of Henry
Bolingbroke and easily gets it. Aumerle's father (who has just been
seen, like some aged buffoon in a comedy, calling for his boots and
arguing with his wife) then rushes in. He demands his own son's
death. Before King Henry can get much of a word in, however, the
Duchess of York enters, and soon she too is on her knees pleading

against her husband for the king to spare her son. Eventually he convinces them all, but the tone is one not of life-or-death high drama but of domestic comedy. Even treason has become a subject for laughter in the fallen feudal world of Henry's court after Richard's self-induced demise.

HISTORY AND POWER

King Henry V believes, or certainly seems to believe, that he is the rightful King of France (II 2 193). The righteousness of his cause both justifies his invasion of France and authorizes the death and devastation that will follow. To the medieval mind, Henry's power would seem to flow through this sense of Providence – of God being on Henry's side. He is always keen to stress that he needs God to ensure his success (e.g. I 2 307; II 2 189–90). When the English forces win so comfortably at Agincourt, it seems that divine intervention really must have played a part. He says of the victory: 'Take it, God, / For it is none but thine!' (IV 8 111–12).

Providence, however, is the necessary *ideological* cover to the actual operation of power in this play, and elsewhere in the histories (by 'ideology', I mean here the widely believed stories in a society which justify the exercise of power by the already powerful; see p. 221). Shakespeare makes clear in the writing of these texts that it is not in fact divine approval, gained because of a ruler's essential virtue, that ensures victory in battle. These plays show, first, that royal power is actually not very different, either in content or in execution, from the actions of thieves and fraudsters; and, second, that such power is very often exercised not through wisdom, or valour in battle, but simply through the convincing performances, and the rhetoric, of the rulers, who get their way because of their skills as speakers, not as warriors. This idea has something interesting to say about modern politics and the political role of theatre.

Many readers and audience members are puzzled by the character of Ancient Pistol in *King Henry V*. Boastful and cowardly, he speaks a strange language which seems entirely made up of bad blank verse taken from other plays. Yet there is also something vaguely familiar about his grindingly heavy-handed rhetoric.

In the first scene we discover that he has married Mistress Quickly, the landlady of the Eastcheap tavern where he and his companions spend most of their time. His claim to her is not unchallenged, however. Corporal Nym claims that she was previously engaged to him. Nym draws his sword on Pistol. Mistress Quickly, the 'hostess', intervenes, but Nym spurns her:

Nym	Will you shog* off ? I would have you solus.*	45
Pistol	'Solus', egregious* dog? O viper vile!	
	The 'solus' in thy most mervailous* face,	
	The 'solus' in thy teeth, and in thy throat,	
	And in thy hateful lungs, yea, in thy maw,* perdy;*	
	And which is worse, within thy nasty mouth!	50
	I do retort the 'solus' in thy bowels,	
	For I can take,* and Pistol's cock is up,*	
	And flashing fire will follow.	

(II 1 45–53)

* [45] *shog* move; *solus* alone (Latin) [46] *egregious* remarkable, a word usually used as praise [47] *mervailous* marvellous; astonishingly ugly [49] *maw* stomach; *perdy* by God [52] *take* strike; *cock is up* the cock of a pistol was the hammer holding the flint which, struck against steel, produced the sparks to fire the gunpowder. He means he is ready to kill, but no doubt Pistol's *double entendre* here is deliberate

But on stage only about five minutes previously, King Henry had been engaged in a dispute over France (which is often referred to as female in the text, e.g. I 2 227) – and had responded to a rude challenge in a passage of strikingly heavy repetition and obscene innuendo. The dauphin, the King of France's son, has sent Henry some tennis balls to play with, because, he says, they are more the kind of thing which Henry is fit to be concerned with than are the affairs of state. King Henry responds to the French ambassador:

King Henry	And tell the pleasant prince this mock of his
	Hath turned his balls to gun-stones,* and his soul
	Shall stand sore-charged for the wasteful vengeance
	That shall fly with them; for many a thousand widows

Shall this his mock mock* out of their dear husbands;   285
Mock mothers from their sons, mock castles down;
And some are yet ungotten* and unborn
That shall have cause to curse the Dauphin's scorn.

(I 2 281–8)

* [282] *turned his balls to gun-stones* converted his tennis balls to bullets, but there is the suggestion that he will shoot him in the testicles [285] *mock mock* here means both to laugh at and to cheat [someone of] [287] *ungotten* unconceived

The parallels between Henry and Pistol are picked up in other places, too. The boy says of Pistol that he 'hath a killing tongue and a quiet sword' (III 1 34). Henry captures the port town of Harfleur, not by assaulting it but by promising terrible rape and slaughter if the French governor does not surrender the town (III 3 1–43). It turns out to be a good thing that he did surrender, for Henry's army was in fact in no condition to make the assault (III 1 55–6) (see pp. 196–7). In the same way Pistol captures the French soldier in Act IV Scene 4 because of his ferocious threats and brutal manner. Pistol is no real threat to anyone, of course. He won't charge into the breach at Harfleur, all he can do is sing a song about the glory of war (III 2 8–11). (But maybe war is glorious *only* in song. Those who do charge into the breach clearly don't come out again.) Pistol leaves London for France with these words:

Pistol   Let us to France, like horse-leeches my boys,
       To suck, to suck, the very blood to suck!

(II 3 55–6)

A few minutes later the King of France uses the same word to describe Henry, even if he is using a different metaphor:

French King   For England* his approaches makes as fierce
       As waters to the sucking of a gulf*.

(III 4 9–10)

* [9] *England* the King of England [10] *gulf* a whirlpool

Why these connections? Pistol is a thief. He is going to France to make what personal profit he can (II 1 111–12). He is able to get his way, up to a point, by his boastful language. At first he impresses both Fluellen (III 6 12–16) and Henry (IV 1 62); but he remains a braggart and a thief. Henry is an English king who has a dubious claim to France that he can enforce only by violence, because its rulers and people do not want him. The question posed is whether he is fundamentally different from a thief like Pistol? Henry's war is a war fought for personal glory. It is a war of aggression, not a war of national defence. He is seeking to pocket up what is not his. In addition, the very theatricality of Pistol's language draws attention to the way Henry uses rhetoric so effectively to get what he wants, and Henry is a king as performer (see below).

The same use of the sub-plot to emphasize this notion of rulers being morally comparable to criminals is built into the early structure of *King Henry IV Part I*. In Act II Scene 2 Falstaff and his gang rob some innocent pilgrims on their way to Canterbury. No sooner have they seized their booty than they are robbed in turn by the disguised Prince Hal and his friend Poins. The point of the jest is to see what preposterous lies Falstaff will tell about the incident that night in the tavern. As Hal expected, Falstaff extols his own bravery when in fact he ignominiously ran away (see p. 168). In the previous scene, however, we had seen Worcester and Northumberland reveal their plot to depose the usurper Henry IV from the throne – the very throne which they had helped him seize in *King Richard II*. The same narrative motif, of thieves being robbed by thieves, recurs here first as serious action, then as comedy. But the comic repetition undercuts and de-heroicizes the noble characters in their original playing of the actions.

It is possible to read this scene in a very conservative way. In a forty-year-old school edition of this play, the editor states with full confidence that '[Shakespeare] wrote to demonstrate that rebellion and usurpation were sinful in the sight of God and unmitigated disasters to the countries that experienced them' (Reese 1965: 5). You could argue that the montage effect here reveals the moral turpitude of the usurper Bolingbroke: authority must never be resisted, even when it is dangerous or tyrannical. But one can also read this scene as a dramatic deflation of all the pretensions of monarchs and nobles who steal and murder but dignify their acts by calling them other things. Power in the history plays comes down to one of three things: first, having the military force to take what you want; second, being able to persuade people; or, third, being able to put on a convincing performance which makes effective use of the most powerful beliefs of the time. Talk of 'divine right', 'just claims' and 'Providence' mystifies these unattractive alternatives; but the dramatic structures of main plot and sub-plot in these plays hint perceptively at the bald truths of power in medieval and early modern England.

Many writings about politics in Shakespeare's time use theatrical metaphors. It was widely recognized that a monarch's actions and demeanour should be such as to inspire belief and obedience. The monarch's speech and costume must possess what writers called 'decorum': appropriateness to the circumstances in which he found himself. This is at the heart of what Machiavelli wrote about politics (see p. 225). Public events (such as the entry of King James I into London for the first time as monarch in 1604) were intricately staged, with painted triumphal arches, specially written poetry and carefully costumed courtiers. King James's court mounted expensive masques which extolled a particular royal virtue or taught some lesson about loyal obedience. Members of the royal family and the court themselves acted in these entertainments.

Prince Hal and Henry IV are very aware of the theatrical element of kingship in the world in which they live. They talk openly about the king having to be a performer (actually, of course, *performers* playing kings and princes are talking about kings and princes having to be performers). Theatricality was very much at the cultural and political heart of early modern England. Power and the theatre interact closely (Howard 1994: 145).

At the end of the very first scene of *King Henry IV Part I* Prince Hal explains to the audience the nature of his part, his act, in this play. He is associating with Falstaff not because he necessarily enjoys it – though his behaviour might well lead one to suspect that this is one of his reasons. Rather, he is making himself look a very unlikely candidate for monarchy, so that when he abandons his old companions, he will *appear* to be totally different from people's expectations. He will therefore be all the more admired as a monarch because his virtues will be so unexpected:

Prince Hal · So when this loose behaviour I throw off
　　　　　And pay the debt I never promised,
　　　　　By how much better than my word I am,　　　　　　　210
　　　　　By so much shall I falsify men's hopes,
　　　　　And like bright metal on a sullen ground
　　　　　My reformation, glittering o'er my fault,
　　　　　Shall show more goodly and attract more eyes
　　　　　Than that which hath no foil* to set it off.　　　　　215
　　　　　I'll so offend, to make offence a skill,
　　　　　Redeeming time when men think least I will.

　　　　　　　　　　　　　　　　　　　　(I 2 208–17)

> * [215] *foil* the metal 'housing' of contrasting colour to that of the jewel
> which it holds. Hal means that if he had always been well behaved, there
> would be nothing to which his conduct could be compared when he
> became king. As it is, the future contrast with his present behaviour will
> make him look all the more impressive when he changes his lifestyle

It is a common dramatic technique to satisfy an audience by making a morally wayward character suddenly turn out to be the hero they all hoped he would be. Here this dramatic technique is used for a blatantly political end. This is an example, at worst, of duplicity and, at best, of deviousness, but kings and politicians in general have a public identity which is not necessarily the same as their private one. King Henry explains very carefully to his son that it was the *image* he presented to the lords and the people that made him preferred to the vain and foolish Richard, who had allowed his *presence* to become too familiar and common. Consequently people tired of him, as his faults, instead of being concealed, became all too clearly revealed (III 2 39–84).

Hal and Falstaff's acting out of two different versions of this scene in the tavern the night before it actually happens (II 4 374–80) underlines, in the sub-plot, the centrality of ideas of performance in the politics of the play. The very fact that this satirical improvisation takes place twice, with two different 'non-scripts', indicates the theatre to be not only no respecter of the dignity of monarchs but also capable of showing that the world need not be as it is. If monarchs are performers who keep their power by pleasing their audiences, theirs is an act that can always be changed. No unchangeable divine law governs their actions and decisions. If the world is unjust, it really can be changed.

The humanity of monarchs beneath the essentially hollow stage conventions and rituals of the institution is also stressed by this focus on kings as performers. As King Henry V, Hal learns this all too well (IV 1 238–69). 'Ceremony' makes a man a king, but he is still a man like any other in every other way. Yet the king must still play his part well and establish his unique claim to the role. When Henry IV dresses up several lords in a copy of his armour at the Battle of Shrewsbury (V 3; V 4), in order to make it appear as if the king is fighting everywhere, it seems as if Henry is cheating. He devalues his own presence, as well as revealing that it does not really matter who is king: as long as the performance is convincing, anyone can do it. Hal makes it clear when he confronts Hotspur at the play's climax that only he is truly qualified to play the role of Prince of Wales (V 4 63–7).

Hal surpasses his father in theatrical skill. When he invades France to claim the throne of France for himself, his very first objective is the port town of Harfleur. He meets with very little success, however. One of his greatest talents is to clothe his own personal ambition in the mantle of nationalism in his great public speeches, such as the one he makes in order to persuade his men to go 'Once more into the breach, dear friends, once more' (III 1 1). But this attack, too, fails. The king then summons the governor on to the walls of the town and makes a series of startlingly blood-thirsty threats. Unless they surrender now, he cannot promise to control the behaviour of his men once they get into the town. The dire consequences which follow will then be the governor's fault for not surrendering, while Henry still has the English army securely under his command. Surrender, he says:

> *King Henry*   If not – why in a moment look to see
> The blind and bloody soldier with foul hand
> Defile the locks of your shrill-shrieking daughters;   35
> Your fathers taken by their silver beards,
> And their most reverend heads dashed to the walls;
> Your naked infants spitted upon pikes,
> Whiles the mad mothers with their howls confused
> Do break the clouds, as did the wives of Jewry   40

At Herod's bloody-hunting slaughter-men.*
What say you? Will you yield, and this avoid?
Or guilty in defence, be thus destroyed?

(III 3 33–43)

* [40–1] In Matthew's Gospel (2:16–18) just after Jesus's birth Herod, King
of Judea, ordered all the first-born babies of the Jews to be killed in an
unsuccessful attempt to kill Jesus, the new 'King of the Jews'

The governor does open the gates of his town. He has heard that no reinforcements are on their way and is convinced by Henry's speech that the English really do have the power to take the town and the will to commit these awful atrocities. It is immediately revealed, however, that it was all a bluff on Henry's part. The English army has taken so long to take the town that winter now approaches. What is more, the soldiers are so enfeebled by sickness that they must abandon the whole campaign and march for Calais and home (III 3 55–6). Even in war, Henry wins as much through virtuoso performance as through combat.

It is interesting that the Chorus in *King Henry V* paints an idealized picture of Henry and his army that is not supported by what we see in the dramatic scenes which follow. The Chorus to Act III depicts a mighty and heroic fleet full of 'culled and choice-drawn cavaliers' (III 0 24). But in the scenes that follow we see only the cowardly Pistol and his cronies or the squabbling officers who discuss the siege: the pompous Fluellen, the taciturn – not to say dim – Gower and two men, Jamy and Macmorris, who, since they come from countries normally at war with England in this period, can only be mercenaries (III 2). The Chorus to Act IV describes how, on the night before the Battle of Agincourt, Henry goes among his troops offering vital encouragement and personal inspiration (IV 0 28–47). Yet, in the scene following, Henry actually adopts a disguise so that he can be alone. When he does meet his men, he seems either to quarrel with them (Pistol, Williams) or to actively suggest that their situation is desperate (IV 1 97–8). In a first long soliloquy he appeals to the sympathies of the audience regarding the difficulties that beset a king (IV 1 269–84). His peasants have it easier, he says.

Why is this? It can be argued that the heroic and theatrical language of the Chorus offers a *poetic* version of history specifically crafted for presentation; the dramatic scenes may be seen as a more prosaic reality with which the poetic version is deliberately juxtaposed. In doing this, the myth-making, which is part of all historical writing, is held up to the audience's gaze. In the same way, Shakespeare's own histories are self-consciously crafted versions of 'real events', and it is the *internal* contrasts of these histories that reveal political ideas and attitudes.

This is not *necessarily* to argue that Shakespeare's exposure of the theatrical pretence of kings constitutes an attack on the very idea of monarchy (although there were some who favoured republican government of various kinds at the time, and Shakespeare seems to be interested in the concept; see Hadfield 2004: 8ff.). Shakespeare demystifies monarchy though without at the same time suggesting a considered alternative. It can be argued that the plays in fact reveal the workings of monarchy while showing also the desirability, indeed the necessity, of the institution in the world of 1600. Shakespeare was a dramatic artist, not a political propagandist. As Stephen Greenblatt puts it, art is 'the source both of settled calm and deep disturbance . . . As a dramatist and a poet, he was simultaneously the agent of civility and the agent of subversion' (Greenblatt 2004: 48). Nevertheless, it can be shown that the very structure of these plays recognizes the voices of the politically excluded, so that the plays raise more questions than they settle about the way power was distributed in early modern England. And of all those groups which at this time could have claimed to be excluded, none had an apparently stronger claim than did women.

HISTORY AND WOMEN

Where are women in Shakespeare's histories? Of the 135 named characters in the *dramatis personae* of the second tetralogy in the 1997 *Riverside* edition of Shakespeare, only ten are women. Nevertheless, they are crucial to the action. In the world of military conflict and male honour presented in these plays, women stand both physically and symbolically as the forgotten centre, or unregarded 'other', of their ideologies.

A crucial issue in these plays is genealogy. Power and property in medieval English society are passed down through the principle of *primogeniture*: everything goes, on the death of the father, to the first-born legitimate son. Richard II has produced no male heir; the question of which of his cousins is to succeed him then becomes vital. The Archbishop of Canterbury in *King Henry V* (I 2 32–95) goes to great lengths to query the reasoning behind the principle (called 'Salic Law' in the play) that prevents princes of France inheriting the throne through female succession. Exeter later presents to the French king a carefully written genealogy to validate Henry's claims, showing his descent from earlier French kings through the male line (I 4 84–95). 'Female succession' means, for example, a claim to the throne based on descent from a king's daughter rather than from his legitimate male heir.

The key word in all this is *legitimacy*. Prior to the development of the kind of scientific testing now available, a man could never be absolutely certain that the son to whom his wife gave birth was actually his own. He would have only his wife's word, and the words of women were not regarded as having the same weight as men's. Female sexuality and female sexual desire consequently have the power to undermine and destabilize the very basis on which male power and property are built. A woman's desire to have sex with another man can destroy the 'house' and thence the honour and family line of her husband. This anxiety keeps surfacing in the plays, and, interestingly, it is here to be put to rest by the display of male violence in battle. The display of fighting by men both impresses and abashes female sexuality. Female qualities are seen as a threat to the male qualities of the warrior.

When Henry V is seeking to motivate his troops before Harfleur, he issues this challenge:

King Henry Dishonour not your mothers; now attest
     That those whom you called fathers did beget you.

(III 1 22–3)

If the English soldiers do not fight bravely, it will suggest that their mothers had been unfaithful and allowed lesser warriors than their valiant fathers to breed by them. They are fighting, then, in what seems a chivalrous way, to demonstrate their mother's chastity; but there is certainly a sub-textual worry about the capacity of English women to have sex with other men, whether they are valiant warriors or not. Furthermore, the British critic Lisa Jardine suggests (1996: 12) that female sexual susceptibility to other (foreign) men actually undermines the notions of national purity and stability, blurring the very distinctions between the English and the French that are at the heart of the play. Women must be controlled, if war between *true* nations is to be possible at all.

As the English army marches unhindered through France, the Dauphin, spoiling for a fight, argues that his soldiers must prove their manhood to French women in battle against the English or the women will turn to the invaders for sexual pleasure:

Dauphin   By faith and honour,
        Our madams mock at us, and plainly say
        Our mettle* is bred out, and they will give
        Their bodies to the lust of English youth   30
        To new-store France with bastard warriors.

                                  (III 6 27–31)

                            * [29] *mettle* heroic quality

In *King Henry IV Part I* Hotspur is so appalled by the effeminacy of King Henry's messenger (I 3 23–69) as to forget himself and fail to pay attention to the emissary of the king himself. Womanliness is an affront to the warrior. Its caring and nurturing values must be shunned because they damage the hero's willingness to kill at close quarters. Indeed, a real warrior like Hotspur seems to get a strange kind of thrill from blood, and, indeed, from breathless physical contact with his male opponent. Look at the way he describes his prospective encounter with Prince Hal at the Battle of Shrewsbury:

Hotspur   The mailed Mars shall on his altar sit
        Up to the ears in blood. I am on fire
        To hear this rich reprisal* is so nigh,*
        And yet not ours. Come let me taste my horse,
        Who is to bear me like a thunderbolt   120
        Against the bosom of the Prince of Wales.

Harry to Harry shall, hot horse to horse,
Meet and ne'er part till one drop down a corse.

(IV 1 116–23)

* [118] *reprisal* prize; *nigh* near; [123] *corse* corpse

Violent soldiers can also abuse women's sexuality and control their bodies when they turn to rape. Rape is threatened disturbingly often in King Henry's speech prior to Harfleur (III 3 11–14, 21–2, 34–5). Hal and Falstaff look forward to 'buying' the scores of maid-enheads that will be made available to them as the war reduces desperate women to prostitution (II 4 361–5).

A common belief at this time was that a woman was an 'incomplete' man. She had been created without the faculties of reason and self-control. Men in Shakespeare's plays are constantly in fear of losing these qualities and so falling back into a state of *womanhood* (Sinfield 1992: 135). But it is not reason that is used in the attempt to control female sexuality: it is military violence, or its modern variant, effective performance. Mortimer, the apparently legitimate heir to King Richard in *King Henry IV Part I*, loses his qualities as a warrior because he so loves his wife (III 1 263–4). Hotspur is so keen to demonstrate that he is not effeminized by love for his wife that he gracelessly and jokily puts her off and mocks her, even when she is upset at not being part of his life (II 3 90–5). Neither of these men shows the ability to win over a woman with the convincing manliness displayed by King Henry in the last scene of *King Henry V*. While claiming to be a bluff soldier, Henry is so charming that he wins Katherine, his wit and apparent affection making him seem the obvious and appropriate bridegroom for her. In fact, as Katherine's reply makes clear, she has no say in the match at all:

King Henry . . . wilt thou have me?
Katherine Dat is as it shall please *de roi mon père*.*
King Henry Nay, it will please him well, Kate; it
        shall please him, Kate.
Katherine Den it sall also content me.

(V 2 246–50)

* [247] *de roi mon père* 'the king my father'

In fact, Katherine had been offered to Henry as a way of buying off the invasion even before Henry reached Harfleur (III 0 29–30). By concluding a dynastic marriage, Henry declares his wish to produce a son who will have genealogical claims to the thrones of both France and England (V 2 206–9). He has, however, to persuade the audience that the courtship succeeds through his and Katherine's mutual affection, and this indeed is the way the scene is usually played. The text, though, would allow the actors to play the scene so that Katherine's lack of choice and, indeed, lack of real power of assent are made obvious. He dominates the conversation, often turning her words back wittily on her (V 2 109–10, 169–73, 195–8). He assumes the right, since he has the power, to decide the meaning of her language in their conversation. The stark reality of power is once more dressed in the pleasing costume of the performer, and the facts of the case almost escape us (Howard 1994: 150).

I say *almost* because, following the wooing of Katherine, there is a passage, often cut from performance, in which Henry and Burgundy, in Katherine's presence, exchange crude and public innu-endos about the shyness of virgins in their first sexual encounter (V 2 291–314). Once the wooing is over, Katherine is immediately treated by Henry as an object of his pleasure, not as an individual woman. She is another French city 'girdled with maiden walls that war hath never entered' (V 2 321–2). This tends to be lost among the general good humour of the scene in performance. As already stated, France has been the female body for which the men have fought, but it has also become the background against which they have sought to prove their masculinity through acts of violence. The skilful monarch is able to justify his power by making his violence appear appropriate and required. That is Henry V's great victory.

History plays were popular throughout the 1590s not just because they gave a clear sense to their audiences that their world was indeed different from what it had been, but because they were in tune with a developing sense of national identity and distinct-ness. England was an embattled Protestant country with its own Anglican Church, faced by an array of Catholic continental enemies. The plays seem to want to draw clear divisions between past and present, England and France. It is perhaps not surprising that the differences between men and women are much less loosely drawn than they seem to be in the comedies (see pp. 165ff.)

IMAGE PATTERNS IN THE HISTORY PLAYS

When Shakespeare began writing the second tetralogy with *Richard II*, it seems that his writing acquired a level of sophistication and artistry which it had rarely achieved before. What is particularly interesting is the way in which his use of imagery (see above, p. 22) becomes not just ornamentation of the play's language, but a subtle and theatrically powerful means by which the play's ideas about the historical changes in England which he depicts can be portrayed.

In *Richard II* there is, as critics have noted (Forker 2002: 65), a recurrent concern with language itself: with speech, words and breath. But the king and Bolingbroke use images which understand the way that language connects to the world in contrasting ways. The medieval notion of how words represent reality held that there was some kind of organic, albeit mystical relationship between a word and the thing that it referred to (see above, p. 30). In Shakespeare's time this 'theory of meaning' was being rapidly superseded by the modern idea that there was no *necessary* connection between a word and its reference: it was a matter of convention, rather than part of the fabric of the universe, as it were. The contemporary philosopher Francis Bacon strove for a language which would be 'congruent' with reality, but thought that it would always remain a discrete entity, separate from the world of things (Elsky 1989: 108). In his introduction to the recent Arden edition of the play, the American scholar Charles Forker argues that Richard talks about language according to the medieval theory of meaning, while Bolingbroke is associated with the modern idea of how words refer to the world. This is because Richard sees his position as king as a 'natural' part of God's creation; the name 'king' can only refer to him, no matter how other men use the term (Forker 2002: 67).

Thus even when faced with the seriousness of Bolingbroke's rebellion, he gives the opinion, you may recall, that 'Not all the water in the rough rude sea / Can wash the balm off from an anointed king' (III 2 54–5). Earlier in the scene Aumerle and Carlisle smile at the spectacle of Richard greeting his land as if it were his child, and of him calling upon its spiders, toads, stinging nettles and adders to attack Bolingbroke's soldiers. But the king protests:

King Richard   Mock not my senseless conjuration,* lords,
        This earth shall have a feeling, and these stones
        Prove armed soldiers, ere her native king   25
        Shall falter under proud rebellion's arms

                                      (III 2 23–6)

* [23] *senseless conjuration* conjuring of that which has no sense or perhaps, to his audience, pointless conjuring

Richard sees himself as the 'native' king whose words consequently have a mystical power to conjure. He is a kind of magician whose words have a real, if occult, connection with the things to which they refer. In context, these words also make him look foolish to the audience at this moment. Later in the scene, he thinks that his title of king has the power of twenty thousand men (III 2 85). When he ceases to become king, he cannot imagine he has an identity, for his name and him were part of the same unity: consequently he keeps referring to himself as 'nothing' (IV 1 201; V 5 38, 41). Even in the prison cell at the end, he imagines that he can summon a world into existence by talking about it (V 5 6–10).

At the beginning of the play Richard believes that his word has the force of reality. If he decrees a term of exile for Mowbray (I 3 150–4), and then shortens Bolingbroke's sentence, his word is simple fact, as Bolingbroke observes (I 3 213–5). But the future king recognizes that this connection between word and the world is not a 'natural' one, but purely the effect of Richard's power. The world is as it is, and words cannot conjure the reality they refer to into existence, no matter who speaks them:

Bolingbroke   O, who can hold a fire in his hand
        By thinking on the frosty Caucasus?*   295
        Or cloy* the hungry edge of appetite
        By bare imagination of a feast?
        Or wallow naked in December snow
        By thinking on fantastic summer's heat?

                                    (I 3 294–9)

* [295] *Caucasus* a mountain range in Asia [296] *cloy* satisfy

Richard's feudal world is one bound together by words: oaths, titles, codes of honour and rituals. It is the reality of action and power which motivates Bolingbroke, a reality which words themselves serve, their meanings determined by that power – but only contingently, and by socially and politically created convention.

In his introduction to the Arden *King Henry IV Part I*, the American critic David Scott Kastan produces an analogous argument about a recurring image pattern concerned with money and market value. The play is full of references to coins and their worth. Falstaff jokingly calls on his creditors to coin the carbuncles on Bardolph's face (III 3 77–9) and later undertakes to 'answer for' the coins which he owes his lieutenant (IV 2 7–8), for example. Hotspur says that the king's friendship is no more than 'half-fac'd' (I 3 208), like the monarch's head on a coin. Scott Kastan points out that Queen Elizabeth strove to make the value of the precious metal equal to the face value of the coin after the debasement of the English currency by her father, Henry VIII (Scott Kastan 2002: 65). But this conception of coinage was already an anachronism at the end of her reign, when Shakespeare was writing the play. The monarch's head on the coin asserted the value of the coin in circulation, but the actual value of the coin in terms of what it could purchase was determined by the laws of supply and demand. In a period of inflation like the 1590s, for example, the coin simply bought less.

King Henry and Prince Hal seem to understand that their own political value is fixed by the market of their subjects' desires, and that there is no 'natural' connection between royalty and political authority as suggested by the medieval understanding of how coinage functioned. Hal's soliloquy at the end of his first scene (see above, p. 194) reveals a strategy like that of a cunning merchant who publicly undervalues the true worth of his goods so that when he 'pay[s] the debt' he 'never promised' and behaves in a princely manner (I 2 209), the worth of those goods is made to seem much greater. His father criticizes King Richard for making himself 'so stale and cheap to vulgar company' (III 2 41), thus devaluing himself through overexposure. Later in the same scene Hal describes Hotspur as merely his 'factor' (buyer, business agent):

Prince Hal   Percy is but my factor, good my lord,
          To engross* up glorious deeds on my behalf;
          And I will call him to so strict account
          That he shall render* every glory up   150
                                              (III 2 147–150)

                    * [148] *engross* buy up [150] *render* pay back

Worcester realizes that the king thinks of himself and
Northumberland as creditors (I 3 286). When Hal confronts Douglas
at Shrewsbury, he presents himself, however, as the royal stamp that
authorizes the value of the coin, even though he knows that to be a
myth: 'It is the Prince of Wales that threatens thee, / Who never
promiseth but he means to pay' (V 4 41–2). This is despite the fact
that the king, in presenting so many 'counterfeit[s]' of himself on
the battlefield (V 4 35), gives away the idea that, as Scott Kastan
puts it, 'kingship itself is always and only a counterfeit, a role, an
action that a man might play' (Scott Kastan 2002: 64). The success of
the king and the prince in the play, however, does reflect their
understanding of the new economic conditions in which they live.

SUMMARY

- These plays show an awareness that the old feudal world
  had gone and that in its place was a new world in which
  monarchs, with the backing of their armies, demanded
  absolute power.
- The plays can also be seen to show royal power to be fundamentally self-serving. While claiming God's support, in
  reality these kings justified their authority by their more or
  less convincing performances in the monarch's role.
- Women's potential for undermining men's right to inherit
  is in these plays kept in check by the threat of violence.
- Patterns of imagery reflect the new ideas about language
  and economics which accompany the political changes
  depicted in the plays.

FURTHER THINKING

- Consider these ideas in relation to the actions of both Prince John and Hal in *King Henry IV Part II* (Act IV Scene 2 and Act V Scene 2, respectively). Do they help explain why Falstaff has to be banished at the end of this play (V 5 41–96)? You might also like to consider the idea of the king as performer in relation to *King Richard III* (look, for example, at Act I Scene 2 and Act III Scene 7).
- If there are certain qualities in the plays which the male warrior strives to possess, how are distinctly feminine qualities depicted in the plays?
- What other image patterns are significant in these plays and how do they add to the overall meaning? For example, blood, gardens, the sun and Christ are recurring images in *King Richard II*.

FURTHER READING

Holderness (1989b) is a good introduction to the perspective on feudalism contained in *King Richard II*. The same writer develops and deepens his perspective on the plays' understanding of history in *Shakespeare: The Histories* (2000). Ideas relating to feudalism in the play are dealt with also in Rackin (1990). Contemporary theories about monarchy in the plays are thoroughly explored in Hadfield (2004). Howard (1994) gives a very thorough exploration of the idea of monarchs as performers, as does Greenblatt (1985) in an important and subtle essay. Connections between sexuality and nationalism in the history plays are interestingly discussed in Sinfield and Dollimore's 'History and ideology, masculinity and miscegenation: the instance of *Henry V*', in Sinfield (1992), and also in the Introduction to Jardine (1996) and in Howard and Rackin (1997). The precise historical context of *King Henry V* is examined in Patterson (1989), and the political context of *King Richard II* is dealt with very lucidly in Healey (1998). Scott Kastan (1991) develops the idea of the 'counterfeit' in *King Henry IV Part I* further. Dutton and Howard (2003) is a compendious and wide-ranging collection of the most up-to-date critical opinion on the histories.

9

UNDERSTANDING TRAGEDY

Hamlet, King Lear, Macbeth and *Othello*

Literary criticism uses the word *tragedy* differently from the way we use it in normal conversation. In normal use, any untimely death is 'tragic'. This is not the way the term is used in literature, however. In literary criticism it is used with a specific, technical meaning.

The first tragedies were written by the ancient Greek dramatists, most notably by Aeschylus, Sophocles and Euripides, who wrote in the fifth century BC. They were imitated by the Roman writer Seneca, whose plays were studied at grammar schools in Shakespeare's time. The conventions of classical tragedy had been identified by the Greek philosopher Aristotle in his *Poetics*. For Aristotle, a tragedy has a main character, a protagonist. This protagonist must be 'noble': not only rich, powerful and strong but possessing certain admirable personal qualities. The play will tell the story of their fall. To have its appropriate effect on the audience this fall must be from a position of eminence and must affect other people who depend on the protagonist. If the protagonist is a monarch, then a whole people are affected. Though fate plays a strong part in these plays, the downfall of the protagonist must be due to some personal error of judgement (*hamartia* is the Greek word). The tragic spectacle depends on the audience being aware of the capacity of even the most powerful of individuals to destroy themselves through their imperfect understanding of our condition in the world, he thought. The experience of this insight, which Aristotle believed conferred moral benefits upon the audience, would not occur if the protagonists were wicked, or if their fall came about by accident. In the first case the audience would feel no regret at their fall, and in the second no perception of mortal frailty would be granted. The point of tragedy, then, was to provide some form of moral and philosophical education for the audience.

There is no evidence that Shakespeare had any direct acquaintance with the *Poetics*. Early modern English tragedies on the public stages of London took the name and an approximation of the tragedic form. These plays did not necessarily set out to explore a moral, social or religious issue, as the Greek writers, and their Roman imitators, sought in their plays. They set out to tell a story in a recognized dramatic genre that would be attractive to London theatregoers, only a minority of whom would have come across classical tragedy in its Senecan form. There was no coherent contemporary idea of what tragedy should be, even if aristocratic writers like Sir Philip Sidney recommended going back to the classical rules.

In telling these stories within the genre of tragedy, the playwrights made statements about many aspects of human life, but perhaps principally about the nature of political power and the problems of the powerful in the world that they knew. They were aware that the feudal society of the fairly recent past had been very different in its organization and in its ideas about how life should be lived (see above, pp. 176–7). They could see a new world coming into being, a world in which individuals had much more opportunity to make their own way; where new forms of power were competing with old ones, and where the role of women was changing.

When powerful historical forces come into conflict, individuals are sometimes the site of that conflict and are destroyed by it. A protagonist who is living within one system of ideas or beliefs has to struggle to come to terms with the forces of another system. But the protagonists cannot understand this other system (usually) because they can see the world only from where they are. Yet, standing outside of the drama, as members of the audience, we can see their predicament and perhaps also see how things could have been different. From the outside we can see that men and women can transform society because the conditions that produce tragedy are shown to be man-made not divinely ordained, as many critics thought in the past. Some critics find the experience of watching the end of a tragedy to be a gloomy confirmation of human powerlessness. Others see there a pointer to a more just world which is perhaps the product of, but separate from, the conflicting forces which have destroyed the protagonist. There is death, waste and destruction at the end of a tragedy; but there is always some hope.

TRAGEDY AND HISTORY

The historical moment of transition between the medieval and modern worlds can be seen to create the nature of tragedy in Shakespeare's work. I want to explain this idea by referring to *Hamlet*, *Othello* and *Macbeth*.

Just after Shakespeare had written *Hamlet*, there occurred a serious political disturbance in London. On Sunday 8 February 1601 Robert Devereux, Earl of Essex, ex-general of the queen's forces in Ireland and one-time royal favourite, seems to have made an attempt to seize power by force. That was certainly the way the old queen's government saw it; Essex was beheaded for treason. Six of the other 140 rebels were executed. Shakespeare's former patron, the Earl of Southampton, had taken part as Essex's lieutenant but was reprieved and released from the Tower after two years. The reasons for Essex's desperate attempt are complex, but the fact that he possessed the mindset of the aristocratic warrior seems to have played some part. In previous centuries heroic men of noble birth and skill in combat were regarded as their country's natural leaders. The king himself was supposed to embody these qualities. Indeed, the ability to kill all your challengers must have been one of the essential qualifications for kingship in the earliest days of that institution. Kings of England led their armies into battle until as recently as the 1740s. Essex certainly had these qualities. He was an accomplished swordsman and a fearless warrior, and he had a very high opinion of his own qualities as a general. The fact that he saw himself as a knightly warrior is suggested by his curiously old-fashioned behaviour. When abandoning the siege of Rouen in 1592, he rode up to the city wall and flung a lance into the wooden gates, bearing on it a challenge to single combat to anyone who claimed their mistress was fairer than his lady, Queen Elizabeth. (The figure of the monarch as military adventurer also haunts Shakespeare's history plays; see Chapter 8.)

By 1600 the existence of men living this way of life was increasingly seen as a problem rather than an asset to the state. Elizabeth set about depriving the lords of their private armies and preventing them from settling their jealousies and grudges in bloody skirmishes on the streets of London. From 1591 the government was effectively run by Robert Cecil. Short, hunchbacked and quietly spoken, his rank as secretary of state (after 1597) and his prestige at court were due to his political vision and administrative skills, not his military valour. That world had passed. At the time of his rebellion Essex was in disgrace and effectively under house arrest. He responded in the only way he knew.

In the first scene of *Hamlet* we are told by Hamlet's friend Horatio that a border dispute between Denmark and Norway in the days of Hamlet's father had been settled by the kings of the two countries in single combat, a fight won by Old Hamlet (I 1 80–95). Now young Fortinbras, the son of that defeated Norwegian monarch, is secretly planning to recover by force the territory lost. Claudius's response to this renewed threat is very different from his predecessor's. He sends ambassadors to the current king of Norway, the defeated king's brother, with very precise diplomatic instructions (II 1 17–41). Their mission is successful, at least temporarily. We can see here that Old Hamlet belongs to the old world of heroic chivalry. Even his ghost appears in full plate armour in Act I. His way of settling the question is the solution Essex might have chosen. Claudius, however, belongs to a recognizably more modern political system, one in which a rational approach is taken to a dispute between nations. Personal military prowess is not the decisive quality in a political leader.

In the Middle Ages trial by combat was a means by which justice was seen to be done. If one nobleman accused another of killing a member of his family, and the other denied it, single combat between the two could settle the matter. Shakespeare depicts just such a conflict between Bolingbroke and Thomas Mowbray, Duke of Norfolk, in Act I of *King Richard II*. It was believed that Providence would ensure that victory lay with the true contestant (by *Providence* was meant the belief that God would ensure that the good are rewarded and the wicked punished, even on earth). Two things changed this. First, people began to rely on their own observations rather than on the decree of an authority. (A truly medieval mind would believe X to have been guilty in some way if he lost the combat, even though their own eyes may have assured them of his innocence.) Second, the state's courts and judges finally succeeded in taking control of *all* disputes, even those involving the aristocracy. Old Hamlet lived in the heroic-chivalric world of trial by combat. The medieval language used by Horatio to describe him reinforces that (I 1 83–95). But Prince Hamlet lives in Claudius's early modern court. What, then, is he to do when his father's ghost comes back from the dead demanding revenge?

Hamlet, like his fellow student Horatio at the University of Wittenberg, would not be expected to believe in ghosts. Denmark, like England, was an officially Protestant country where the idea that ghosts were the unsettled spirits of the dead was regarded as a foolish Catholic superstition. The ghost can be seen as a manifestation of the old feudal values which Hamlet's father held. Hamlet loved his father, but he is a modern sceptical rationalist. He even, famously, doubts that there is life after death (III 1 55–85). He lives in a state where justice is not to be privately settled but publicly resolved. We can see the reasons for this in Laertes' behaviour. Hamlet kills the hidden royal minister Polonius, mistakenly thinking that he is stabbing his uncle. Laertes, Polonius' 'noble' son, returns furious at his father's death and threatens the safety of the king himself in his desire for revenge. Laertes' reaction reminds us that blood feuds lead only to further bloodshed. There will never be peace or justice while they are allowed to flourish.

And yet we can also see the problem with the modern system of state justice. What does an individual do when the state itself is corrupt and secretly carries out actions that its own laws define as crimes? How can Hamlet call on Claudius to arrest himself for the secret murder that only the two of them know Claudius committed? Once the framework of the rule of law is violated, through revolution or assassination, perhaps, the lawless territory of the blood feud and personal revenge returns. The character of Hamlet can be seen as tragic because he is caught in this double-bind between, on the one hand, the loved father whose ghost demands a medieval revenge that Hamlet's modern mind wants to, but cannot, accept; and, on the other, the modern state that he wants to believe in but knows to be corrupt. The Marxist critic Arnold Kettle described Hamlet as 'the first modern intellectual in our literature' because he realizes that 'power is in the hands of a class whose values humane people feel they must repudiate' (Kettle 1964: 156). In the end, he has to fall back on letting events take their course. Despite his scepticism about matters of religious belief, Hamlet falls back on the workings of Providence. Let God decide when and how Claudius dies; Hamlet himself cannot affect his fate:

Hamlet   If it* be now, 'tis not to come; if it be not to come, it will be now; if it be not now, yet it will come – the readiness is all. Since no man, of aught* he leaves, knows what is't to leave betimes,* let be.

(V 2 220–2)

* [220] *it* his death [222] *aught* anything; *knows what is't to leave betimes* knows what he misses if he leaves early

Most contemporary critics do not like to talk about character at all. They take the view that both stage characters and real people aren't actually unified coherent individuals. We are never consistent enough to be talked about as if there were an essential core to our identity. We talk differently and act differently depending on whom we are with and what we are doing – and that does not take account of our subconscious. Indeed, some critics believe that it is the *language* we use in these particular circumstances that creates who we are. Furthermore, language exists societally outside of the individual; we don't create it for ourselves. Such critics ignore character and are more interested in looking at how a role in a Shakespeare play is constructed from the social and political relationships of the time in which the play was written. Hamlet's *subjectivity*, as they put it, is produced by the conflicts and stresses in his society. The play does not either approve of or condemn revenge, but it does present to the audience, both then and now, important problems with certain political principles. These principles are the underlying ideas about revenge in each of the conflicting ways of life in which Hamlet must live.

One of Hamlet's key concerns is his identity. He seems unsure whether he is a madman or a coldly sane individual; a real avenger or an actor playing a role in a revenge play (II 2 571–87); a lover of Ophelia and his mother or a hater of women in general. But this may be because the tragic protagonist always goes through a process of losing his identity. In the medieval world social status was identical with political power. A man's position within the feudal hierarchy at birth – as prince, duke, earl, knight or peasant – told him who he was, who he remained and how he should conduct himself. It established his relationships with others, too. There is, however, in Shakespeare's time a new fluidity. It is possible to be a prince, as Hamlet is, but to have no power because the cunning politician Claudius keeps him sidelined and under surveillance. He cannot see clearly who he is any more. That is another distinctly tragic feature of the role. Hamlet is an intelligent and perceptive man struggling to live among the deceptions, contradictions and stupidities of the only society he can know. That is what makes him a tragic figure. But he sees that the world could be otherwise. Claudius recognizes this too, I think, but decides to accept the present situation for his own selfish advantage (III 3 3–72). It is the time in which Hamlet has to live that is actually 'out of joint' (I 5 188), not the prince himself. That is why he has no stable identity in a disjointed and contradictory society.

Othello, on the other hand, has power but no status. Venice is happy to employ mercenaries to lead its forces. Noble Italian birth is not a qualification in this modern situation; military proficiency is what matters. Yet Othello is black and foreign, so he cannot be accepted in the hierarchy of the Venetian state. Brabantio, Desdemona's father, cannot accept him as a suitable husband for his daughter because of his colour. Yet Othello does not come across, in either his language or his attitudes, as foreign. His foreignness and blackness are, however, emphasized by others. There is a certain grand pomposity to his language, but this is to do with Othello's vision of himself. He sees himself as a noble, almost legendary, warrior. Only a minute or so after he first comes on stage he tells Iago 'I fetch my life and being / From men of royal siege' (I 2 21–2), a most unusual, archaic use of the word 'siege', meaning 'seat' and therefore social status. The story of his life, which he tells to the duke and the senators, is a story of desperate adventures straight out of a 'romance' (a medieval tall story of the unlikely adventures that a wandering knight meets on his quest). It was the same story that he had told to Brabantio and which had made such an impression on Desdemona:

Othello   Wherein I spoke of most disastrous* chances:
        Of moving accidents* by flood and field,*   135
        Of hair-breadth stapes i' th'imminent deadly breach,*
        Of being taken by the insolent foe
        And sold to slavery, of my redemption thence
        And portance* in my travel's history;
        Wherein of antres* vast and deserts idle,   140
        Rough quarries, rocks and hills whose heads touch heaven,
        It was my hint to speak – such was my process* –
        And of the Cannibals that each other eat,
        The Anthropophagi,* and men whose heads
        Do grow beneath their shoulders.   145
                               (I 3 134–45)

* [134] *disastrous* unlucky [135] *accidents* events; *by flood and field* on sea and land [136] *i' th'imminent deadly breach* in the deadly danger of leading an attack through a gap made in a castle wall [139] *portance* conduct [140] *antres* caves [142] *process* proceeding [144] *Anthropophagi* man-eaters

In the medieval romances a knight's feats of heroism win the lady's love. Chivalric prowess is actually inseparable from the love of the knight's lady who dignifies and sanctions his deeds. And it is for these very adventures that Desdemona loves Othello. He tells the duke and senators:

Othello   She loved me for the dangers I had pass'd,
        And I loved her that she did pity them.

                               (I 3 167–8)

Desdemona's love for Othello is founded on his qualities as a warrior and his history of noble deeds. These heroic qualities even override his blackness:

Desdemona My heart's subdu'd 250
        Even to the very quality of my lord.*
        I saw Othello's visage* in his mind,
        And to his honours and his valiant parts*
        Did I my soul and fortunes consecrate.

(I 3 250–4)

> * [250–1] *subdu'd* / *Even to the very quality* 'my heart has been conquered completely by his way of life and the character which that way of life gives him' [252] *visage* face – here she means his real face [253] *parts* qualities

This is a love from the world of stories and legends, an idealized version of courtly love in feudal chivalry. It is completely at odds with imperialist, pragmatic, money-driven Venetian society (Holderness 1989a: 58).

Both lovers become dupes of the worldly Iago. Othello is an outsider in Venice and unsure of its ways. Desdemona is a young noblewoman who has been kept apart from male society and politics. Their love is not grounded in the reality of how their society operates, and so it founders when it comes into contact with that world in its most pure form: Iago. Not that the nature of their love is shown to be admirable. Indeed, the contradictions of this sort of courtly love are quickly exposed. If the warrior's qualities are dependent on the steadfast love of a woman, and that woman proves unfaithful, then the warrior loses his status. Once Othello is convinced that his wife is having an affair with Cassio, 'Othello's occupation's gone' (III 3 357). The capacity for violence which gives the warrior his suitability as an object of love is then turned against the woman: 'I will chop her into messes. Cuckold [i.e. be unfaithful to] me!' (IV 1 200). She must be destroyed because she is a threat to male integrity: 'she must die, else she'll betray more men' (V 1 6). For her part, Desdemona cannot understand how a woman's love can be unfaithful, since she understands love to be the complete surrender of the woman to the warrior ('My heart's subdu'd / Even to the very quality of my lord' [I 3 250–1]). This explains her naive question to Iago's wife Emilia (IV 3 61–3), when she asks if there really are women who are unfaithful to their husbands. It explains also her strange claim to be responsible for her own death, and her continuing love for her 'kind lord' at the moment of her death at his hands (V 2 124–5). If the woman loves a man because of his ability to use violence against his enemies, she can only approve – crazily – of that violence being turned against her, should she become a suitable target in his eyes. Otherwise she betrays his love and deserves his hatred. The man's love in this sort of relationship is all-subduing and allows no argument once you accept it.

Othello's tragedy is that he lives according to a set of stories through which he interprets the world – an ideology – but it is a world that has been superseded. He cannot see that this is so, and the contradictions within his ideology destroy him (Holderness 1989a: 58). He is living the life of a chivalric warrior in a world run by money and self-interest. A woman's love inspired by violence will itself fall prey to that same violence when, thanks to Iago, the chivalric code by which he once lived fails to provide him with an understanding of the real world of the Venice in which Othello lives.

Yet we can see, from our perspective outside of the world both of Othello and of the Venetians, that the play points forward to an order of living in which people should be free to love whoever they want; where marriage with anyone outside your country, class or colour is not seen as 'unnatural' (as Iago says at III 3 229–31). Othello's tragedy can also be seen to be the product of being trapped in a period of history where such egalitarian values are unachievable. The play, however, *hints* powerfully to the audience at the possibility of such values, as Emilia's speech at the end of Act IV indicates (see p. 234).

In a similar way, *Macbeth* can be seen to dramatize the contradictions that lie within the feudal society (see pp. 176–7) of medieval Scotland. On the one hand, the language used to describe both the king (I 7 16–20) and his relationships with his loyal nobles (I 4 14–29) makes Scotland sound a gentle place, where social bonds rest on mutual affection and genuine respect (Holderness 1989a: 60–1). On the other, it is clear that violent challenges to the authority of the king are actually the normal state of affairs in this country. In the course of the play, Macdonald, Macbeth and Malcolm make violent attempts to seize the throne. But it is to be noticed that bloodthirsty violence (I 2 16–23, 35–40) in support of the king is praised in the highest terms (I 3 89–93); violence directed against the king is condemned utterly (I 2 9–14). As the

British critic Alan Sinfield points out, Macbeth kills a rebel and a king at the beginning of the play and is condemned. Macduff kills a rebel and a king (who happen to be the same person) at the end and is to be praised (Sinfield 1992: 100). Critics often assume Malcolm to have been the legitimate king and Macbeth the usurper; but it is by no means clear that being 'Prince of Cumberland' ensured succession to the throne: kings in medieval Scotland, it seems, were sometimes elected (Sinfield 1992: 102).

King James I, to whom *Macbeth* is sometimes seen as a kind of tribute, was not, of course, a feudal king. He sought, rather, to rule as an *absolutist* monarch, one who legitimately does not defer to the authority of any other person or body in any area, such as the Church, the landowners or parliament, as he explained and tried to justify in his 1599 book of advice for his son, *Basilikon Doron* ('Royal Gift' in Greek). James denied that a legitimate monarch could be a tyrant. Conventionally critics have argued that the supernatural forces which seem to conspire against Macbeth in the play indicate that Shakespeare wanted to show that the lawful monarch had God on his side, whereas nature itself revolts against the usurper. But as Sinfield pointed out, there are rational, material explanations for the moving of Birnam Wood and the birth of Macduff (Sinfield 1992: 102). Furthermore, is Malcolm, whose army kills Macbeth, to be any more legitimate than his predecessor? When Malcolm 'tests' Macduff in England, by saying he will debauch Scotland's women (IV 3 60–5) and steal the nobles' property (IV 3 76–84), Macduff accepts that he can tolerate such vices if the king has other 'graces' (IV 3 90). Even if he lacks all the kingly graces, Macduff's response is self-exile, not rebellion (IV 3 111–13). Of course, Malcolm says he will rule as justly as he can, but the scene exposes a contradiction in absolutism: a lawful ruler can be a tyrant, too, who needs to be overthrown, as one of Shakespeare's sources, the Scottish historian and political theorist James Buchanan, argued (Sinfield 1992: 101). James tried to ban Buchanan's works, but his ideas suggest an interesting contemporary reading: *Macbeth* may actually show us that there is no reason why a legitimate monarch may not also be a tyrant, or even that the more absolute he is (Macbeth destroys the power of the nobles), the more likely he is to become one.

The historical evidence would indicate that in medieval Britain it was usually violence which ensured succession. In the feudal Scotland of *Macbeth* violence is the means by which power is achieved and held; but the value system by which the nobles claim to live says that loyalty and faithfulness are what keeps the political order intact and functioning. There is, in a feudal society, what Sinfield calls 'a split between legitimacy and actual power – when the monarch is not the strongest person in the state' (Sinfield 1992: 96–7). The stories about their society told by Duncan and Macbeth are evidently at odds with how these men actually live their lives. For there is this second set of values – a cult of masculine military prowess among the nobles – that is in conflict with the first one of steadfast loyalty.

Acts of valour and daring are what make a man worthy in this society. A real man, as Lady Macbeth successfully argues, keeps his word and is not afraid even to murder the king (I 7 39–59). The most worthy man is he who will challenge the strongest authority in the country: the king. Yet the king is the very man in whose interest Macbeth is supposed to use violence, the person to whom he owes ultimate loyalty. This contradiction within feudal society is what divides and destroys Macbeth. Macbeth cannot avoid living on the line of division running through his society; his fate is therefore tragic.

It can also be argued that the tragedies do not merely embody the ideologies (see p. 190 and p. 221 below) of the past, but that they point towards a more humane future. The tragic contradiction can be seen in the figure of Macbeth himself, rather than in the principles of the society in which he lives. Macbeth's feudal loyalty to Duncan can be seen to be in conflict with an emergent kind of masculinity. According to the British critic Kiernan Ryan:

> Macbeth is the tragedy of a man driven, despite the resistance of a new kind of self awakening within him, to become a savage individualist, whose defiant creed is 'For mine own good / All causes shall give way' (III 4 134–5). The play affords an unflinching demonstration of the cost of that creed, with whose less eloquent, latter-day slogans ('me first', 'look out for number one', 'every man for himself') most of us are all too familiar.
>
> (Ryan 2002: 90)

The play shows that the result of this modern, ruthless individualism is that by the end of the play Macbeth is isolated, hated and hopeless, his life, as he says,

> a tale
> Told by an idiot, full of sound and fury,
> Signifying nothing.

(V 5 26–8)

But Malcolm's triumph is not the reimposition of a divinely approved feudal order, or even of a self-contradictory order which itself approves of savage violence, as Holderness argued (see above, p. 217), and which, as Lady Macbeth explains, demands that a real man is one who dares to kill the king (I 7 49). Instead, the play presents to the audience, in its feudal context, a 'new kind of awakening' that 'the individual's true interests and those of the human community are ultimately identical' (Ryan 2002: 94). For Macbeth's wife fears that he may be 'too full o' th' milk of human kindness' (I 5 17) to stoop to murder. Before the assassination it is pity, figured as a 'naked new born babe' (I 7 21), which is the most powerfully imagined, clinching factor that makes him temporarily lose his resolve to kill the king, not the sin of regicide (I 7 12). What haunts him is not Duncan's death, but that 'Macbeth does murther sleep' (II 2 33), 'the common blessing that linked him to his kind' (Ryan 2002: 94). He is haunted by the shedding of blood (III 4 121), the fluid which makes us all human, whatever our class. This realization, of the moral claims of our common humanity, looks forward to a possible better future where individualism is revealed to be as cruel and empty a way of living as feudalism is now realized to be.

TRAGEDY AND POWER

Because Shakespeare's tragedies are concerned with people who have a share in the exercise of power and authority in their societies, understanding these plays will involve looking at what is being said about the nature of power.

Power is sometimes exercised through physical force. State power exerted in this way depends on the firm loyalty of the police and the armed forces, and is therefore expensive and of questionable reliability. If loyal armed forces are the only means by which power is sustained, one's hold on it is unlikely to last very long.

In 1600 there was neither a police force nor a standing army in England, so that kind of state power was not a real option for its rulers. It is not clear that rulers at this time would have wanted such forces, either. A better way to exercise power is to convince the ruled that it is in their interest to obey their rulers, even if it actually is not. If people in a society believe a set of statements and stories that explain and justify the exercise of power by one group over others in this society, then that power will be much more secure. This 'set of statements and stories' is a better definition of the word *ideology*. The powerful themselves will no doubt believe these stories – unless, that is, they are 'machiavels' (see pp. 225f.).

The most secure exercise of power is that which is seen as *natural*, even by those who are exploited by that power. Shakespeare is very interested, it seems to many modern critics, in power that is exercised in this ideological way. He seems particularly interested in how power is connected with justice. In all the tragedies this is perhaps nowhere more evident than in *King Lear*.

Edmund is the character who at first glance has some very perceptive insights into how power operates. He is the illegitimate son of the Duke of Gloucester, and he has a grudge. All of Gloucester's property will be inherited by Edgar, the legitimate son and heir. Edmund realizes that the law which denies the father's property to the illegitimate son is merely 'custom' (I 2 3). By this he means that it is a man-made rule; there is nothing *natural* about it. He is just as much a man as his brother. Why, then, should bastards be regarded as inferior people (I 2 6–15)? Rationally speaking, one can see the truth of what he says. His father's affection for him is the same as it is for Edgar (I 2 16–17), but the law will not permit that affection to be reflected in inherited property. Thus Edmund has seen that the relationship between affection and property is purely *arbitrary*: there is no natural or essential reason why the amount of love a parent holds for a child, or a child holds for a parent, should have any connection with how much property that parent passes on to his children. Love is love and property property. In a humane society, love is not love when it depends on external factors that have nothing to do with it – as the king of France remarks in the first scene of the play (I 1 238–40).

This is an insight that has certainly escaped Lear in the same scene. The aged Lear has decided to 'retire' and divide up his territory between his three daughters. He invites each of them to say how much they love him so that he can reward their affection accordingly. The two older sisters, Goneril and Regan, strive to outdo each other in their declarations of love (I 1 54–61; 69–76). The youngest, Cordelia, refuses to play along. She says she loves her father as much as she ought, in duty. She refuses to speak a great deal of words which she knows are bluster and exaggeration (I 1 86–105). Lear is furious and disowns Cordelia, banishing her without a dowry to become the wife of the king of France, who is happy to accept her nevertheless. Thus he loses, simultaneously, that 'love' of his false daughters which was his only for so long as he retained kingly power and the company of his true daughter, who loves him simply because he is her father. Lear is trapped in a way of thinking that defines who he is but no longer fits the world in which he lives.

Edmund, too, is aware that we tend to hide the actual causes of events in the world behind abstractions and religious dogma and so lose sight of our ability to change the world for ourselves. Astrology is a typical example of this:

Edmund   An admirable evasion of whoremaster* man, to lay his goatish
           disposition on the charge of a star! My father compounded
           with* my mother under the Dragon's tail, and my
           nativity* was under Ursa Major,* so that it follows,   130
           I am rough and lecherous. Fut, I should have been
           that I am, had the maidenliest star in the firmament
           twinkled* on my bastardising.

                                       (I 2 127–33)

* [127] *whoremaster* literally a pimp, but here it must mean someone lecherous [128] *compounded with* slept with [130] *nativity* birth; *Ursa Major* the Great Bear – a constellation, like the 'Dragon's tail' [131–3] I *should have been . . . bastardising* 'I would have been just as I am, had the most virginal star in the sky twinkled on the moment of my illegitimate conception'

If our natures were laid down by the position of the stars in the sky at the moment of our conception, there would be nothing we could do to change the way the world is. In that sense astrology is part of a distinctly conservative ideology. But Edmund sees that this is a story that we tell, like the one about 'legitimacy' and 'illegitimacy', to mask the real facts of individuals and groups seeking to exert power over others. They are just stories, and the more that those stories involve the mystical or the 'natural', the more powerful they are likely to be. Edmund sees all this; he sees the fact that justice in the world of the play is simply what the powerful say it is. This is the message that Lear is going to learn to his cost.

Lear thinks that he can give away all his property to his daughters Goneril and Regan and still retain the authority and respect due to a king and the affection due to a father. He has not seen that all these things are the direct product of the land he possesses, which gives him economic power. He does not realize that in the world of the play love and respect flow towards possessions, but do not belong to people as individuals. He is loved as a king because he is powerful. Without his power there is (apparently) nothing there to love. Cordelia tries to reveal this 'truth' to him, but the story he had told himself, that kings are loved and obeyed for their personal qualities – which he confuses with their power – makes him regard her statement as treasonable. Only on the heath, when he has been deserted by nearly everyone, can he see the truth about power.

Just before he is found by Cordelia's attendants, Lear meets Edmund's father Gloucester. Gloucester has been cruelly blinded by Regan's ruthless husband Cornwall for helping Lear to escape from their clutches. He, too, is destitute and wandering. Lear tells him that he does not need eyes to see the truth about justice in the world:

Lear	What, art mad? A man may see how this	150
	world goes with no eyes. Look with thine ears; see	
	how yond* justice* rails* upon yond simple thief. Hark	
	in thine ear: change places, and handy-dandy,* which is	
	the justice which is the thief? Thou hast seen a	
	farmer's dog bark at a beggar?	155
Gloucester	Ay, sir.	

Lear   And the creature run from the cur?* There
          thou mightst behold the great image of authority: a
          dog's obeyed in office.*

(IV 6 150–9)

* [152] *yond* that; *justice* judge; *rails* abuses, shouts at [153] *handy-dandy* a
    child's guessing game in which an object is hidden in one hand or the
    other. Lear means here: 'You can take your pick – the same thing can be
    hidden in either hand. The same man could be either judge or thief' [157]
    cur dog [158] *a dog's obeyed in office* the authority of an official has nothing
    to do with the personal virtue or qualities of the person holding the office

Because the dog belongs to a landowner, a beggar will recognize its
authority even though it is only a dog. In the same way, Lear has
realized that a king is obeyed and loved only because of his position
as monarch. Any man could be a king, in fact. Who is to say that
the man sitting in judgement has not himself at some time robbed
another? So long as the public remains ignorant of the fact, his
ability to pass judgement is, to the public mind, unimpaired. He has
no personal virtue just because he is a judge. Or maybe stealing
itself is socially defined: if an employer lowers wages in a time of
high unemployment, is he or she not stealing his or her employee's
labour just as much as if the employee were to take one of the
employer's possessions without paying for it?

Yet Lear has to be stripped of all his office and power before he
can see through the ideology of kingship, in this case the idea that
monarchs rule because they personally have the particular qualities
that befit them to exercise power over the rest of us, or because God
has chosen them to have this power. He sees now that monarchs are
just ordinary men and as such need to pay attention to the basic
humanity they share with the poorest of their subjects. As the rain
lashes down upon him on the heath, he has this realization:

Lear   Poor naked wretches, wheresoe'er you are,
          That bide* the pelting of this piteous storm,
          How shall your houseless heads and unfed sides,   30
          Your loop'd and window'd* raggedness, defend you
          From seasons such as this! Take physic,* pomp,*
          Expose thyself to feel what wretches feel,

That thou may'st shake the superflux* to them,   35
And show the heavens more just.

(III 4 28–36)

* [29] *bide* suffer [31] *loop'd and window'd* full of holes [32] *physic* medicine; *pomp* the rich and powerful [35] *shake the superflux* redistribute your excess of wealth – the image is of a man shaking off something un-needed that has stuck to him

He would have had no idea that the redistribution of wealth from the rich to the poor was what needed to be done, had he not experienced what it was to be destitute himself. There seems, then, to be a suggestion here that wealth and position prevent the powerful from ever understanding the lot of the poor. The society of the play is organized in such a way that the rich will never understand what needs to be done if social justice is to prevail. The poor are, it seems, more likely to have a clear idea of what justice is. This is emphasized by the fact that one of Cornwall's servants had earlier been prepared to fight his own master and die in an attempt to prevent the torture of Gloucester, simply because he saw it as wrong and cruel (III 7 72–82).

Edmund, as already observed, can see through the stories which are told to justify power, but so powerful is his desire for ownership of land and property that he is prepared to go along with what he knows to be purely conventional (I 2 1–22). People's relationship to land and property in the play defines their identity and establishes their power, irrespective of their personal virtue. That is clearly the power structure of the Britain of *King Lear*.

Characters in early modern English plays who see that the moral and political stories told by the powerful to justify their position amount to no more than a cover for their naked exercise of power, and act accordingly, are sometimes called *machiavels*. The teachings of the Italian statesman and philosopher Niccolò Machiavelli (1469–1527) were understood to advocate deception and ruthlessness in order to maintain a ruler's power, recognizing Christian humility and truthfulness as qualities to be shunned by an ambitious and successful politician in the real world. Though officially demonized, Machiavelli's books were privately recognized by many intellectuals as a ground-breaking analysis of power that broke away from medieval pieties. As Edmund demonstrates, however, an understanding of how ideology works does not seem to lead to any radical desire to make the world a more just place for all (Dollimore 2004: 201). It should be pointed out also that Machiavelli believed 'the Prince' (the title he uses for the ideal ruler) had a right to rule because the mass of his subjects lacked the intelligence and virtue to ensure the general good. Only on stage, it seems, do the insights which escape the powerful get suggested to the audience.

Rituals, processions and plays themselves are of course also stories. An important way in which early modern – and indeed modern – rulers make their right to rule seem natural is by taking possession of the symbols that society regards as being the markers of valid power.

Crowns, thrones and rich robes on public display were of course important parts of this, but so were the rituals and the formal language of power. As a new ruler, Claudius in *Hamlet* has to establish his power by symbolic display as much as by any other means. His first entrance, in what is clearly a formal court occasion, is marked by a fanfare of trumpets. The actors would enter in order of their precedence in the hierarchy of the state:

> *Flourish.** *Enter* CLAUDIUS, KING OF DENMARK, GERTRUDE THE QUEEN; COUNCIL: *as* POLONIUS; *and his son* LAERTES, HAMLET *cum aliis** [*including* VOLTEMAND *and* CORNELIUS].
>
> (I 2 0, sd)

> * *Flourish* a fanfare of trumpets; *cum aliis* Latin, meaning 'with others'

As discussed above (see p. 72), Hamlet's position in the procession entering the stage is clearly different from that designated for his rank. It is also clear from dialogue later in the scene (I 2 68, 77–8) that his black mourning-clothes are not in tune with the bright and expensive ceremonial robes worn by the king and queen. This obvious symbolic dissent must be visually reconciled with the royal ritual or it will be apparent to any onlooker that Claudius's power over his court and kingdom is incomplete, and therefore in reality less effective. After a carefully crafted speech, the rhetoric of which seeks to justify his optimistic outlook in the face of the general mourning for his recently deceased brother (I 2 1–16), he instructs his diplomats to deal with the threat from Fortinbras. Then he hears a request from Laertes, his chief minister's son, before addressing Prince Hamlet – a clear snub in terms of Hamlet's rank in the court. The entreaties of both king and queen succeed in wringing from Hamlet a grudging promise to obey his mother's authority. Claudius, having re-established his authority, announces that he will celebrate by having cannons fired as he drinks that evening:

> *King*   This gentle and unforc'd accord of Hamlet
>   Sits smiling to my heart, in grace whereof,
>   No jocund health* that Denmark* drinks to-day,   125
>   But the great cannon to the clouds shall tell,
>   And the King's rouse* the heaven shall bruit* again,
>   Respeaking earthly thunder. Come away. *Flourish. Exeunt*
>   *all but Hamlet*

(I 2 123–8)

* [125] *jocund health* joyful toast; *Denmark* the King of Denmark [127] *rouse* a full glass drunk down in one; *bruit* echo noisily

The audience then hear the cannon firing off-stage to mark Claudius's drinking, while Hamlet awaits his appointment with the ghost later that evening (I 4 6 sd). The public symbolism of this custom seems clear. The echoing of the king's delight in the skies shows divine approval of his happiness. The heavens concur with his power to wish good health and fortune as he drinks. The king is a consumer of goods on behalf of the people; in fact his unequal consumption of goods is clearly marked as for their benefit. The cannon-fire indicates his military power. The fact that the heavens re-echo the noise shows that God's judgement, in its traditional form of the thunderbolt, is completely in agreement with Claudius. Privately, Hamlet says the custom is actually read by other nations as proof that the Danes are drunks (I 4 17–21). But this sort of subversive reading of ceremonial display is what the sheer spectacle is supposed to disarm.

The fencing match of the play's final scene is also part of a formal display to validate Claudius's power. The fact that he can stage a symbolic duel between two of the kingdom's most powerful young men symbolizes publicly his ability to control and neutralize conflicts within Denmark. The same ritual of the cannon and the drinking takes place during the duel, once more showing who has the real authority (V 2 283, sd). However, Claudius has distorted the ritual from a symbolic to a material exercise of power by giving Laertes a sword tipped with a deadly poison so that he can *accidentally* kill Hamlet. When we hear a cannon announcing the entrance of Fortinbras, it remains unclear whether it is a symbolic ceremonial salute or a piece of artillery fired in anger. The symbolic is here sliding into the actual. And indeed Fortinbras, whose name means 'strength in arms', seems to symbolize the supremacy of armed force in political conflict. Claudius might scheme and connive; Hamlet might put on a subversive play; but the man who rules Denmark at the end of the play is the man who has an army on stage to support his claim. Military ceremonial looks as though it will set the symbolic tone, too, of the new regime.

> *Fortinbras*   Let four captains   395
>   Bear Hamlet like a soldier to the stage,
>   For he was likely, had he been put on,*
>   To have prov'd most royal; and for his passage*
>   The soldiers' music and the rite of war
>   Speak loudly for him.   400
>   Take up the bodies. Such a sight as this
>   Becomes the field,* but here shows much amiss.
>   Go bid the soldiers shoot.
>   *Exeunt marching; after the which a peal of ordinance* are
>   shot off*
>
> (V 2 395–403)

* [397] *put on* become king [398] *passage* i.e. death [402] *Becomes the field* would suit the battlefield [403, stage direction (sd)] 'a peal of ordinance' means a number of cannon fired simultaneously

Although Hamlet has adopted several identities in the play, there is precious little evidence in the text to suggest that 'soldier' appropriately describes him. If the 'his' in line 398 is taken to refer to the dead Claudius (see Hawkes 1986: 118), not the dead prince, the same consideration would apply. The point is, however, that it suits the aim of the military adventurer Fortinbras to portray the previous legitimate rulers as military men just like himself; it is now a way of securing power.

An important question arises from all of this. If the plays show public display used to legitimize the power of monarchs, what then was the political function of the *plays themselves* in the public theatres of London? Perhaps they had none, and that is why they were tolerated, as some critics argue (Yachnin 1997: 3). There is an important school of criticism which argues that because the acting companies were licensed by the monarch, and indeed could exist only under the patronage of an aristocrat, the function of the theatre was always to affirm and consolidate the power of the monarchy. Of course, it is true that the plays show monarchs acting unjustly; it also shows them overthrown and punished. Many of the theatre's Puritan critics argued that the plays actually taught their audiences disobedience and a willingness to defy authority through a sort of 'copy-cat' effect. But the American *new historicist* critics argue that, even though the plays do show authority challenged and overthrown, the drama always ends with monarchical power re-established; and, indeed, all the more strongly established because it allowed subversion to flourish but has contained it successfully. The right of a king or queen to rule absolutely was under threat all the way through the period in which Shakespeare wrote for The King's Men. Indeed, it collapsed altogether when war broke out between king and parliament twenty-six years after Shakespeare's death; and, of course, parliament immediately closed down all the theatres. Absolute monarchical power in the person of Fortinbras, argues Leonard Tennenhouse (1986), an important American new historicist, has shown itself more secure than ever at the end of the play. Neither of the regicides (king-killers), Claudius and Hamlet, has shown, in the way they stage themselves and their concerns, the ability to be the rightful ruler of Denmark. Legitimate monarchy, when it is descended from royal blood and uses military force openly and effectively, is irresistible. Neither Claudius nor Hamlet uses force in this way, and each is defeated.

It can also be argued that there is something obviously unsatisfactory about the succession of Fortinbras. This is something you feel when watching the end of the play. Perhaps it is because we are seeing 'power nakedly materialized' in the figure of Fortinbras. Stories about what makes kings sacred, and the monarchy an enduring and unifying paternal reassurance in an unstable world, are embarrassingly and revealingly stripped away in this moment (Barker 1993: 51).

The new historicists' ideas are opposed by the British school of Shakespeare critics known as the *cultural materialists*. They see in the plays subversive ideas that not only deny the 'naturalness' of absolute monarchy, but even speak up for the marginal and dispossessed – the poor, the outcast and women. They contest the idea that the historical and tragic drama of the time always represents the total dominance of male power, the court and the monarch. They see within the ideology a *series of conflicting stories*, not a *single* story that will always finally contain the others. For the cultural materialists there are *dissident* stories that undermine and call into question (or subvert) that story which supports the powerful and is most widely believed (i.e. is dominant). That story, however, according to the new historicists, will always ultimately endorse the rule of the king in the state and of the father in the family (a simple definition of the term *patriarchy*). We can look at these two theories about how power works by examining the depiction of women in the tragedies.

TRAGEDY AND GENDER

Many feminist critics have written about the tragedies' portrayal of women and their relationships with men. Feminist critics are not all of a type. Here by 'feminist critics' I mean those who feel that literature, like our society, is, and has been, unjustly dominated by men. In their writings, these critics seek to show the nature of that male dominance as it appears in different forms in the texts being studied. *Gender* is, for them, part of that dominance, because it is seen as socially created; *sex*, on the other hand, is a biological fact (though there are obviously grey areas here too). Thus women naturally have breasts, are equipped to conceive, bear and nurture children, and so on. These are sexual characteristics. Most feminists, on the other hand, would say that being submissive, gentle and taking trouble over your appearance are qualities that society tends to make women want to have; they are not 'naturally' female, as are the sexual characteristics of female bodies. Gender relates to a set of ideas and assumptions that are attributed variously to men and women, but have no *necessary* connection to their bodies' sexual characteristics. In a society dominated by men, the qualities of the female gender will reflect that power imbalance and place women at a disadvantage.

There is, of course, no doubt that women's position in society was considerably worse in Shakespeare's time than it is today, though there is some debate about how bad it actually was (see above, p. 141). Unmarried women and widows, for instance, had independent rights over property superior to those enjoyed by females in the late eighteenth century. The restrictive sexual prud-ishness of the mid-nineteenth century did not exist then. Yet women were generally regarded as inferior. Some influential authorities held them to be incomplete men, as earlier observed. The rational and logical element believed to distinguish the male was lacking in the woman. Women were governed by the moon, as their menstrual cycle revealed. Consequently, they were inconstant and changeable. Women could never shake off the responsibility of mother Eve for the Fall of mankind in the Garden of Eden. Once their virginity was lost, they were likely to be sexually demanding and to lead men into sin. A gentlewoman was supposed to be a virgin at marriage so that her husband could be sure that the chil-dren she bore were his own, and he could then control her sexuality. Legitimate birth was, after all, the principal qualification for the transfer of property in this society (see Box 3.2, p. 65). Silence and obedience were politely regarded as the highest of female graces. All these ideas are evident, perhaps dominant, in Shakespeare's plays; but there are also female characters who clearly present quite different qualities.

The power of men over women can be seen not only in the way women are represented but in the assumptions that the plays make about the nature and place of women in society. The response from its audience that *King Lear* expects would seem to be based firmly on an idea of female subordination. Goneril and Regan's treatment of their father can be seen as wrong not just because it is cruel but, crucially, because it reverses the 'natural' and unchangeable law that daughters must always obey their fathers and husbands. In Act I, the now-retired Lear and his troop of badly behaved knights are staying at the home of his daughter Goneril. For Lear the first concrete sign of resistance from his older daughters is when Goneril requests that he slims down this riotous crew. He is angry with her not for her lack of respect, or because she went back on the terms under which her power was established; what rouses him to fury is that *his daughter* could *disobey* him. He immediately denies that she is really his daughter (I 4 218) and keeps repeating the idea; he pretends he cannot recognize her (I 4 236), then says she cannot have been fathered by him (I 4 254). Female disobedience is to him unthinkable. Finally, in a horrible curse, he calls upon 'nature' herself to make Goneril incapable of bearing children:

Lear	Hear, Nature, hear, dear goddess, hear!	275
	Suspend thy purpose, if thou didst intend	
	To make this creature fruitful.	
	Into her womb convey sterility,	
	Dry up in her the organs of increase,*	
	And from her derogate* body never spring	280
	A babe to honour her!	

(I 4 275–81)

* [279] *organs of increase* her womb [280] *derogate* debased, or perhaps incomplete, disabled

Not only does Lear think that as a (retired) king he has the right to command a goddess, but he also thinks nature will agree to go against her own course (i.e. render a fertile woman infertile) as a punishment for a daughter disobeying her father. Female disobedience is depicted by him as more unnatural than infertility. The speeches that condemn Goneril and Regan concentrate on their *unnaturalness*. Albany, Goneril's weak but honest husband, calls them 'tigers, not daughters' (IV 2 40); the heavens themselves must surely quickly punish such a subversion of the natural order, or else 'Humanity must perforce [i.e. of necessity] prey on itself / Like monsters of the deep' (IV 2 49–50). 'Proper deformity shows not in the fiend [i.e. the devil] / So horrid as in woman' (IV 2 60–1). In fact the devil, the bringer of all evil into the world, is overtly connected with female sexuality in Lear's shockingly vicious description of the female genitals (IV 6 118–29). This may be seen as prophetic. It is the lust they share for Edmund that leads to the destruction of them both: Regan is poisoned by Goneril, and Goneril, in despair when Edmund is mortally wounded, kills herself.

It might be objected that Cordelia shows disobedience to her father but is nevertheless presented as virtuous. At first glance, this looks true, but Cordelia is actually only standing up for the right of a husband to take some of the love that a daughter, prior to her marriage, owes solely to her father. And, indeed, even though disowned by her father, by the end of Act I Scene 1 Cordelia, as the betrothed of the king of France, has a new master. Unlike her sisters, she has never challenged patriarchy at all:

Cordelia	Good my lord,	95
	You have begot* me, bred me, loved me: I	
	Return those duties back as are right fit,	
	Obey you, love you and most honour you.	
	Why have my sisters husbands if they say	
	They love you all? Happily, when I shall wed,	100
	The lord whose hand must take my plight* shall carry	
	Half my love with him, half my care and duty.	

(I 1 95–102)

* [96] *begot* fathered [101] *plight* wedding vow

When the two are finally reconciled, she even denies that she has a reason to resent the way he has treated her (IV 7 75). The whole dramatic development of the play seems slowly to build up our sympathy for Lear and never seems to put us in a position to question the play's subordination of women. A feminist critic may therefore condemn the play altogether. Alternatively, the critic may continue to take pleasure in the play as drama, while withholding approval of what the play may be saying (McLuskie 1985: 98).

Or, again, the critic may actually find readings of the plays that subvert the apparent sexist assumptions of early-seventeenth-century plays. These readings might not detect a hidden feminism in Shakespeare – though some critics, like Juliet Dusinberre (1996a), claim to have done so (see p. 142). Rather, they uncover the social and economic roots of injustice and inequality and expose the contradictions within them. Or they find clearly expressed in the plays a plea for treating everyone fairly, simply because we are all human.

Such a project can be conducted for *King Lear*, but I would like to discuss it with relevance to *Othello*. Emilia, Iago's wife, puts in context much of the play's male behaviour in a speech she makes at the end of Act IV. Desdemona is getting ready for bed, for the last time – though she does not know this, of course. When Othello comes to bed, he will kill her because he has been persuaded by Iago that she has slept with Cassio. Are there women, she asks Emilia, who would be unfaithful to their husbands? She would not be so for the whole world. If you had the world, replies Emilia, it would be up to you whether or not it was wrong (IV 5 61–82). And this is the play's point about male jealousy and possessiveness: it is the men who have the power and make the rules. But if men realized that women were the same as them and treated women as equals, not as possessions, the catastrophe which is about to occur would never arise. That whole code of behaviour which makes men feel that they must use violence to defend their collective honour against a treacherous and rebellious womankind would fall away, to everyone's advantage (Ryan 2002: 88). Thus some feminist critics read Othello's violent jealousy as the product of a social system where women are dominated and possessed by men. More equal relationships between men and women, in which one party did not see the other as their property, would make such actions seem absurd.

Desdemona   Beshrew me, if I would do such a wrong
           For the whole world.

Emilia   Why, the wrong is but a wrong i'th' world;   80
           and having the world for your labour, 'tis a wrong in
           your own world, and you might quickly make it right.

Desdemona   I do not think there is any such woman.

Emilia   Yes, a dozen; and as many to th' vantage* as
           would store the world they play'd for.*   85
           But I do think it is their husbands' faults
           If wives do fall. Say that they slack their duties,*
           And pour our treasures into foreign laps;*
           Or else break out in peevish* jealousies,
           Throwing restraint upon us; or say they strike us,   90
           Or scant our former having in despite:*
           Why, we have galls;* and though we have some grace,
           Yet have we some revenge. Let husbands know
           Their wives have sense* like them; they see, and smell,
           And have their palates both for sweet and sour,   95

As husbands have. What is it that they do
When they change us for others? Is it sport?*
I think it is. And doth affection* breed it?
I think it doth. Is't frailty that thus errs?
It is so too. And have we not affections,   100
Desires for sport, and frailty as men have?
Then let them use us well; else let them know,
The ills we do, their ills instruct us so.

(IV 3 78–103)

* [84] *to th' vantage* in addition [85] *store the world they play'd for* populate
the world they wanted to win [87] *slack their duties* neglect their wives in
bed [88] *into foreign laps* into other women [89] *peevish* childish [91] *scant
our former having in despite* spitefully reduce how much money they allow
us [92] *galls* the capacity to feel resentment [94] *sense* physical senses [97]
sport fun [98] *affection* emotion

It worth noting that this speech does not appear in the Quarto
version of the text, but only in the Folio (see Box 1.2, p. 23). No one
knows why this is, but it may be connected to the controversial
power and directness of Emilia's argument here.

Such feminist readings of the plays do not seek to prove that
Shakespeare was a feminist, or indeed a sexist. Instead they try to
reveal the ways in which ideology operates both to oppress women
and to trap men into a way of behaving that entails violence.
Sometimes this violence can even be directed against themselves, as
we see in *Othello*.

TRAGEDY, THEATRE AND ETHICS

Some modern critics, however, feel that we can be too hasty to
assume that the representation of women in the tragedies will
always make a political or even psychological statement of some
sort. Perhaps the theatre sometimes examines its *own* nature. In
considering the issue of witchcraft in *Macbeth*, for example, the
American new historicist Stephen Greenblatt suggests that when
Shakespeare chose to put witches on the stage in that play, he was
participating in a public debate and concern over how such women
'should be conceived of, or even whether they should be said to

exist at all' (Greenblatt 1993: 115). An early modern writer, Reginald Scot, thought the idea of witchcraft to be a mere creation of poetic language, a delusion of our imaginations. What he feared and despised in humans was 'this imaginative capacity to make what is absent present, to give invisible things the force of embodied realities' (Greenblatt 1993: 123). This, he thought, was the source of the witch craze of the time. But it is also the nature of what Shakespeare and other dramatists were doing on the stage, making the 'absent' (imaginary characters) 'present' with 'the force of embodied realities' (actors).

The precise identity of the witches is very unclear. Banquo cannot decide if they are earthly – though they seem to be on the earth (I 3 41–2) – or whether they are just 'fantastical' (I 3 53). It is also unclear whether they have any *direct* impact on the play at all. But just like in the theatre, 'virtually everything that follows in the play transpires on the border between fantasy and reality' (Greenblatt 1993: 125), a place where a mental image can make men behave 'unnaturally'. The first thought of Duncan's murder might still be 'fantastical', thinks Macbeth, but it

> Shakes so my single state of man* that function* 140
> Is smother'd in surmise,* and nothing is
> But what is not.
>
> (I 3 141–3)

> * [140] *single state of man* personal coherence, integrity [140] *function* proper operation of a sane human mind [141] *surmise* imagined action

If the witches and their prophecies, the dagger (II 2 33), Banquo's ghost, Lady Macbeth's vision of blood that cannot be washed off (V 1 43) and so on could all be explained supernaturally, or all 'dismissed as fantasy or fraud' (Greenblatt 1993: 125), we could feel secure. But in the play the secular, ordinary world is infected by the demonic, and the demonic by the secular. This sense of existence on the border between the imagined and the real is perhaps what Macbeth means when he sums up his life:

> *Macbeth* Life's but a walking shadow, a poor player,
> That struts and frets his life upon the stage, 25

And then is heard no more. It is a tale
Told by an idiot, full of sound and fury,
Signifying nothing.

(V 5 24–8)

But to the audience these lines are far from empty. The simile of Macbeth as a performer can be read to suggest that this play acknowledges that there is something 'demonic' in the nature of theatre itself. As Greenblatt puts it, for Shakespeare 'his theater is the space where the fantastic and the bodily . . . touch' (1993: 130). In another place Greenblatt argues that Hamlet's father's ghost brings to the stage a distinct echo of the suppressed Catholic rites for the souls of the dead, and, in fact, 'Hamlet immeasurably inten-sifies a sense of the weirdness of the theater, its proximity to certain experiences that had been organized and exploited by religious institutions and rituals' (Greenblatt 2001: 253). The gender of the witches, in this reading, is far less important than their role in conveying in some analogous sense the strange, semi-magical ritual and unspoken communal significance of the theatre.

Greenblatt locates the meaning of the play very much in the ideas and concerns of its time. This generally historicist approach is typical of contemporary attitudes to the tragedies. They are not about heroic individuals with 'flawed' characters whose lives are lived out in a world where good and evil are engaged in a mighty struggle. Rather, critics look at how tragedies show human suffering to be the result of society's contradictory forces – forces that we can recognize on stage and therefore, perhaps, seek to change in the world.

The 'ethical' criticism of the last ten years, on the other hand, is no less political in its concerns with how we should live, but it is less concerned with precise historical forces and more with fundamental insights which exist *in* history – but are not perhaps so entirely unique to a precise historical moment. What we feel at the end of a great tragedy like *King Lear*, for example, is often more than just an insight into the nature of raw political power. The British critic Ewan Fernie has argued that 'true perception of the other [person], as this tragedy reveals, is the revolutionary move, the foundation of all ethical and political projects' (Fernie 2002: 206).

It was often argued in the past that the play was distinctly *humanist*: it showed the heroic struggle of the flawed human individual against cosmic forces greater than itself (this sense of the word is distinct from its early modern usage: see pp. 179 and 270). An individual protagonist found salvation and dignity in a final and futile act of resistance to those forces, what the mid-twentieth-century critic G. Wilson Knight called 'the thing that man dares scarcely face: the demonic grin of the incongruous and absurd in the most pitiful of human struggles with an iron fate' (Knight 2001: 198). For Fernie the play is anti-humanist in that it reveals that if there is any kind of salvation, it lies not in the struggle of the *individual* but in the recognition that we live in and through *others*: the play shows that if there is hope for the future, it is to be achieved through the denial of our own egos. For most of the play Lear feels shame that he has not acted as he feels a king should act. But even when he realizes in the storm scene (see p. 224 above) that he could have ruled more justly, he still has not completed his tragic journey to ethical enlightenment: he still glorifies himself as a king. But a tragic king in this play must offend against all decorum and see that he is the same as all other humans. Lear sees this when he tries to be naked like poor Tom ('Off, off you lendings!', III 4 108–9), and when he contemplates the blind, lost figure of Gloucester in Act IV Scene 5. But even when captured after the battle, he still wants Cordelia for himself (V 3 8–19). Only, finally, at her death does he painfully recognize her life as separate and independent of his need of her, and thus achieves a state of knowledge and love. As Fernie puts it, 'carrying his child, he at last becomes a father, instead of an aged dependent ... His unique distinction among tragic heroes is that he dies pointing away from himself, at someone else' (Fernie 2002: 206–7):

Lear And my poor fool is hang'd! No, no, no life!
        Why should a dog, a horse, a rat have life,
        And thou no breath at all? Thou'lt come no more,
        Never, never, never, never, never.
        Pray you undo this button. Thank you, sir.   310
        Do you see this? Look on her! Look her lips,
        Look there, look there!   *He dies.*
                                                                (V 3 306–12)

SUMMARY

- Shakespeare lived at a time when the medieval world was giving way to the modern one. The principal characters in tragedies can be destroyed because they are trying to live in a world that no longer has any secure basis, or, more often, because the contradictions within the way they understand the world make their lives impossible.
- The tragedies show the operations of power in society by revealing how the stories and displays of those in authority convince those without power of their superiors' right to rule, baseless though these stories may well be.
- In particular, the tragedies reveal the ideological means by which men at this time ensured dominance over women.
- The tragedies have also recently been seen as telling us something about other philosophical issues: the nature of representation in the theatre itself, or general ethical principles about how we should live our lives now.

FURTHER THINKING

- How might you apply the idea of a character destroyed by a changing or contradictory ideology to Antony and / or Cleopatra in *Antony and Cleopatra*? Or Brutus in *Julius Caesar*? Or Coriolanus in *Coriolanus*?
- What might you gain by applying this sort of feminist reading to the depiction of Tamora and Lavinia in *Titus Andronicus*?
- With the multiple historical perspectives available in a play like *Macbeth* or *King Lear*, are there any values and ideas which can be seen to be common to all the perspectives, including that of the present?
- It is sometimes asserted that we live in an age when it is not possible to write tragedy. If this is true, why might that be?

FURTHER READING

O'Toole (2002) is a lively and radical re-reading of the tragedies in their historical context and is a very good place to start. I have made extensive use here of Holderness (1989a), a paper written for pre-university students in Britain. More difficult, but certainly accessible, is Belsey (1985a), which deals very interestingly with tragedy and gender. Also difficult, but important in the recent history of criticism, are Dollimore (2004) and Barker (1993). Two good modern collections of essays on the tragedies are those edited by Drakakis (1992) and Zimmerman (1998). Challenging and exciting feminist criticism includes Newman (1987) and Wayne (1991) on *Othello,* and Jardine (1996) on *Hamlet.* As with the other genres, Dutton and Howard (2003) is a compendious and wide-ranging collection of the most up-to-date critical opinion. This book does not attempt to deal with the psychoanalytical tradition of criticism, which has been very important in the study of the tragedies. Key texts here are Adelman (1992) and Rose (1995). Finally, undergraduate students should find the Routledge Sourcebooks invaluable. They exist on *Othello,* edited by Hadfield (2003), *King Lear,* edited by Ioppolo (2003), *Macbeth,* edited by Leggatt (2006), and *Hamlet,* edited by McEvoy (2006).

10

UNDERSTANDING ROMANCE

The Winter's Tale and *The Tempest*

John Fletcher was the dramatist who became The King's Men's principal writer after Shakespeare retired in about 1613. In 1610 he published his play *The Faithful Shepherdess*. Though not a success in the theatre, it heralded a new fashion, which Shakespeare himself was following at the end of his career. Fletcher's play, like its imitators, features shepherds and shepherdesses engaged in amorous misunderstandings, sometimes comically presented, which nearly lead to tragic conclusions. The happy resolution is effected with the help of magic herbs, a satyr and the god of the river. As the genre developed, the more serious roles were filled by noble characters, but the importance of magic and divine intervention in the plot remained.

Shakespeare's four plays in response to this new genre of *tragicomedy* are generally known today as his 'romances': *Pericles* (1607–8), *Cymbeline* (1609–10), *The Winter's Tale* (1611) and *The Tempest* (1611). The term 'romance' here has nothing to do with its modern sense. It was first used in the thirteenth century to refer to Old French poems that told tales of daring deeds done by the knights of King Arthur and Charlemagne, or by the heroes of Greek and Roman mythology (see the discussion of *Othello* above, p. 215). It became the name for tales about heroes on quests in which magic and improbable coincidence would lead to a happy resolution, and where sundered families and lovers are eventually reunited, often after much suffering on the way. In Shakespeare's plays the protagonists, similarly, must travel, be shipwrecked, or be lost. The movement of the plot is from sorrow to joy, from division to unity.

It should be stated that the term 'romance' is a label attached to these plays by later critics, notably the Victorian writer Dowden in 1877 (Orgel 1996b: 2). In the early seventeenth century these plays would have been regarded as 'tragicomedies' (though both *The Tempest* and *The Winter's Tale* are actually classified as comedies in the First Folio). As Orgel says (1996b: 3), critics talked about genres as a way of identifying the elements of a play, rather than as fixed pigeonholes in which to file a play. It remains, however, a useful observation that these plays share many of the conventions of romance.

The medieval versions often sought to illustrate a moral point. Shakespeare's romances can also be seen as making a statement of some sort. The plays seem to demonstrate an awareness of the improbability of their own stories. The combination of myth and fantasy characteristic of this genre gave a writer as sophisticated as Shakespeare, now late in his career, two tempting opportunities. It gave him a pretext to reflect upon the way art and the imagination operate in creating our understanding of the world. It also provided an appropriate context in which to show the world not only as it is but as it could be, were its potential to be fulfilled.

In Shakespeare's romances it seems to be the role of children to make good the errors of their parents and bring harmony where once was discord. The loves of Perdita and Florizel in *The Winter's Tale*, and of Miranda and Ferdinand in *The Tempest*, are the means by which the courts of Sicilia and Bohemia, Milan and Naples, are reconciled. For the future to be better than the past in these plays daughters must fall in love with other men's sons, with or without their fathers' permission. Women and their relationships with men are therefore central to these plays.

ROMANCE AND GENDER

In the tragedies there seem to be two types of woman: the chaste and virtuous (Ophelia, Desdemona) and the sensual and apparently untrustworthy (Gertrude, Emilia). These female stereotypes are even more obvious in the romances, where the mythical nature of the stories and the tradition of courtly love from which they sprung tend to produce female characters who, at least on the surface, are seen to fit what some early twentieth-century critics called two 'archetypes' of femininity: the submissive and chaste wife / daughter on the one hand ('the angel'), and the garrulous, sexually promiscuous harridan on the other ('the whore'). By 'archetype' I mean more than a stereotype. 'Archetypes', said some critics and psychological theorists, are symbols or ideals that correspond to profound and eternal truths about the nature of human beings; they last from generation to generation, unchanging over time. The psychologist Carl Gustav Jung (1875–1961) thought they lived in the 'collective unconscious' of humanity. In Celtic mythology, for example, the three 'phases' of woman were the virgin, the wife and the crone, and certain characteristics went with these archetypal phases.

Of course, if something is said to come from the 'unconscious', then by definition it cannot be known to be there because one is not consciously aware of it. Consequently many critics and readers find these archetypes to be rather dubious notions with which to work. One of the philosophical bases of the contemporary criticism with which much of this book is concerned says that all symbolic representations are produced by particular historical, social and political circumstances at actual moments in time. Nothing is outside time and history. It makes more sense and is much more useful, it is contended, to ask in whose interest these views of the nature of women actually *are*. Early modern writers didn't have the concept *archetype*, but they did think women had a very distinctive *nature* which was different from that of men. But these plays reveal their own ideas about that nature in interesting ways. In fact, their views about gender were perhaps not as rigid as some twentieth-century ideas.

In *The Winter's Tale*, Hermione, the wife of Leontes, the King of Sicilia, is suddenly and unjustly accused by her husband of being pregnant by his best friend Polixenes. Polixenes is the King of Bohemia and has been staying with them for the last nine months. The innocent Polixenes flees home, accompanied by Camillo, the nobleman ordered by the madly jealous Leontes to kill his guest.

Hermione's reaction to her husband's accusation and her general demeanour when put on trial for her life baffle many modern women. Though she shows great dignity and composure, she never once directly responds to her husband's mad behaviour with a counter-charge of gratuitous cruelty. When first accused, she blames the configuration of the planets (II 1 105–7), not him; she immediately obeys his command and goes meekly to jail. On trial for her life she resolves that her best defence actually lies in not offering any testimony at all; she will rely on the gods to make her false accusers feel ashamed (III 2 22–32). One of the reasons she is not afraid of death at his hands is that she has lost the main joy in her life, his love (III 2 91–6). To many modern women her passive reaction is not exactly a source of inspiration. On stage, however, her patience and forbearance convince everyone other than the king himself of her innocence. Indeed, in the case of Hermione, chastity is closely connected with saying little, with suffering everything but doing nothing, as we will see.

There is, on the other hand, a woman, Paulina, who does speak out against the king's absurd accusations. But Paulina is quickly accused of sexual infidelity *because* she speaks out. She brings Hermione's new-born child into Leontes' chamber, in front of all his lords, in the hope that when he sees his new daughter, he will be moved to realize his error. When he is not, she lets him know exactly what she thinks of him. Antigonus, Paulina's husband, is also present.

Leontes   A nest of traitors!
Antigonus   I am none, by this good light.*
Paulina   Nor I, nor any
       But one that's here – and that's himself; for he
       The sacred honour of himself, his queen's   85
       His hopeful son's,* his babe's, betrays to slander,
       Whose sting is sharper than the sword's . . .

                                           (II 3 83–7)

* [83] *this good light* Antigonus swears by the sun [86] *His hopeful son's* Leontes already has a son, by Hermione, called Mamillius

The king calls her a 'bawd' (II 3 69) and a 'callat [whore] of boundless tongue' (II 3 91–2). She is a 'gross hag' (II 3 78) whose tongue cannot be silenced. She is also accused of being a witch (II 3 68, 114). Her husband, Antigonus, is ridiculed by Leontes because he cannot control her (II 3 75–6, 108–9); she is like a horse, says Antigonus, who won't always obey the pull of the reins (II 3 51).

But why should female silence and patience in the face of injustice be regarded as chaste and virtuous, and the willingness to speak out against injustice be seen as a sign of sexual looseness, or even of witchcraft?

To call early modern English society *patriarchal* is to say that it was ruled by men and, in particular, by fathers (*pater* is the Latin word for 'father'). Patriarchy as an ideology (see pp. 221), then as now, is sustained by a number of philosophical and political beliefs as well as by myths, stories and associations of ideas. The philosophical view of men in power in this period is well represented in Sir Thomas Elyot's *The Book of the Governor*:

> A man in his natural perfection* is fierce, hardy, strong in opinion, covetous of glory, desirous of knowledge, appetiting by generation to bring forth his semblable.* The good nature of woman is to be mild, timorous, tractable, benign, of sure remembrance,* and shamefast.*
>
> (Quoted in Orgel 1996a: 107)

> * *natural perfection* state of completeness; *appetiting by generation to bring forth his semblable* eager to produce children in his image; *of sure remembrance* never forgets her duties and her place; *shamefast* modest and afraid of shame

As regards women in fiction and myth, the moral of story after story emphasized the virtues of silence and patience in the face of suffering: patient Griselda, for example, in Chaucer's *Clerk's Tale*. Low-born Griselda endures her children being taken away by her noble husband, apparently to be killed, because of his shame at marrying so humble a woman. She then must suffer her impending replacement by the new young bride of her husband, to whom she must act as a servant (he claims to have obtained permission from the Pope to annul their marriage). When the husband reveals that he did all this to test Griselda's virtue, she accepts it all meekly: he is her husband, and she will do as he wishes.

Audiences would also be reminded of Lucretia (Lucrece), whose story is told as a model of virtue in Chaucer's *The Legend of Good Women*, the Italian writer Boccaccio's collection of stories *The Decameron* and in Shakespeare's own *The Rape of Lucrece*. Having been raped by Tarquin, Lucretia kills herself in front of her husband and her father so that she can bring no more shame on her family now her body has committed adultery, albeit against her will; Antonio's wife in Cyril Tourneur's *The Revenger's Tragedy* (published 1607) suffered the same fate and took the same action:

> Antonio   her honour forced,
> [She] Deemed it a nobler dowry for her name*
> To die with poison than to live with shame.
>
> (Tourneur 1967: I 4 46–8)

* *Deemed it a nobler dowry for her name* thought it better to ensure a good reputation for the future by . . .

Dying is the ultimate way of remaining silent. Male power over women rested partly on their physical ability to restrain and hurt them. Military and legal power were entirely in the hands of men; before a state prison system of any size had come into being, the sentence of law was enforced physically on the bodies of those whom it found guilty, by whipping, pillorying, mutilating or hanging. Women literally could not fight back, even had they wanted to. They could talk, however; as Vittoria explains while on trial in John Webster's *The White Devil* (published 1612): 'O Woman's poor revenge / Which dwells but in the tongue' (Webster 1972: III 2 285–6). *Talking* was the way in which women could assert their needs and wants, and for that reason had to be controlled under patriarchy. Female speech, it was thought, if unrestrained, could become a torrent of scolding and nagging which could wear men down. For this reason 'scolds' could be sentenced by magistrates to be physically bridled with an iron bit, the branks, to prevent them from talking. It was Eve's tongue, after all, that had persuaded Adam in Eden and led to the Fall of mankind.

Female attributes in general seemed to patriarchal attitudes to be *unrestrained*. Compactness, hardness and closeness were features of the male body which seemed particularly appropriate in a world where being an emotionless, fit and skilful warrior was one definition of virtue. Female bodies were soft and expansive, and given to the production both of extra fluids (milk, menstrual flow) and children. Their sexual appetite was supposed to be insatiable compared with that of men. One of the stories which used to be told of our culture was that it was usually the men who were after sex and the women who tried to avoid it. Popular culture in the early modern era portrayed it exactly the other way round. The never-ending desire which a woman acquired once she lost her virginity was always provoking men to sin. Were it not for gold and women, says the cynical Vindice in *The Revenger's Tragedy*, 'there would no damnation – / Hell would look like a lord's great kitchen without fire in't' (Tourneur 1967: II 1 254–5). Again and again female speech is described as the woman's 'tongue'; its sensual, fluid quality and the fact that it is both a site and a giver of pleasure is so often implied. As Ferdinand tells his sister the duchess in Webster's *The Duchess of Malfi* (published 1623), women 'like that part, which ... / Hath nev'r a bone in't ... I mean the tongue ... ' (Webster 1972: I 2 257–60). Promiscuity and talking too much were connected.

Though men were certainly dominant in this society, female sexuality was a powerful threat to men. Hence chastity was the principal female virtue. It was argued that chastity and sexual fidelity were the female equivalents of male heroism in battle: both required physical courage in order to win glory against powerful natural instincts. Here the male view of woman's sexual nature is abundantly clear. By elevating female chastity to the peak of moral behaviour, men's anxiety about the sexual threat to them is made very plain. An adulterous wife had the power to turn a man into a ridiculous beast, the cuckold, whose symbol was a man with horns growing from his brows. In the case of men of property she could also undermine the system of inheritance by the first-born *legitimate* son, which was the basis of the vast majority of property transfers. If men could not be sure of their wife's fidelity, the stability of society itself would be threatened (see Box 3.2, p. 65). Both the mouth and the vagina are focal points of male insecurity about women, and are associated one with the other in the patriarchal discourse of the period. Unruliness in both must be checked: unruliness in one can lead to unruliness in both.

And yet the scold was accepted as a character in literature who was allowed to get away with more than one, at first glance, would imagine. A woman might also be a prophetess. Women's talkativeness *could* become privileged, like that of the fool who is allowed to be impertinent because in his ramblings there might be some profound truth. It is this kind of privilege that allows Paulina to get away with the accusations she aims at the king. It might be thought perhaps that, because she was a woman, what she had to say would not be taken too seriously. But her pleadings seem to move Leontes to back off from the immediate destruction of the child. And there is a further paradox here: in the end, it is Paulina and her 'witchcraft' with the 'statue' that bring harmony and reconciliation to Leontes' court.

It is too easy, in fact, to see misogyny (hatred of women) as a single simple force running through all of society in Shakespeare's time. It clearly was not like that. England was after all ruled by a woman, Queen Elizabeth I, from 1558 to 1603, and ruled very successfully. How did that fit in with patriarchal ideology?

In the British feminist critic Lisa Jardine's *Still Harping on Daughters* (1983: 169–79) it is suggested that Elizabeth was proclaimed, indeed proclaimed herself, an exceptional woman whose rule served only to demonstrate by comparison the frailty and failings of other women. Thus her learning and knowledge placed her beyond her sex and reminded everyone of how women were normally incapable of such achievement. More significantly, she created herself not as a woman at all, but as an emblem or symbol of perfection in womanhood. She embodied qualities that were female ideals, but which no real woman could possess. Thus her chastity, the paramount female virtue, became the centre of the state cult around her. She became the idealized object of courtly-love literature and fantasies; she was closely associated with the classical goddess of chastity, Astraea. Furthermore, the public celebration of her person in progresses (official visits), tournaments and ceremonies was seen by many to have replaced the worship of the Virgin Mary, a powerful and ancient cult which had been suppressed only twenty years before she came to the throne, in Protestant England. Thus her political success was not the product of the actions of a *real* woman at all. This, at any rate, is how one argument has it.

Finally back to *The Winter's Tale*. Hermione, in her obedience and chastity, can be seen as a sort of Griselda or Virgin Queen (or *maybe not*: she does insist in her trial on her dignity as a woman – see III 2 91–123, for example – and, I suppose, has the determination not to return to her husband until the loss of her daughter has been made good, even after sixteen years). But the actions and words of Paulina are the agents of renewal and harmony. The play does not pretend that she is some kind of female beyond the ordinary. In Act V Leontes no longer regards her as a 'mankind witch', but now sees her as a trusted adviser. He even allows her to take liberties with him (V 1 1–84; V 3 1–3). At the moment when he thinks he has lost his wife, he is happy to give her free rein to speak, in fact: 'Go on, go on: / Thou canst not speak too much' (III 2 214–15). Some might think it is magic that she employs in the final scene (V 3 89–91, 96–7, 105), but if it is, says Leontes, 'let it be an art / Lawful as eating' (V 3 110–11). She not only brings a statue to life, as it seems, she apparently even brings Hermione back to life. But she is no witch, as Hermione explains (V 3 125–8). If patriarchy is so strong, how can representations like this be performed in public, and, indeed, before the king, as the play was on 5 November 1612?

Strict 'sumptuary' laws forbade the wearing of certain rich fabrics and colours by those whose income and status did not warrant them. But why was no law passed or legal action taken against the fashionable young women who cut their hair and went around in men's clothes in the first decade of the seventeenth century? They adopted male dress the better to show off their figures in unbuttoned doublets (jackets) and tight hose (tights). Why was it that trade guilds at this time had so many women in trades like carpentry and masonry (48 per cent in Southampton in 1600 [Orgel 1996a: 73])? Why did men accept the authority women had over them in very many social and domestic situations as mothers, nurses, housekeepers, estate managers and the like?

An ideology, even a powerful and dominant one, is not a set of rules to be universally applied; nor is it a rigid mindset applying across all classes and peoples. One way of understanding it is as a myth of the 'norm', a set of ideas which indicate normal behaviour in a society; the perfect example may not actually exist, but it is a story that seems 'natural' and seems to tell the truth about that society to those who live in it. How do we then explain these cases, both in literature and in life, that so startlingly seem to contradict it? English society in Shakespeare's time was patriarchal, after all.

The new historicist (see pp. 229) explanation is to say that in order for a dominant idea to stay dominant it has to create threats to itself so that it can be seen to accommodate and absorb those threats: it has to reveal its nature in conflict in order to show its teeth, even if in this case patriarchal power is not actually under serious threat. For the cultural materialists (see pp. 230), on the other hand, these cases are examples of contradictions within this ideology that expose the arbitrary (not 'natural' or God-given) and unnecessary power structure which is patriarchy. Furthermore, cultural materialist analysis points out the material forces (actual people and events, representational and otherwise) whose challenge will one day damage that power structure and overthrow it. Patriarchy may not be dead, but its grip on women in 2005 is certainly not that of 1605. In this play, then, Paulina, and perhaps even Hermione, can be seen as *utopian* figures. By this I mean that, as the intellectual and moral equals of men, they look forward self-consciously to a much fairer world than the one depicted in the play, or even known by the author and original audiences (a *utopia* is an ideal society).

I do not think the same kind of utopian undercurrent is evident in the depiction of Miranda in *The Tempest*. She does not look forward at all. In fact she is there to be looked at, as her name (the Latin means 'worthy to be wondered at') suggests. In addition, now that she has reached the age (of about 15, it seems) at which she can produce children, she has become the object of several men's desires to produce offspring by her.

Prospero, her father, was once Duke of Milan. Twelve years earlier than the action depicted in the play he had been overthrown by his brother Antonio, with the help of Alonso, King of Naples. Prospero and the infant Miranda were set adrift in the Mediterranean with the barest of provisions, their clothes and Prospero's books of magic spells. Coming ashore on an island, Prospero soon took control of both the environment and its inhabitants. These comprise Ariel, a spirit who had been imprisoned in a pine tree by the witch Sycorax because he would not obey her commands, and Caliban, a 'savage and deformed slave' (as he is described in the *dramatis personae* – 'characters of the play' in the

Folio). Caliban is Sycorax's son. Now a ship carrying Antonio and Alonso is passing the island and Prospero uses his powers to 'wreck' the vessel. He does this without harming crew, passengers or ship. He disperses them around the island so that he can take his revenge upon the appropriate people by his own chosen means. The first of the shipwrecked to come to his attention is Ferdinand, son and heir of Alonso. He arranges for Miranda and Ferdinand to meet and fall in love. Thus they will produce an heir who will unite the city of Milan and the kingdom of Naples in future peace and harmony.

But there are others who have designs on Miranda as a sexual partner. Caliban had attempted to rape Miranda in the hope that he could people the island with his own kind (I 2 349–51). Stephano, Alonso's drunken butler, teams up with Caliban in a comic attempt to seize the island for himself and become king, with Miranda as his consort (III 2 106–7). Caliban's enslavement to Stephano through drink can be seen as an undercutting parody of the magic power by which Prospero enslaves him. It mocks Prospero's power through a comic replication of the main action, as happens in the history plays (see pp. 68–9 and 190–3). But Prospero (acting through Ferdinand), Caliban and Stephano all see Miranda's body as a piece of property to be cultivated, from which each hopes both to produce a future for himself and to establish his own identity, at the same time cementing his authority over some territory in the future: Milan or the island, and, by the same token, Miranda's body. Prospero will win. He has magic; he is the father.

Miranda, then, stands symbolically for the island itself. This maiden is the virgin territory that is to be conquered so that the conqueror may establish his identity and authority over part of the world.

Contemporary critics often write about *The Tempest* as a narrative of colonialism. Shakespeare's source material clearly draws on the recent adventures of an English fleet in Bermuda, and the play was written in a period when there was considerable investment and settlement taking place in the English colonies in the New World, particularly Virginia (in what is now the southern USA). Though geography, strictly speaking, would indicate a Mediterranean location (Alonso's ship is *en route* from Tunis to Naples), Caliban's name is clearly some sort of corruption of the word 'cannibal' or maybe 'Carib', the name of the original West

Indian islanders wiped out by European disease and genocide. A New World colonial setting is often assumed by critics. (Though, as the British critic Jerry Brotton has argued, to assume this is to ignore so much of the play's Mediterranean geography. The play is actually set in an area which was a point of conflict between Catholic Europeans and Muslim Turks. In this struggle the Protestant English pursued profitable, but embarrassing, commercial alliances with the Turks. The play, he argues, totally ignores this subordinate relationship to the 'infidel' and looks westwards to easier pickings, perhaps [Brotton 1998: 36–7]). There was also, of course, the continuing struggle to establish English rule in Ireland, over a people regarded by many English writers and colonizers as scarcely, if at all, human. 'Masterless men', like Stephano and his sidekick the jester Trinculo, were also seen as a threat to order and good government, even in the heart of London. The play can be seen to explore, with various degrees of explicitness, the issues of colonization and legitimacy of government current at the time. What gives one people the right to dominate another? What makes a government the just authority in a particular territory?

The association of the land to be colonized with the female body is an interesting one, and one which tells us much about male attitudes to women and women's sexuality. As Paul Brown points out (1985: 51), it is common in the discourse of colonialism to talk about 'opening up virgin territory' or 'making the land fruitful'. But there are also the temptations of the wilderness, which might lead the virtuous and saintly European astray. The colonizers will encounter the amoral and anarchic lives of the 'savages', whose careless enjoyment of nature's gifts and sexual licentiousness might lead the settler astray. Stories told about the uncivilized often made their lives seem like a tempting utopia, even if the Europeans knew it was actually a myth – see Gonzalo's account of his imaginary commonwealth, and Sebastian and Antonio's justifiable response to it (II 1 141–64). There is something tempting and mysterious about this unknown world, which drives the authorities to place it all the more fiercely under their control. This wild and anarchic utopia is figured as female in the symbolic function of Miranda, and the subversive delight of female sexuality as an ungovernable threat to male power runs through *The Tempest* in various forms. Prospero knows in his heart that his power is a dream ('an insubstantial pageant' [IV 1 155]) which might any moment dissolve into noth-ingness. Yet his nagging fear seems to be that he will lose control over his own daughter's sexuality (IV 1 14–23, 511).

Prospero admits, half jokingly, that he has only his dead wife's word that Miranda actually is his daughter (I 2 56–7). Leontes in *The Winter's Tale* is actually driven to the edge of madness by his suspicion that he may not be the father of Hermione's child. Neither he nor Prospero can know for sure. Richard Wilson (1993: 158–83) argues that the late plays expose, among other things, historical moments at which men have sought to gain control over what, until then, had been a dark mystery presided over entirely by women: conception, pregnancy and childbirth. Doctors began to take precedence over midwives in supervising births. They began to adopt a new scientific medical practice based on the observation of women and the anatomy of corpses, animal and human, rather than the employment of folklore and quasi-magical operations based on the old medieval theories of resemblances (see pp. 26ff.). No one knew exactly how the man's seed becomes the child; no man could ever have proof, apart from his wife's word, that her child really was also his own. Men didn't attend the birth of children. The attempt by doctors and lawyers to regulate the practices of midwives was an attempt by men to bring light (the male gaze) to a darkness which they had obviously found alluring, but also constituted a threat to their power and sense of identity. Shakespeare's son-in-law, John Hall, was one such doctor.

Miranda wields power over men, first because she is sexually attractive to men of all classes (both Stephano and Ferdinand) and cultures (Caliban) and, second, because she is the one with real magic in the play: the mysterious power to produce new versions of the man who is her lover. This is why she must be controlled by the man who seeks political dominance in the play, just as the new science had to replace the folk medicine of the past to establish its authority, even when such methods actually worked. The domina-tion of women by men, a domination based on both desire and fear of the mysterious but essential 'other', is the model for domination by class, culture and race in the society of the time. It is an unstable state of affairs.

Strangely, Prospero's account of how he arrived safely on the island makes it seem as if he were courting a mistress who took pity on his distress (Brown 1985: 60). Miranda and he were left on their rotting boat

> To cry to the sea that roared to us, to sigh
> To the winds, whose pity, sighing back again,
> Did us but loving wrong.

(I 2 149–51)

The winds became his lover in pity at the romance hero's troubles on his quest – a little like Desdemona in *Othello* (II 1 167–70). The goddess Fortune herself (luck, chance) and the very stars become lovers whom he must woo, if his plan to take revenge on his brother and the Neapolitans is to come to fruition, as he tells Miranda:

> *Prospero*   Know thus far forth:
>   By accident most strange, bountiful Fortune,
>   Now my dear lady, hath mine enemies
>   Brought to this shore; and by my prescience*   180
>   I find my zenith* doth depend upon
>   A most auspicious* star, whose influence*
>   If now I court not, but omit,* my fortunes
>   Will ever after droop.

(I 2 177–84)

> * [180] *prescience* foreknowledge [181] *zenith* high point, moment of greatest opportunity [182] *auspicious* a force for success; *influence* astrological power to affect life on earth [183] *omit* ignore

A man's whole future, it seems in Prospero's case, depends on his successful courtship of the female forces of chance and the stars that govern life. In the romances, the future is female. Male power has to come to terms with this fact. In *The Winter's Tale* Leontes learns this lesson over the course of sixteen years. It is the tender affection Ariel wants to feel for the vanquished and confused Neapolitans in *The Tempest* that makes Prospero decide to forgive rather than take vengeance (V 1 11–28). Tender feelings are usually unmanly in the culture of the period. But at this moment in the play they become 'human' (V 1 20), not womanly. Prospero recognizes female qualities in himself; their exercise becomes the exercise of male 'noble reason' (V 1 26). Tender female feelings, even so, don't reign at the end of this play. But they have, for Prospero, replaced the male desire to dominate.

In the romances, then, despite the portrayal of women as either unruly creatures or merely beautiful and fruitful possessions, it can nevertheless be argued that there is a powerful undercurrent of 'female' qualities that will ultimately redeem the destructive 'male' desire to dominate.

ROMANCE AND UTOPIA

> *Jonson* [to Shakespeare] Your recent stuff's been pretty peculiar. What was *The Winter's Tale* about? I ask to be polite.
>
> (Bond 1987: 44)

How, then, can the romances be explained? In the twentieth century one reading was fairly dominant, both among the conservative critics of the first part of the century and among the American new historicists of recent years. That view sees the romances as showing the God-given hierarchical social order being disturbed only so that it can be triumphantly reinstated, and thereby strengthened, at the end of Act V. Triumph, or even cosy reassurance, however, is not the feeling I ever get in the theatre at the close of these plays. At the end of *The Winter's Tale* there is a sense of wasted years. Hermione is no longer as young as she was when Leontes last saw her (V 3 27–9), and there is also a feeling of unease about Paulina's sudden marriage (V 3 136–8). In *The Tempest*, Antonio is neither repentant nor contrite. It is true that Caliban, the would-be rapist and savage murderer (III 2 88–91), is now under control again, awed at Prospero's authority and feeling suitably abashed for having acquired such unworthy new masters (V 1 261–2, 296–8). But there is something also in the crushing of Caliban and in the reinstatement of the old order that makes the reader or spectator feel a sense of loss. The recollection of the freedom and energy of the magic island, or of the joyously affirmative life of rural Bohemia in *The Winter's Tale*, leaves one feeling that a better world has been glimpsed in these plays, even if palpably not achieved.

From where does our sympathy for Caliban come? Modern awareness of the wrongs done in the name of white imperialism, of course, prompts us to be more sympathetic to Caliban than many European audiences would have been in the past. Indeed, in Shakespeare's time the dominant attitude towards the original inhabitants of the Americas, if that is what he represents, regarded them as semi-animals who had no language, or at best a defective one. Alternatively, the native languages were thought by some to be fundamentally the same as the European ones, describing the world according to the same concepts and the same social, political and religious ideas as the invading Spanish, Portuguese, French or English (Greenblatt 1990: 17–19). The former view seems to apply to Caliban; he has to be taught to talk, according to Prospero and Miranda (I 2 353–8). Yet he retains some sort of integrity and dignity. He has not become totally their creature, even though he is forced to think in their words. He is not an animal.

The invaders control the island by virtue of the violence threatened by Prospero's magic. Theirs is a language that contains the violence of their way of life, as Caliban immediately reminds them:

Caliban   You taught me language, and my profit on't
Is, I know how to curse. The red-plague rid* you
For learning me your language!

(I 2 363–5)

* [364] *rid* kill

When Prospero and Miranda first came to the island, Caliban had no knowledge of their language, yet they treated him with affection and he treated them with love and care in return (I 2 332–9). The attempted rape seems to have happened after their concepts and ideas had been imparted to him more fully. Prospero and Miranda told him what his own words meant, and so had power over him. They gave him a language which replaced his 'brutish . . . gabble' (I 2 355–8). But they blame the rape attempt on his own savage nature (I 2 358–60), not on the view of the world which their acquisitive language has given him.

What Prospero has not quite managed to do, however, is destroy Caliban's capacity to think for himself. Stephano and Trinculo might sing that 'Thought is free' (III 2 123), but it is Caliban who knows the real tune, even if Prospero's spy Ariel knows it as well (III 2 124–5) (Patterson 1989: 161). Even under such surveillance, Caliban is not totally trapped by the system of hierarchy and oppression the invaders have brought to his island. Prospero is a usurper in Caliban's kingdom just as much as Antonio is in Milan, but it is still Caliban who appreciates the beauty of his home and can speak the play's most tranquil lines, looking forward to future peace and happiness:

Caliban	Be not afeared, the isle is full of noises,	135
	Sounds, and sweet airs, that give delight and hurt not.	
	Sometimes a thousand twangling instruments	
	Will hum about my ears; and sometimes voices,	
	That if I then had waked after long sleep,	
	Will make me sleep again, and then in dreaming,	140
	The clouds methought would open, and show riches	
	Ready to drop upon me, that when I waked I cried to dream again.	

(III 2 135–43)

The text seems to go out of its way to make us see how different is the ugly, violent and vengeful Caliban from the 'civilized' invaders, while still being totally human. Caliban has his own distinctive view of the world, his own sense of beauty and of what it is to be alive. We are aware of what Stephen Greenblatt means when he refers, in relation to another passage, to 'the independence and integrity of Caliban's construction of reality' (Greenblatt 1990: 31).

Caliban's ultimately independent view of the world, even if achieved in only a few places, stands out against the structurally oppressive language and ideas of the Italian invaders. Kiernan Ryan has pointed out (2002: 152–4) that Prospero's language is full of threat, aggression, violence and demands; even the love-promises of Miranda and Ferdinand are expressed in the language of master and slave (III 1 63–6, 84–6). As Ferdinand says, Prospero is 'composed of harshness' (III 1 9). Yet the voices of Caliban (and of Ariel, I 2 242–9) speak out for liberty, and we are given an even more startling anti-hierarchical perspective in the face of physical realities in the play's first scene. As the storm created by Ariel threatens the

King of Naples' ship, the courtiers come up on deck only to be firmly put in their place by the boatswain:

Alonso   Good boatswain, have care. Where's the master?
        Play the men.*
Boatswain   I pray now, keep below.   10
Antonio   Where is the master, bos'n?
Boatswain   Do you not hear him? You mar our labour.*
        Keep your cabins – you do assist the storm.
Gonzalo   Nay, good, be patient.
Boatswain   When the sea is. Hence! What care these roarers   15
        for the name of king? To cabin! silence! Trouble us not.
Gonzalo   Good, yet remember whom thou hast aboard.
Boatswain   None that I love more than myself. You are a
        councillor;
        if you can command these elements to silence, and work the
        peace of the present*, we will not hand a rope more.   20
        Use your authority.

                                     (I 1 9–21)

* [9–10] *Play the men* 'Act like men' [12] *You mar our labour* 'You're getting in the way' [20] *work the peace of the present* 'make everything quiet immediately'

The courtiers presume that their superiority is natural and will apply even over professional seafarers struggling to save the lives of everyone in the teeth of a vicious storm. The scene shows such superiority to be far from natural and prepares for the other challenges of the play that suggest the foundations of hierarchy to be violence, not a God-given right to rule at all.

Yet the play's ending sees the courtiers back in charge. Where then does the egalitarian energy come from in these plays? Kiernan Ryan suggests (2002: 109–10) that in this play history is, so to speak, speeded up, so that the guilt and wickedness of the present are suddenly seen from the perspective of the future, and seen not to matter so much. Forgiveness becomes possible, and we see human suffering from a different viewpoint, becoming less entrenched in our passions and dogma. The world from this later perspective is a more understanding and harmonious one, not so passionately vengeful as it used to be. It is a better place in which to live. In *The Winter's Tale* the figure of Time acts as a chorus between the two halves of the play. He moves the action on sixteen years and reminds us exactly of his function:

Time   . . . it is in my power
        To o'erthrow law, and in one self-born hour
        To plant and o'erwhelm custom.

(IV 1 7–9)

Thus the world in the first half of the play is one where passionate jealousy, in the hands of a man of power, destroys the lives of his wife, his son and two of his courtiers; his best friend is alienated and lost. A ship is wrecked and those on board drowned. A bear kills an old man carrying out an heroic act of kindness to a baby. These disasters are too much like the world as it is. After sixteen years, however, the original passions matter far less than the love which had existed previously. The folly of inflexible and selfish human action is revealed. A new generation has grown to maturity which is not destined to repeat the errors of the past. In *The Tempest* Ariel's perspective on Prospero's vengeful outlook has the same effect. Standing outside the action, like Time, Ariel can remind Prospero what it actually means to be human (V 1 20).

Ryan's argument *is* fundamentally humanistic. By this I mean that it has the premiss that all people are basically the same and have ultimately the same needs, no matter to what period in history they belong. All of us should be treated with respect and dignity, and no one group can have a claim to special privileges simply by virtue of who they are. Injustice and suffering are produced by failure to recognize these facts. Time overwhelms the arbitrary divisions among people which we use to justify inequality (e.g. being a woman, being a Roman citizen, being homosexual, being the descendant of a Norman duke, being Jewish, etc.), showing all of them to be temporary. So seeing things from Time's perspective is always going to make us realize the folly of our excessive passions, unjust actions and special pleadings. Ariel, standing outside humanity and being able to see the similarities rather than the differences between us, has the same perspective. When romance relocates action to another part of the world, where things are viewed differently, we have the same shift in the point of view. Extramarital sex that produces unwanted offspring is the subject for a humorous aside among the shepherds of Bohemia (III 3 71–6). In the court of Sicilia it is a capital offence against the state.

Ryan's political project is fairly apparent. A non-humanistic sceptic, on the other hand, might argue that all time actually does is replace one set of arbitrary divisions between people with another set. Ryan is assuming that we can envisage a human society in which no one group of people is exercising power unjustly and to its own advantage over another group. There never has been such a society, it could be argued, since power and its exercise are everywhere in our lives; society simply cannot function without it – it is 'inscribed' (see p. 154) in the very nature of social life. This would be a more *postmodern* view, one that is argued by critics influenced by the French philosopher Michel Foucault. Power is in constant circulation around the world, flowing now here, now there. No one really possesses it: it is simply active in every social exchange. We are all special pleaders in our own interests, all of the time. There can be no utopia according to this view.

The humanist argument does not suggest, however, that these plays show any sort of blueprint for the future. In fact the plays go out of their way to stress the provisional and outrageously fictional nature of the solutions they find to the problems of the narrative. When Antigonus was pursued off stage by a bear at The Globe or Blackfriars in 1611 (III 3 58, sd), it would have been by either a man in a bear-suit or a tame performing bear familiar to the audience from the Southwark entertainments. Both would no doubt have drawn laughter or cheers of a derisively affectionate nature. The mortal danger that the character of Antigonus is in would be immediately defused as a painful spectacle by the blatant fictionality of the moment. It is not scary or dangerous, this bear. Shakespeare is signalling that the play is shifting mood and genre in a big way.

Paulina never ceases to stress the preposterousness of the plot's conclusion, even though she has engineered it herself. Shakespeare won't show us the obvious conclusion of the narrative from which we would expect to get our emotional satisfaction. We expect to see the tearful reunion of Leontes and Polixenes and the greeting by Leontes of his long-lost daughter, and her realization of her true identity. But in fact this is relayed to us by two 'Gentlemen', one of whom has the cheek to tell us that we 'have lost a sight which was to be seen, which cannot be spoken of' (V 2 42–3). Instead of the expected dramatic denouement we get the scene where the 'statue' comes to life. It is an ending that some might attribute to 'wicked powers' (V 3 91), 'unlawful business' (V 3 96). Certainly it breaks many of the rules of decorum, just as the play breaks the unities (see p. 64). More to the point, however, were this outcome to be recounted to an audience, it 'should be hooted at / Like an old tale' (V 3 115–16). A 'winter's tale', indeed, was an improbable story with which to pass a long dark evening.

By giving us a scene like this, however, the play highlights the *provisional* nature of its ending. This isn't the way the plot would end in the real world, and we know it. It's a symbolic fiction only. But by the same token it's not pretending that Providence (see p. 212) really exists. It's not even an ideal ending, as I have just argued. It is therefore not escapism. Its fictionality underscores the fact that it is an ending *made* by humans, not by God or the gods. It shows that just and humane resolutions are possible, if we have the moral *imagination* and humanity to create them; but *we* have to make them.

The ending of *The Tempest* is even less ideal, as we have seen. But throughout the last part of the play Prospero seems to strive, at a level partly outside the drama of the play, to excuse himself from his own involvement in the injustice of the world in which he lives. Ryan (2002: 152) suggests that Gonzalo's speech about his ideal kingdom, and Sebastian and Antonio's response to it (II 1 144–67), foreground a paradox about power in the play. It draws attention to an interesting contradiction in the rulers' ideas. Prospero seeks to bring about liberty and justice through his use of absolute hierarchical power, but without any notion of his responsibilities to a wider community. By the last part of the play, however, he knows his power is arbitrary in its nature; it can be discarded at his will, and he chooses to discard it. In his speech after the end of the masque he reminds us of the insubstantial fictionality both of what we are watching and of his authority (IV 1 146–58), an estrangement device (see p. 59) in itself. But most of all he calls on us, the audience, at the end of the play to release him from the island and his role there by our action of approval: applause (V 1 Epilogue). Just as we have committed injustices, he too seeks freedom from guilt; but it is a freedom he can only achieve outside his roles as duke and magician in the play:

Prospero   As you from crimes would pardoned be,
            Let your indulgence set me free. *Exit*

(V 1 Epilogue 19–20)

The fictional exists in real historical time, just as the self-consciously fictional and the recognizably historical exist together in these plays. Our hopes for a more just world are there, realizable in the fiction; but the fiction is part of the real world, too. Plays happen in real time, in real places, and they affect the way we see reality. Romance gives us hope that our ideals can be brought to actuality, despite everything. Prospero says that we will, however, have to do it through our own actions.

SUMMARY

- Women and their relationships with men are central to these plays especially, because in romance it is through the production of the next generation that the errors of the older generation will be redeemed.
- Though women are seen either as unruly and uncontrollable individuals or as beautiful and fertile objects to be possessed, they nevertheless have qualities that will make the world better, because they save men from the harshness and injustice of the masculine desire for power and control.
- By their very obvious fictional contexts, and by showing how time can undermine all deeply held beliefs and structures except those that relate to our common humanity, these plays have a utopian vision, according to humanist critics, which looks forward to a more equal and fair world. Other critics would dispute this and say nothing has really changed at the conclusion to these plays.

FURTHER THINKING

- Can the same arguments about the roles of women, time and the utopian vision also be applied to *Cymbeline* and *Pericles*? What comparisons can you draw between the portrayal of Perdita in *The Winter's Tale* and Miranda in *The Tempest*? What is their function in the renewal of the worlds of the latter two plays?

- What might these plays suggest about 'romantic' love as the basis for marriage in early modern England and, indeed, now?

- Why is magic and the fantastical so central to these particular plays?

FURTHER READING

Orgel's introductions to the Oxford editions of both *The Tempest* (1987) and *The Winter's Tale* (1996b) are very good places to start. There is brief and accessible information on genre, historical context, performance and criticism. Important new historicist work on *The Tempest* includes the title essay in Greenblatt (1990) and, at a slightly more demanding level, Brown (1985). An insightful cultural materialist reading of *The Winter's Tale* and *Cymbeline* can be found in Belsey (1999). I have drawn extensively on Jardine (1983) for the discussion here on 'shrewish' women. A very influential Marxist-humanist reading of the romances as utopian plays is Ryan (2002). Ryan has edited a collection of relevant and useful essays (1999), as has Thorne (2003). See Dutton and Howard (2003) for a thorough overview of the most contemporary criticism.

CONCLUSION

For many years in Great Britain the government has seen Shakespeare's plays as part of our common language and national heritage, as something essentially 'English' that will unite young people in a common culture. The plays will also, many have argued, provide a model of beautiful and memorable language. The plays are often praised for their 'universality', their ability to stand outside time and history and to 'speak' to all people, past, present and future.

A similar function seems to be performed by these plays in other English-speaking countries, such as the United States, Australia, Canada and New Zealand, where their high cultural status makes them central to the study of English at high-school level. The plays are often described as part of a common cultural heritage which transcends the issues of national origin and politics. In other former British colonies such as South Africa, India and parts of the Caribbean Shakespeare's works seem to have a different educational status; but the notion of Shakespeare's *universality* and trans-cultural value is often employed as a reason for studying the plays.

I hope you can see from this book that at the higher levels of the education system the academic study of Shakespeare tends to march to a very different tune. Instead of the idea of Shakespeare as the creative genius who stands outside time, Shakespeare has often come to be seen as a writer whose plays are the product of the time in which they were written. Similarly, the meaning of the plays tends to be seen to depend on the circumstances – the time and place – in which they are seen or their texts read. It so happens that this current academic agenda seeks to promote neither a sense of national unity nor some timeless values whose purity is untouched by the fashionable opinions of today or tomorrow (except, perhaps, in those critics who find deep ethical values in the text such as Fernie [p. 237ff.] and Ryan [p. 258ff.]). Much contemporary Shakespeare criticism looks instead at issues of power and social injustice; it is interested in gender, race and sexuality as concepts that are not only alive in the plays but important in the lives of those who read, teach, study or act Shakespeare. Shakespeare criticism has become *social* and *political*. It is also interested in the plays not just in the classroom, but in the theatre and on the screen.

I hope this book has helped you to see how much more enthralling the study of Shakespeare can be when it is part of this wider social and political picture. There are many things in this book which I hope you would want to contest, or think are misreadings or miss the point. That is the way Shakespeare studies moves forward. Time moves on, and new styles of Shakespeare studies will emerge. In the six years since this book was first published, a less political kind of 'ethical' criticism has begun to emerge, as has a concern with the minutiae of Shakespeare's own life and the production of his own works, what Lisa Hopkins has called 'New Factualisms' (Hopkins 2005: 111). Performance criticism continues to grow more and more significant, and feminist criticism is often now known as 'gender' criticism as the focus turns to the nature of masculinity, as well as of heterosexuality and homosexuality in these texts. There also continues to be much fascinating work in types of criticism barely touched on in this book: post-colonial criticism and psychoanalytical readings, for example. I hope this book will provide a secure foundation to your studies so that you will wish to explore new approaches and to develop new arguments. Most important of all, I hope that it will add to the enjoyment you will derive from watching and reading the plays.

CHRONOLOGY

Year	Events	Shakespeare – the theatre
1564	Gypsies expelled from England	William Shakespeare born.
1576	Dutch rebellion against Spanish rule	James Burbage builds The Theatre, London's first purpose-built theatre, in Shoreditch
1581	Laws against Catholics passed	Worcester's Theatre Company play at Stratford-upon-Avon
1582	Plague in London	Shakespeare marries Anne Hathaway
1583	Rebellion in Ireland	Birth of Susanna, daughter to Anne and William
1585	War with Spain	Birth of twins, Hamnet and Judith, to Anne and William; Shakespeare leaves Stratford?
1587	Mary Queen of Scots beheaded by Elizabeth I	Philip Henslowe builds The Rose theatre on Bankside
1588	Spanish Armada defeated	Shakespeare now in the London theatre?
1589		First play: *King Henry VI Part I*

(continued on next page)

Year	Events	Shakespeare – the theatre
1592	Successful English attacks on Spanish treasure fleet; plague in London	*King Richard III, The Comedy of Errors;* Marlowe's *Dr Faustus, Edward II*
1593	Anglican church attendance made compulsory; plague continues	Marlowe murdered
1594	Two plots on Queen Elizabeth's life; rebellion in Ireland	*The Taming of the Shrew, Titus Andronicus;* Lord Chamberlain's Company founded
1595	War abroad, unrest at home	*A Midsummer Night's Dream, Romeo and Juliet, King Richard II;* The Swan theatre built
1596	Essex destroys Spanish fleet; food shortages	Coat of arms granted to Shakespeare's father John; *The Merchant of Venice* and *King Henry IV Part I;* Hamnet dies
1598	Rebellion in Ireland	*King Henry IV Part II* and *Much Ado About Nothing*
1599	Essex fails to put down Irish rebellion	The Globe theatre built; *King Henry V, Julius Caesar* and *As You Like It*
1600	East India Company founded	*Hamlet*
1601	Essex's rebellion and execution	Death of John Shakespeare; *Troilus and Cressida, Twelfth Night*

(continued on next page)

Year	Events	Shakespeare – the theatre
1603	Death of Queen Elizabeth and accession of James I	Shakespeare's last recorded stage performance, in Ben Jonson's *Sejanus*; Lord Chamberlain's Company becomes The King's Men
1604	Catholic priests banished	*Othello* and *Measure for Measure*; Marston's *The Malcontent*
1605	Gunpowder Plot	*King Lear*; Shakespeare makes land purchases in Stratford
1606	Expedition to colonize Virginia	*Macbeth* and *Antony and Cleopatra*; Jonson's *Volpone*
1607	Defeated Irish earls flee to the Continent	Susanna Shakespeare marries Stratford doctor John Hall; *Coriolanus*
1608	Conflict between king and parliament	The King's Men lease the indoor Blackfriars Theatre
1610	Parliament petitions the king with 'Grievances'	Jonson's *The Alchemist*; Heywood's *The Fair Maid of the West*
1611	Parliament dismissed by King James; Scots Protestants settled on Catholic land in Ulster; translation of the Bible authorized by King James	*The Winter's Tale* and *The Tempest*. Shakespeare now living mostly in Stratford?
1613		*The Two Noble Kinsmen* written by Shakespeare and John Fletcher; The Globe theatre burns down
1616		Susanna Shakespeare marries Thomas Quiney; William Shakespeare dies
1623		Publication of First Folio

GLOSSARY

Absolute monarch A king or queen who claims the right to rule without consulting the opinions of their subjects or their representatives.

Catholic The form of Christianity dominant in Western Europe until the Reformation of the early sixteenth century. Salvation for the individual soul is achieved through good works, by receiving the sacraments of the Church and by recognizing the authority of the Church hierarchy. The rituals of worship tend to be elaborate. In Shakespeare's time English Catholics were subject to persecution by the Protestant state if they practised their faith openly.

Decorum The doctrine that the form of a work of art should be appropriate to its content: a 'high' poetic style was thought to suit the language of princes, but comic prose to be appropriate for shepherds, for example. The actions of characters should suit their nobility and social position, too.

Early modern A term used to describe the sixteenth and seventeenth centuries. It lacks the value-judgement about previous centuries contained in the term 'Renaissance' and stresses the continuity of this period with the modern world.

Feudalism The economic and social system dominant in Europe during the Middle Ages. The different ranks of society were bound together by bonds of loyalty, with the superior ranks in theory bound to protect their inferiors in return for service, originally military in nature. Social mobility was very limited and the economy principally agricultural. Although the king was supposed to stand at the apex of the feudal pyramid, his position was often vulnerable since lands were held in his name rather than by the monarch himself.

Folio A book composed of sheets of paper folded once only, forming four large printed pages. Shakespeare's friends John Hemmings and Henry Condell published a collection of thirty-six of his plays in this format in1623, the so-called 'First Folio'. Many of the plays only survive in this version.

Humanism An intellectual movement in Europe in the late-fifteenth and sixteenth centuries which drew its inspiration from a revival of interest in Greek and Roman texts. Humanists wished to study human nature and to advance the human condition, rather than adhere to the medieval view that mankind was a fallen creature subject to God's will.

Ideology The term has several different meanings. In the type of literary criticism found in this book it means the dominant set of beliefs held by a society about itself which makes the distribution of power in that society seem 'natural'.

Machiavel An amoral and opportunistic character who apparently follows the teachings of the Italian political theorist Niccolò Machiavelli (1469–1527). Machiavelli was realistic about power politics and thought that if a prince were to rule in peace and harmony, it would be necessary to be secretly ruthless in action. The exercise of Christian humility and a reliance on the workings of Providence might well lead to the overthrow of a conventionally 'virtuous' prince.

Mise-en-scène The term in film studies used to refer to the setting, costumes, props, lighting, etc. of the production itself.

Providence The Christian belief that God will ensure that the virtuous are rewarded and that the wicked are punished even in this life.

Protagonist The principal character of the drama, who is not necessarily a 'hero'.

Protestants Those Christians who, from the Reformation of the early sixteenth century onwards, rejected the teachings of the Catholic Church. Protestantism stresses the individual relationship of the soul with God, without the intercession of priests, bishops or of saints in heaven. All beliefs must have their foundation in the Bible itself, rather in the teachings of any church hierarchy. It prefers plain and simple forms of worship. The state Church of England in Shakespeare's time was Protestant.

Puritans Protestants who rejected the moderate religious stance of the state Church of England and wanted a more thoroughly reformed church according to what they saw as scriptural principles. Many were followers of the Swiss reformer Jean Calvin (1509–64), who believed that only a predestined 'elect' would be saved. Most were opponents of the theatre.

Quarto A pamphlet-style play-book composed of single sheets of paper folded four times and thus half the size of a folio page. Most individual editions of plays in this period were 'quarto' texts. Those quarto texts of Shakespeare's plays which were published in his lifetime are never completely identical with their 1623 Folio versions.

Renaissance The 'rebirth' of western thought and literature in the late-fifteenth and sixteenth centuries; a movement encompassing scientific discovery and advance, the development of humanism in the arts and an abandonment of many medieval ways of thinking about religion and the world.

Soliloquy A speech spoken by one character alone on stage to the audience.

Subjectivity The term 'subject' in contemporary literary criticism means an apparently individual consciousness which thinks of itself as unified and self-governing, but which is in fact constructed by language ('subject' in the grammatical sense) and by social and political forces ('subject' in the political sense).

REFERENCES

Adamson, S., Hunter, L., Magnusson, L., Thompson, A. and Wales, K. (eds) (2001) *Reading Shakespeare's Dramatic Language: A Guide*, London: Thomson.

Adelman, J. (1992) *Suffocating Mothers: Fantasies of Maternal Origin in Shakespeare's Plays, 'Hamlet' to 'The Tempest'*, London and New York: Routledge.

Albanese, D. (2001) 'The Shakespeare film and the Americanization of culture', in J.E. Howard and S. Cutler Shershow (eds) *Marxist Shakespeares*, London and New York: Routledge.

Almereyda, M. (2000) *William Shakespeare's 'Hamlet': A Screenplay Adaptation*, London and New York: Faber and Faber.

Barker, F. (1993) *The Culture of Violence: Essays on Tragedy and History*, Manchester: Manchester University Press.

Bate, J. (1996) 'Introduction' to J. Bate and R. Jackson (eds) *Shakespeare: An Illustrated Stage History*, Oxford: Oxford University Press.

Bate, J. and Jackson, R. (eds) (1996) *Shakespeare: An Illustrated Stage History*, Oxford: Oxford University Press.

Belsey, C. (1985a) *The Subject of Tragedy: Identity and Difference in Renaissance Drama*, London and New York: Routledge.

——(1985b) 'Disrupting sexual difference: meaning and gender in the comedies', in J. Drakakis (ed.) *Alternative Shakespeares*, London and New York: Routledge.

——(1998a) 'Love in Venice', in M. Coyle (ed.) *New Casebooks: The Merchant of Venice*, London: Macmillan.

——(1998b) 'Shakespeare and film: a question of perspective', in R. Shaughnessy (ed.) *Shakespeare on Film*, Basingstoke and London: Macmillan [1983].

——(1999) *Shakespeare and the Loss of Eden*, Basingstoke and London: Palgrave.

Blake, N.R. (1983) *Shakespeare's Language: An Introduction*, Basingstoke: Macmillan.

Blakemore Evans, G. (ed.) (1997) *The Riverside Shakespeare* (second edition), Boston, MA: Houghton Mifflin Company.

Bond, E. (1987) *Bingo: Scenes of Money and Death*, in *Bond Plays: Three*, London: Methuen [1974].

Boose, L.E. and Burt, R. (eds) (1997) *Shakespeare, The Movie: Popularizing the Plays on Film, TV and Video*, London and New York: Routledge.

——(2003) *Shakespeare, The Movie II: Popularizing the Plays on Film, TV, Video and DVD*, London and New York: Routledge.

Brook, G.L. (1976) *The Language of Shakespeare*, London: Andre Deutsch.

Brotton, J. (1998) '"This Tunis, sir, was Carthage": contesting colonialism in *The Tempest*', in A. Loomba and M. Orkin (eds) *Postcolonial Shakespeares*, London and New York: Routledge.

Brown, J. (2003) 'Becoming Falstaff', online. Available: http://www.pbs.org/newshour/bb/entertainment/jan-june04/falstaff_01-07.html> (accessed 6 February 2005).

Brown, P. (1985) '"This thing of darkness I acknowledge mine": *The Tempest* and the discourse of colonialism', in J. Dollimore and A. Sinfield (eds) *Political Shakespeare*, Manchester: Manchester University Press.

Bulman, J.C. (1996) 'Shakespeare and performance theory', in J.C. Bulman (ed.) *Shakespeare, Theory and Performance*, London and New York: Routledge.

Burnett, M.T. and Wray, R. (eds) (2000) *Shakespeare, Film, Fin de Siècle*, Basingstoke: Macmillan.

Byrne, C. (2003) 'Crowning achievement: Dakin Matthews' Shakespeare adaptation triumphs', online. Available: http://www.gaycitynews.com/gcn_250/crowningachievement.html (accessed 6 February 2005).

Ceresano, S.P. (ed.) (2004) *William Shakespeare's 'The Merchant of Venice': A Sourcebook*, London and New York: Routledge.

Coyle, M. (ed.) (1998) *New Casebooks: A Midsummer Night's Dream*, London: Macmillan.

Crowl, S. (2000) 'Flamboyant realist: Kenneth Branagh', in R. Jackson (ed.) *The Cambridge Companion to Shakespeare on Film*, Cambridge: Cambridge University Press.

Davies, A. (1988) *Filming Shakespeare's Plays*, Cambridge: Cambridge University Press.

Davies, A. and Wells, S. (eds) (1994) *Shakespeare and the Moving Image: The Plays on Film and Television*, Cambridge: Cambridge University Press.

Davies, S. (1995) *William Shakespeare: The Taming of the Shrew*, Harmondsworth: Penguin Books.

Dawson, A.B. (1996) 'Performance and participation: Desdemona, Foucault and the actor's body', in A.C. Bulman (ed.) *Shakespeare, Theory and Performance*, London and New York: Routledge.

Dessen, A.C. (1986) 'Shakespeare and the theatrical conventions of his time', in S. Wells (ed.) *The Cambridge Companion to Shakespeare Studies*, Cambridge: Cambridge University Press.

Dollimore, J. (2004) *Radical Tragedy: Religion, Ideology and Power in the Drama of Shakespeare and His Contemporaries* (third edition), Basingstoke: Palgrave.

Drakakis, John (ed.) (1992) *Shakespearean Tragedy*, London: Longman.

Dusinberre, J. (1996a) *Shakespeare and the Nature of Women* (second edition), London: Macmillan.

——(1996b) 'Squeaking Cleopatras: gender and performance in *Antony and Cleopatra'*, in A.C. Bulman (ed.) *Shakespeare, Theory and Performance*, London and New York: Routledge.

Dutton, R. (ed.) (1996) *New Casebooks: The Merchant of Venice*, London: Macmillan.

Dutton, R. and Howard, J.E. (eds) (2003) *A Companion to Shakespeare's Works; vol. 1: The Tragedies; vol. 2: The Histories; vol. 3: The Comedies; vol. 4: The Poems, Problem Comedies, Late Plays*, Oxford: Blackwell.

Dymkowski, C. (2000) *Shakespeare in Production: 'The Tempest'*, Cambridge: Cambridge University Press.

Elsky, M. (1989) *Authorizing Words: Speech, Writing and Print in English Renaissance*, Ithaca and London: Cornell University Press.

Escolme, B. (2005) *Talking to the Audience: Shakespeare, Performance, Self*, London and New York: Routledge.

Fernie, E. (2002) *Shame in Shakespeare*, London and New York: Routledge.

Forker, C.R. (2002) *The Arden Shakespeare: 'King Richard II'*, London: Thomson.

Foulkes, R. (2002) *Performing Shakespeare in the Age of Empire*, Cambridge: Cambridge University Press.

Gay, P. (2003a) 'Introduction', in E. Story Donno (ed.) *Twelfth Night*, Cambridge: Cambridge University Press.

——(2003b) *'Twelfth Night*: "The babbling gossip of the air"'', in R. Dutton and J.E. Howard (eds) *A Companion to Shakespeare's Works vol. 3: The Comedies*, Oxford: Blackwell.

Gilbert, M. (2001) *Shakespeare at Stratford: 'The Merchant of Venice'*, London: Thomson.

Greenblatt, S. (1985) 'Invisible bullets: Renaissance authority and its subversion, *Henry IV* and *Henry V'*, in J. Dollimore and A. Sinfield (eds) *Political Shakespeare*, Manchester: Manchester University Press.

——(1990) *Learning to Curse: Essays in Early Modern Culture*, London and New York: Routledge.

——(1993) 'Shakespeare bewitched', in *Shakespeare's Tragedies: Contemporary Critical Essays* (1998), ed. S. Zimmerman, London and Basingstoke: Macmillan; originally in J.N. Cox and L. Reynolds (eds) *New Historical Literary Studies: Essays on Reproducing Texts, Representing History*, Princeton, NJ: Princeton University Press.

——(2001) *Hamlet in Purgatory*, Princeton, NJ, and Oxford: Princeton University Press.

——(2004) *Will in the World: How Shakespeare Became Shakespeare*, London: Jonathan Cape.

Griffiths, T.R. (1996) *Shakespeare in Production: 'A Midsummer Night's Dream'*, Cambridge: Cambridge University Press.

Gurr, A. (1992) *The Shakespearean Stage 1574–1642*, Cambridge: Cambridge University Press.

Hadfield, A. (ed.) (2003) *William Shakespeare's 'Othello': A Sourcebook*, London and New York: Routledge.

——(2004) *Shakespeare and Renaissance Politics*, London: Thomson.

Hapgood, R. (ed.) (1999) *Shakespeare in Production: 'Hamlet'*, Cambridge: Cambridge University Press.

Hawkes, T. (1986) *That Shakespeherian Rag*, London and New York: Methuen.

——(1991) 'Comedy, orality and duplicity: *Twelfth Night*', in G. Waller (ed.) *Shakespeare's Comedies*, London and New York: Longman.

——(2002) *Shakespeare in the Present*, London and New York: Routledge.

Hazlitt, W. (1906) *Characters of Shakespeare's Plays*, London: J.M. Dent [1817].

Healey, M. (1998) *Richard II*, Plymouth: Northcote House.

Holderness, G. (1989a) 'Are Shakespeare's tragic heroes fatally flawed? Discuss', *Critical Survey*, 1(1).

——(1989b) *King Richard II*, Harmondsworth: Penguin Books.

——(1992) *Shakespeare Recycled: The Making of Historical Drama*, Hemel Hempstead: Harvester.

——(2000) *Shakespeare: The Histories*, Basingstoke and London: Palgrave.

Holland, P. (1993) 'Professional productions in the British Isles, January to December 1990', *Shakespeare Survey 45*, Cambridge: Cambridge University Press.

——(1994) *The Oxford Shakespeare: A Midsummer Night's Dream*, Oxford: Oxford University Press.

Honan, P. (1998) *Shakespeare: A Life*, Oxford: Oxford University Press.

Hopkins, L. (2005) *Beginning Shakespeare*, Manchester: Manchester University Press.

Howard, J.E. (1984) *Shakespeare's Art of Orchestration: Stage Technique and Audience Response*, Urbana and Chicago: University of Illinois Press.

——(1994) *The Stage and Social Struggle in Early Modern England*, London and New York: Routledge.

Howard, J.E. and Rackin, P. (1997) *Engendering a Nation: A Feminist Account of Shakespeare's English Histories*, London and New York: Routledge.

Howard, T. (2000) 'Shakespeare's cinematic offshoots', in R. Jackson (ed.) *The Cambridge Companion to Shakespeare on Film*, Cambridge: Cambridge University Press.

Ioppolo, G. (ed.) (2003) *William Shakespeare's 'King Lear': A Sourcebook*, London and New York: Routledge.

Jackson, R. (2000a) (ed.) *The Cambridge Companion to Shakespeare on Film*, Cambridge: Cambridge University Press.

——(2000b) 'Introduction: Shakespeare, film and the marketplace' and 'From play-script to screenplay', in R. Jackson (ed.) *The Cambridge Companion to Shakespeare on Film*, Cambridge: Cambridge University Press.

Jardine, L. (1983) *Still Harping on Daughters: Women and Drama in the Age of Shakespeare*, Hemel Hempstead: Harvester Wheatsheaf.

——(1996) *Reading Shakespeare Historically*, London and New York: Routledge.

Jonson, B. (1983) *Volpone*, ed. B. Parker, Manchester: Manchester University Press [1606].

Jorgens, J.A. (1998) 'Realising Shakespeare on film', in R. Shaughnessy (ed.) *Shakespeare on Film*, Basingstoke and London: Macmillan [1977].

Kermode, F. (2000) *Shakespeare's Language*, Harmondsworth: Allen Lane.

Kettle, A. (1964) 'From *Hamlet* to *Lear*', in A. Kettle (ed.) *Shakespeare in a Changing World*, London: Lawrence & Wishart.

Kiernan, P. (1996) *Shakespeare's Theory of Drama*, Cambridge: Cambridge University Press.

Kliman, B.W. (1995) *Shakespeare in Performance: 'Macbeth'*, Manchester: Manchester University Press.

——(2001) 'The unkindest cuts: flashcut excess in Kenneth Branagh's *Hamlet*', in D. Cartmell and M. Scott (eds) *Talking Shakespeare*, Basingstoke: Palgrave.

Knight, G. Wilson (2001) *The Wheel of Fire*, London and New York: Routledge [1930].

Krieger, E. (1979) '*A Midsummer Night's Dream*', in R. Dutton (ed.) *New Casebooks: A Midsummer Night's Dream* (1996), London: Macmillan.

Leggatt, A. (ed.) (2006) *William Shakespeare's 'Macbeth': A Sourcebook*, London and New York: Routledge.

McDonald, R. (2001) *Shakespeare and the Arts of Language*, Oxford: Oxford University Press.

McEvoy, S. (ed.) (2006) *William Shakespeare's 'Hamlet': A Sourcebook*, London and New York: Routledge.

McKernan, L. and Terris, O. (1994) *Walking Shadows: Shakespeare in the National Film Archive*, London: British Film Institute.

McLuskie, K. (1985) 'The patriarchal bard: feminist criticism and Shakespeare: *King Lear* and *Measure for Measure*', in J. Dollimore and A. Sinfield (eds) *Political Shakespeare*, Manchester: Manchester University Press.

McMillin, S. (1991) *Shakespeare in Performance: 'King Henry IV Part 1'*, Manchester: Manchester University Press.

Massai, S. (ed.) (2006) *William Shakespeare's 'Twelfth Night': A Sourcebook*, London and New York: Routledge.

Montrose, L.A. (1996) '"Shaping fantasies": figurations of gender and power in Elizabethan culture', in R. Dutton (ed.) *New Casebooks: A Midsummer Night's Dream*, London: Macmillan [1983].

Murray, M. (2003) 'Henry IV theatre review', online. Available: http://www.talkinbroadway.com/world/Henry4.html (accessed 10 January 2005).

Neill, M. (1994) *The Oxford Shakespeare: 'Anthony and Cleopatra'*, Oxford: Oxford University Press.

Newman, K. (1986) 'Renaissance family politics and Shakespeare's *The Taming of the Shrew*', in G. Waller (ed.) *Shakespeare's Comedies*, Harlow: Longman.

——(1987) 'Femininity and the monstrous in *Othello*', in J.E. Howard and M.F. O'Connor (eds) *Shakespeare Reproduced: The Text in History and Ideology*, New York and London: Methuen.

——(1998) 'Portia's ring: unruly women and structures of exchange in *The Merchant of Venice*', in M. Coyle (ed.) *New Casebooks: The Merchant of Venice*, London: Macmillan.

Orgel, S. (1987) *The Oxford Shakespeare: The Tempest*, Oxford: Oxford University Press.

——(1996a) *Impersonations: The Performance of Gender in Shakespeare's England*, Cambridge: Cambridge University Press.

——(1996b) *The Oxford Shakespeare: The Winter's Tale*, Oxford: Oxford University Press.

O'Toole, F. (2002) *Shakespeare Is Hard, but So Is Life: A Radical Guide to Shakespearean Tragedy*, London: Granta.

Patterson, A. (1989) *Shakespeare and the Popular Voice*, Oxford: Basil Blackwell.

Picard, L. (2003) *Elizabeth's London*, London: Weidenfeld & Nicolson.

Piesse, A. (1996) 'Self-preservation in the Shakespearean system: gender, power and the New History', in N. Wood (ed.) *Measure for Measure*, Buckingham: Open University Press.

Puttenham, G. (1936), *The Arte of English Poesie*, ed. Gladys Doige Willcock and Alice Walker, Cambridge: Cambridge University Press [1589].

Rackin, P. (1990) *Stages of History: Shakespeare's English Chronicles*, London and New York: Routledge.

Reese, M. (ed.) (1965) *King Henry IV Part One*, London: Edward Arnold.

Rose, J. (1995) '*Hamlet*: the Mona Lisa of literature', in D.E. Barker and I. Kamps (eds) *Shakespeare and Gender: A History*, London and New York: Verso.

Ryan, K. (2002) *Shakespeare*, Basingstoke and New York: Palgrave.

——(ed.) (1999) *Shakespeare: The Last Plays*, London: Longman.

Sanders, J. (2000) 'The end of history and the last man: Kenneth Branagh's *Hamlet*', in M. Thornton Burnett and Ramona Way (eds) *Shakespeare, Film and Fin de Siècle*, London and Basingstoke: Macmillan.

Schafer, E. (2003) *Shakespeare in Production: 'The Taming of the Shrew'*, Cambridge: Cambridge University Press.

Scott Kastan, D. (1991) 'The king hath many marching in his coats', in I. Kamps (ed.) *Shakespeare Left and Right*, London and New York: Routledge.

——(2002) *The Arden Shakespeare: King Henry IV Part I*, London: Thomson.

Shaughnessy, R. (ed.) (1998) *Shakespeare on Film*, London and Basingstoke: Macmillan.

Sinfield, A. (1992) *Faultlines: Cultural Materialism and the Politics of Dissident Reading*, Oxford: Oxford University Press.

Smith, E. (2002) *Shakespeare in Production: 'King Henry V'*, Cambridge: Cambridge University Press.

——(ed.) (2004) *Shakespeare's Comedies*, Oxford: Blackwell.

Sommer, E. (2003) 'A Curtain Up review: *Henry IV*', online. Available: http://www.curtainup.com/henry4beaumont.html (accessed 6 February 2005).

Stern, T. (2004) *Making Shakespeare: From Page to Stage*, London and New York: Routledge.

Tatspaugh, P.E. (2002) *Shakespeare at Stratford: 'The Winter's Tale'*, London: Thomson.

Tennenhouse, L. (1986) *Power on Display: The Politics of Shakespeare's Genres*, London and New York: Routledge.

Thomson, P. (1983) *Shakespeare's Theatre*, London and New York: Routledge.

Thorne, A. (ed.) (2003) *Shakespeare's Romances: Contemporary Critical Essays*, Basingstoke and London: Palgrave.

Tourneur, C. (attrib.) (1967) *The Revenger's Tragedy*, ed. B. Gibbons, London: A & C Black [1607].

Vaughan, V.M. (1994) *'Othello': A Contextual History*, Cambridge: Cambridge University Press.

Vickers, B. (1971) 'Shakespeare's use of rhetoric', in K. Muir and S. Schoenbaum (eds) *A New Companion to Shakespeare Studies*, Cambridge: Cambridge University Press.

Waller, G. (ed.) (1991) *Shakespeare's Comedies*, London: Longman.

Wayne, V. (1991) 'Historical differences: misogyny and *Othello*', in V. Wayne (ed.) *The Matter of Difference: Materialist-Feminist Criticism of Shakespeare*, Harvester Wheatsheaf: Hemel Hempstead.

Webster, J. (1972) *Three Plays*, ed. D. Gunby, Harmondsworth: Penguin Books.

Weimann, R. (1978) *Shakespeare and the Popular Tradition in the Theater: Studies in the Social Dimension of Dramatic Form and Function*, trans. and ed. R. Schwartz, Baltimore, MD, and London: Johns Hopkins University Press.

——(2000) *Author's Pen and Actor's Voice: Playing and Writing in Shakespeare's Theatre*, Cambridge: Cambridge University Press.

Wells, S. (ed.) (1997) *Shakespeare in the Theatre: An Anthology of Criticism*, Oxford: Oxford University Press.

——(2004) *Looking for Sex in Shakespeare*, Cambridge: Cambridge University Press.

White, M. (1998) *Renaissance Drama in Action*, London and New York: Routledge.

Willems, M. (2000) 'Video and its paradoxes', in R. Jackson (ed.) *The Cambridge Companion to Shakespeare on Film*, Cambridge: Cambridge University Press.

Williams, C. (1933) *A Short Life of Shakespeare with the Sources Abridged from Edmund Chambers's 'William Shakespeare. A Study of Facts and Problems'*, Oxford: Oxford University Press.

Williams, P. (1995) *The Later Tudors: England 1547–1603*, Oxford: Oxford University Press.

Wilson, R. (1993) *Will Power: Essays on Shakespearean Authority*, Hemel Hempstead: Harvester Wheatsheaf.

——(2004) *Secret Shakespeare: Studies in Theatre, Religion and Resistance*, Manchester: Manchester University Press.

Yachnin, P. (1997) *Stage-wrights: Shakespeare, Jonson, Middleton and the Making of Theatrical Value*, Philadelphia: University of Pennsylvania Press.

Zimmerman, S. (ed.) (1998) *Shakespeare's Tragedies: Contemporary Critical Essays*, London and Basingstoke: Macmillan.

INDEX

Literary Theory: The Basics
Hans Bertens

Part of the successful *Basics* series, this accessible guide provides the ideal first step in understanding literary theory. Hans Bertens:

- leads students through the major approaches to literature which are signalled by the term 'literary theory';
- places each critical movement in its historical (and often political) context;
- illustrates theory in practice with examples from much-read texts
- suggests further reading for different critical approaches;
- shows that theory can make sense and that it can radically change the way we read.

Covering the basics and much more, this is the ideal book for anyone interested in how we read and why that matters.

0-415-35112-X

Available at all good bookshops
For ordering and further information please visit www.routledge.com